Surprised by Truth

Patrick Madrid

Editor

Surprised by Truth

ELEVEN CONVERTS GIVE
THE BIBLICAL AND HISTORICAL
REASONS FOR BECOMING CATHOLIC

Basilica Press

San Diego

Published by Basilica Press
P.O. Box 85152-134
San Diego, CA 92186

Cover design by Gerald L. Gawronski/The Look Design
    98 99 00 01 30 29 28 27 26 25 24 23 22 21 20 19 18 17

Printed in the United States of America
ISBN 0-9642610-8-1

*"If you continue in my word, you are
truly my disciples, and you will know
the truth, and the truth will make you free."*
(John 8:32-33)

I dedicate this book to the glory and honor of Jesus Christ, the Blessed Virgin Mary, and the Catholic Church; and with love and gratitude to my parents, Bernard and Gretchen Madrid, who gave me the greatest gifts of all: life and the Catholic faith. May God reward you.

To my wife Nancy, our children, Jonathon, Bridget, Timothy, Hillary, Maximilian, Madeline, Judith, and Baby Number Eight (due in early 1995), and to Sr. Judith, O.C.D. Thanks for your patience and encouragement. I love you.

I thank the contributors for being willing to share the details of their conversions with me and with the world. I pray that their testimonies to the truth will help many come to Christ. My thanks to Scott and Kimberly Hahn; to Mark and Martha Matia, Gerry and Nell Hackbarth, and Patrick and Rosemary Trask, for their efforts to see this book to completion; to Gerry Gawronski and John Gecik, for their vital technical assitance; and special thanks to my colleague Karl Keating.

Contents

Foreword

T HE PRACTICE of telling the story of one's conversion has been around as long as Christianity has. Since Paul's testimony in Galatians 2 (cf. Acts 9:1-9) of his experience with Christ on the Road to Damascus, to Augustine's *Confessions,* to our own day, thousands have recounted their journey to Christ and his Church. Yet we seem always to be asking for more. "So, what made *you* decide to become Catholic?" is a question I never tire of asking. And from every convert I hear a different story.

None of the conversion testimonies you're about to read is like another. These people come from different backgrounds. They're scholars, pastors, teachers, preachers, and writers. They have different personalities. They followed different roads to Rome. Yet the title of this book, *Surprised by Truth,* sums up every one of these stories, because each relates the earnest quests of persons seeking the whole truth about Christ, and each describes the surprise discovery that the truth of Christ — in Scripture, history, and logic — lies in the Catholic Church.

When C.S. Lewis wrote of his personal passage from atheism to Christianity, the title, *Surprised by Joy*, reflected his emotion at finding himself a Christian. As he mentions in the preface to that book, he wrote his conversion testimony partly in response to the frequent experience of people asking him his reasons for converting. They'd listen and then say, "What! Have you felt that too? I always thought I was the only one!" As I read this book you now hold, I kept having the same sense of "What! You too?"

I've often thought of my own journey to Rome as a mystery story, a horror story, and a love story. Sometimes being surprised by truth is initially being horrified by truth. The *Catholic* Church has the truth? The *fullness* of the truth? Confronting this fact is a gut-wrenching agony for staunch, Bible-based Evangelical Protestants who've thought and taught, largely because of misunderstandings and prejudice, that Catholics are not even Christians. And beyond the interior struggles are the external obstacles: career derailment; loss of salary, benefits, pension, and financial security; alienation from family, friends, and colleagues. Conversion to Catholicism means hardship, sacrifice, and often loneliness. It means following Jesus all the way to the Cross.

And for what? Once someone snidely remarked to Steve Wood that he became Catholic "for the money."

"No, not for the money," Steve replied. "But I did do it for the riches."

We converts have been made so rich. We have been given wealth beyond our wildest dreams! What words can express the sense of the child who, after passing through a series of orphanages and foster homes, finds himself standing in the doorway of an unfamiliar mansion staring into the loving faces of long-forgotten family members? He is reintroduced to his Father, Almighty God, and to Mary, his mother and queen, who is standing, arms outstretched in welcome, next to his elder brother, King Jesus — in the midst of that glorious company of angelic and saintly siblings who stretch forth from heaven to earth and under the earth. Can you imagine a holier homecoming or a more royal reunion? Few joys surpass the ones related here by these former theological step-children who have finally come home.

The anguish endured is not worth comparing to the riches gained: the Holy Eucharist, the pope, the magisterium, the sacraments, Mary, the saints — the splendor

of Christ mirrored in his Church. "Indeed, I count everything as loss because of the surpassing worth of knowing
Christ Jesus my Lord" (Phil. 3:8).

Then the horror turns to surprise, and surprise turns
to delight, and bliss, and fire, and a desire to share all this
with others. Loneliness fades away as one discovers more
and more people who have also been surprised by truth.

While reading each of these incredible journeys I
laughed, cried, grunted affirmations, and basically relived my own journey into the Catholic Church. I heard
echoes of my own struggles in their words. I relived the
anguish I experienced on that lonely and sometimes
frightening path of conversion, and I relived the deep,
abiding joy of coming home.

But enough. Read these stories. They're prayerful,
heavy-on-doctrine, evangelical, scriptural witnesses of
people who discovered that what they had once thought
was the most "unbiblical" church is really the Church of
the Bible.

Scott Hahn

Introduction

CONVERSION is a form of martyrdom. It involves the surrender of oneself — body, mind, intellect, and faith to Christ. It requires docility and a willingness to be led to the truth, and for many the truth lies in a direction "where you do not want to go" (John 21:18-19).

Each of us is called to embrace this martyrdom. Catholics, who have been given the great privilege of membership in Christ's Church, are called to the daily surrender of living its teachings and striving, by God's grace, to grow in virtue and holiness. Non-Catholics are called to this also, but they must first heed Jesus Christ's invitation to enter into the fullness of his truth — the Catholic Church. For some, this particular act of surrender to Christ — becoming Catholic — is joyful and easy. For others it is frightening and difficult. For many, it is abhorent.

But martyrdom is also joyful. The Lord Jesus promised, "Unless a grain of wheat falls into the earth and dies, it remains alone; but if it dies, it bears much fruit. He who loves his life loses it, and he who hates his life in this world will keep it for eternal life. If anyone serves me, he must follow me; and where I am, there shall my servant be also; if anyone serves me, the Father will honor him" (John 12:24-26).

The following allegory, an ancient Chinese parable, is a favorite of mine. It paints a vivid picture of what it means to surrender oneself to Christ. Each of the converts in this book went through this on his journey into the Catholic Church:

Once upon a time, there was a beautiful garden. There in the cool of the day the Master of the garden would walk. Of all the denizens of the garden, the most beloved was a gracious and noble Bamboo. Year after year, Bamboo grew yet more noble and gracious, conscious of his Master's love and watchful delight, but he was always modest and gentle.

Often, when Wind came to revel in the garden, Bamboo would cast aside his grave stateliness, to dance and play merrily, tossing and swaying and leaping and bowing in joyous abandon, leading the garden in the Great Dance which most delighted the Master's heart.

Now one day, the Master drew near to contemplate his Bamboo with eyes of curious expectancy. Bamboo, in a passion of adoration, bowed his great head to the ground in loving greeting. The Master spoke:

"Bamboo, I wish to use you."

Bamboo flung his head to the sky in utter delight. The day had come, the day for which he had been made, the day to which he had been growing hour by hour, the day in which he would find his completion and his destiny. His voice became low. "Master, I am ready. Use me as you will."

"Bamboo," the Master's voice was grave, "I will have to take you and cut you down."

A trembling of a great horror shook Bamboo. "Cut me down? Me, whom you have made the most beautiful in all your Garden? Cut me down? Oh, not that! Use me for your joy, Master, but please do not cut me down."

"Beloved Bamboo," the Master's voice grew even more grave, "If I do not cut you down, I cannot use you."

The Garden grew still. Wind held his breath. Bamboo slowly bent his proud and glorious head, and he whispered, "Master, if you can't use me unless you cut me down, then do your will and cut."

"Bamboo, beloved Bamboo, I will have to cut your leaves and branches from you also."

"Master, spare me. Cut me down and lay my beauty in the dust, but would you also take from me my leaves and branches?"

"If I do not cut them away, I cannot use you."

The Sun hid his face. A listening butterfly glided fearfully away. Bamboo shivered in terrible expectancy, whispering low, "Master, cut away."

"I will also have to cleave you in two and cut out your heart, for if I do not cut so, I cannot use you."
Bamboo bowed to the ground in sorrow. "Master," he whispered, "then cut and cleave."

So the Master of the garden took Bamboo and cut him down and hacked off his branches and stripped him of his leaves and clove him in two and cut out his heart, and, lifting him gently, carried him to where there was a spring of fresh, sparkling water in the midst of his dry fields. Then, putting one end of broken Bamboo in the spring and the other end into the water channel in his field, the Master laid down gently his beloved Bamboo. The spring sang welcome, and the clear, sparkling waters raced joyously down the channel of Bamboo's torn body into the waiting fields.

Then the rice was planted, and the days went by, and the shoots grew, and the harvest came.

In that day Bamboo, once so glorious in his stately beauty, was yet more glorious in his brokenness and humility. For in his beauty he was life abundant, but in his brokenness he became a channel of abundant life to his Master's world.

If you're a non-Catholic, I pray that this book will help you come to the realization that the Catholic Church is the Church established by Jesus Christ and that he is calling you to enter into it. We will welcome you with open arms!

If you're a Catholic, it's my hope that this book will inspire you to a greater zeal and love for our Holy Catholic faith and that it will help equip you to share that faith with others. Let us rejoice at God's mercy and kindness as we read and reflect upon these testimonies, keeping ever in our prayers all those who have yet to be surprised by truth.

Patrick Madrid

His Open Arms Welcomed Me

Paul Thigpen

I WAS QUITE young the first time I saw him, so I don't remember where it happened. But I do remember being terrified by the sight: that tortured man, thorn-crowned, blood-bathed, forsaken. The sculptor had spared no crease of agony; the painter, no crimson stroke. He was a nightmare in wood.

Yet I was strangely drawn to him as well. His open arms welcomed me; his uncovered breast stretched out like a refuge. I wanted to touch him.

Of course, I knew who he was. After all, I'd won the big prize — a Hershey Bar — for being the first kinder-gartner in our little Southern Presbyterian church to memorize the books of the Bible. And my parents had busted with pride on the morning when I stood before the congregation to recite the grand old affirmations of the Westminster Confession: "Man's chief end is to glorify God and to enjoy him forever. . . ."

But in our church the cross on the wall was empty and clean. We read about the blood, we sang about the blood, but we didn't splash it on our walls and doorposts.

In the years to follow, the man on the cross haunted me. When I found out that a schoolmate wore a crucifix around his neck, I asked my father to get me one. But he shook his head and said, "That's just for Catholics." There was no malice in his words; he simply spoke matter-offactly, in the same way he might have observed that yarmulkes were just for Jews.

One day my aunt from New York came south to visit. She was always inheriting odd items from boarders in the residential motel where she worked, and this time she shared them with us. In a box of assorted old treasures calculated to fascinate a little boy for hours, I found him.

He was plaster of Paris, unfinished, maybe a foot long, cross and all. I ran my fingers over the smooth surface. The details were remarkable for so humble a work, though he had a flaw in his right foot. He was beautiful. But he was too white, too clean. So I found some old watercolors and painted every detail lovingly, with crimson dominating the whole. Then I kept him under my bed and took him out regularly so I could look at him, touch him, and wonder why he should be in some Catholic home instead of mine.

I don't remember when I lost that plaster body, but it must have been sometime after I became an arrogant little atheist at the age of twelve. Some school teacher I've long forgotten encouraged me to read Voltaire, the Enlightenment rationalist, who convinced me that all religion was delusion. At the time I didn't need much convincing; the adolescent season of rebellion against my parents had begun, and skepticism was for me the weapon of choice. No doubt I tossed out the man on the Cross in the same trash can with the Westminster Confession.

For six years I ran from him, though I thought I was running to truth. I had no choice about attending the Presbyterian church with my family, but every week I repeated a quiet, private act of defiance: Whenever the congregation said the Apostles' Creed, I remained silent.

My heart was hungry but my head turned away from anything that could have nourished my spirit. So I began to feed on spiritual garbage instead. A science fair project on parapsychology introduced me to supernatural forces. But I thought they were only unexamined natural powers of the human mind.

Before long, I was trafficking in spirits, though I would never have dreamed they were anything other than my own psychic energies. They would sometimes tell me what others were thinking, or whisper of events that were taking place at a distance. The more power they gave me, the hungrier I became for it. I began to experiment with seances, levitation, and other occult practices — all, of course, in the name of "science." I wanted to become an expert in parapsychology.

From time to time I saw him again, usually hanging beyond the altar in the church of my Catholic girlfriend. His open arms still welcomed me. But since I was convinced there was no God, the most he could represent to me was a suffering humanity. And in those heady days of the '60s, when American youth were so certain they could transform the world, I didn't want a reminder of human brokenness.

We were out to forge our own bright destiny in the new Age of Aquarius, and the crucifix was an unwelcome relic of the old order. Like some child of the eighteenth-century Enlightenment, born just a few centuries too late, I was convinced humanity could perfect itself through education. So I set out to prove the thesis in the human laboratory of my high school.

Our particular campus was an odd mix of peril and promise. As a first step in fully desegregating the public schools of our Southern city, the school board by fiat turned an all-black high school into a racially mixed one. Amazingly, those of us with a vision for racial harmony were able to build more of it than many critics had expected: Out of the chaos of a totally new student body gathered from utterly different social and racial backgrounds, we forged well-oiled student organizations that helped smooth the process of integration.

In a short time, blacks and whites were becoming friends and working hard to build a community. We became the city's first model of a school that had been forced to desegregate totally, yet had come out of the process racially integrated as well — and all without violence. As student body president and a central actor in the drama, I felt as if my "Enlightenment" strategy for changing the world had been validated.

Nevertheless, reality at last bumped up against my carefully crafted visions. First to go was the Aquarian illusion. After a massive transfer of students city-wide in my senior year to complete the desegregation process in all the high schools, the make-up of our student population was radically altered. Some of the new students were militant racists and troublemakers, both black and white. When other campuses in the city began closing down because of rioting, we were put on alert that angry students from other schools were planning to infiltrate our student body and provoke violence there as well.

One lovely fall afternoon, after our homecoming rally, it happened. A riot broke out on campus as I watched helplessly. Black and white friends who had once shared my hopes for a new, peaceful world attacked one another with knives, chains, and tire irons. I naïvely ran around campus from one little mob to another, trying to break up fights and restore calm. My watch was knocked off my wrist in the struggle, but I was miraculously spared injury — to my body, that is. My soul was quite another matter.

The sight of one young man in particular was branded on my memory. He lay sprawled cruciform in the dust, his arms extended, his face bloody. The wooden nightmare of my childhood had become flesh and blood, and I wept bitterly for the death of a dream. The idol I had made of humanity was shattered, and nothing could put it back together.

Next to die were my delusions about psychic powers. One starless summer night a chilling demonic force, grown tired of its human plaything, commandeered my body. It physically pushed me toward the edge of a

POSSESSED
BY A DEVIL

nearby river to throw me in. I've never learned to swim, so if a couple of muscular friends who were with me hadn't pinned me down, it would have drowned me.

The next morning I told my English teacher, a Christian who had been praying for me, what had happened. She said I'd had a brush with the Devil.

I laughed at her and scoffed: "Don't be so medieval." Even so, I had to admit something was out there, and it wasn't a friendly ghost. My teacher gave me C.S. Lewis to read — at last, an antidote for the poison of Voltaire — who in turn sent me back to the Scriptures.

A BIG
INFLUENCE
ON
HIM

It was there that I learned about angels, fallen and unfallen. I found dark references to the powers that had tormented me and the evil mastermind behind them, the "god of this world." In the Bible I rediscovered a multi-tiered model of the universe, of nature and supernature, that fit the realities of my recent experience in ways that parapsychology and the Enlightenment never could.

These were my first faltering steps back toward reality, and with a sobering irony, I came to believe in the Devil before I believed in God. Yet that inverted order of my emerging creed had its purpose in the divine intention: So devoid was I of the fear of God that I had to work my way into it by stages, starting with a fear of demons. The pleasure I'd taken in declaring myself an atheist, unfettered by the rules of any creator, began to crumble: If there was indeed a devil but no God to save me from him, I was in deep trouble.

Yet Scripture was teaching me much more than fear. In the gospels especially, I encountered a man whose wisdom and compassion arrested me. He was the same man I'd sung hymns about as a child, the man on the cross who had stirred me with his suffering; but he was becoming real in a way I'd never imagined possible.

Years before, he'd been much like the hero of a fairy tale: a bright legend that embodied the noblest human traits, but only a legend after all. Now he was entering history for me, breathing the air and walking the soil of a planet where I also breathed and walked. I was still scandalized by the thought that he could actually have been more than a man. But the possibilities were opening up. After all, once you grant the existence of supernature, you can't rule out God; and if there's a God, what's there to stop him from invading nature? If there's a God, I knew, then the rest of the story, however shocking — Virgin Birth, miracles, the Resurrection — surely becomes possible.

Meanwhile, I began trying prayer as an experiment. My requests were concrete and specific; so were the swift, undeniable answers that came. The evidence was mounting, and though I felt threatened by the prospect of having to submit to the will of Another, a part of me also longed for that submission.

Soon I was getting to know believers whose lives convincingly enfleshed the gospel — or, to use Merton's haunting line, "People whose every action told me something of the country that was my home." When one of them invited me to a small prayer meeting, I came, however awkwardly, and sat silently for most of the evening. But I came back the next week, and the next, because I sensed that these people genuinely loved me, and I was hungry for their love.

A fresh, new breeze was blowing through my mind, sweeping out the cobwebs and debris that had accumulated through six years of darkness. The light of Christ was dawning inside, and all the frayed old arguments of the skeptics soon rotted in its brilliance. The more I knew of the world and myself, the more I found that Christian faith made sense of it all, and the more I longed to meet this man whose followers I had come to love.

Just after my high school graduation, at a massive nationwide rally of evangelical Christians in Dallas sponsored by Campus Crusade for Christ, he came to me — not in a vision or even a dream, but in a quiet, unshakable confidence that he was alive and knocking at the door of my heart. I repented of my unbelief and all its devastating consequences. I confessed to God that Jesus Christ was his Son, and asked him to become my Savior and Lord. My mind at last had given my heart permission to believe, to obey, and to adore.

When I took up Scripture again to read, the centuries were suddenly compressed, and the historical Figure that had replaced the noble Legend was himself now replaced with a living Friend. In my hands were letters he had addressed personally to me, written two millennia ago yet delivered to my home at this moment, so fresh that it seemed the ink should still be wet. He read my thoughts, nailed my sins, told my story, plumbed the depths of my pain.

Overwhelmed, I asked him to fill me with himself.

Two months later I was sitting alone in our Presbyterian church's sanctuary, late in the evening after a service had ended. I'd opened my Bible to the book of Acts — no one had warned me that it was an incendiary tract — and I read about the day of Pentecost. I'd never been taught about the baptism of the Holy Spirit or his gifts. But I told God that if what happened to those first believers on that day long ago could happen to me this evening, I wanted it. And I was willing to sit there all night until it happened.

I didn't have to wait long. Suddenly a flood of words in a tongue I'd never studied came bursting out of me, followed by a flood of joy that washed over me for a week. The Holy Spirit baptism was for me a baptism in laughter; I giggled like a fool for days over this sweet joke of God. It was a liberation from the chains of the Enlightenment. This irrational — or perhaps I should say para-rational — experience opened my eyes to realms that soared beyond my understanding, and left me face-to-face with mystery. For years, reason had masqueraded as a god in my life, but now I saw it for what it truly was: only a servant, however brilliantly attired.

That realization served me well in the following years when I majored in religious studies at Yale. That school's great, Neo-Gothic library best illustrates the spirit I encountered there: Painted on the wall high above the altar of its massive circulation desk is an awesome icon of Knowledge — or perhaps Wisdom, though I rarely heard her voice in the classrooms of that campus. She was personified as a queen enthroned above us lowly student mortals, and though we freshmen were tempted to genuflect, I owed my first allegiance to another sovereign.

In the twenty years that came after, faith grew, establishing itself as the heart of the vocations that consumed me: I went on to a graduate school program in religion, and I served as a missionary evangelist in Europe, an associate pastor of a charismatic congregation, and a writer and editor for several Christian publishers.

Those were good years, years of settling into a deep relationship with the God I'd once abandoned. He gave me a beloved Christian wife and two children who learned to seek his face from a tender age. But at last the time came for yet another conversion in my life — and another baptism of joy.

A Perennial Longing

I had found the Lord, or rather the Lord had found me, in the Evangelical Christian community. I'd been trained to think in that community's categories, to speak its language, to hold its assumptions, to cherish its traditions. It had been for me a life-giving stream, a place of awesome grace and glory: There, I learned to feed on Scripture, to celebrate the Lord's presence, to seek the way of holiness, to enjoy the fellowship of those who are devoted to him.

But in quiet moments, I sometimes felt a longing sweep over me. It washed across my heart whenever I heard a recording of tranquil Gregorian chant or Schubert's aching "Ave Maria."

It erupted inside me when I visited the great cathedrals of Europe — humbled by the grandeur of their architecture and the sweaty devotion of all the forgotten saints who had labored to raise those stones to the sky.

I felt it when I read St. Augustine's *Confessions*, St. Catherine's *Dialogue*, and St. John's *Dark Night of the Soul.* These were more than books — they were doorways into a communion with the saints who had written them. I felt their presence as I read; I even found myself talking to them, though my theological training told me that such conversations weren't permitted.

Most of all, I ached when I knelt quietly in the sanctuaries of Catholic churches. I felt drawn to the tabernacle and the altar. And I sometimes wept at the longing I felt as I lifted my gaze to behold him, hanging there, broken and bloody. After so many years, his open arms still welcomed me.

But my mind rebelled against the attraction. Those matter-of-fact words from so long ago always returned to dampen my desire: "That's just for Catholics."

The result was a long, thirsty wandering from one Protestant tradition to another: Presbyterian, Baptist, Methodist, Episcopalian, classical Pentecostal, independent charismatic. Each had something solid to offer, each taught me critical lessons in walking with God. But sooner or later I had to admit that none of them was home.

I'd had healthy encounters with the Catholic Church, of course. My childhood girlfriend and her family, and other friends as well, had earned my respect for Catholic faith. The charismatic renewal had shown me how much in common I could have with Catholic believers; I'd even written my senior essay in college on a Catholic charismatic community in Rhode Island. Two good friends, evangelicals from InterVarsity, a college group I'd belonged to, had themselves entered the Church, challenging me to consider why.

But Protestant ways of thinking were so deeply engrained in my mind that I found it impossible to reason my way out of them. The legacy of Voltaire and the

Enlightenment was farther-reaching than I'd ever imagined: I was so confident of all that can be verbally communicated, so suspicious of all that cannot. I knew that the truth of God could be revealed through a book. But could the power of God really reside in a dusty relic, the presence of God in a fragile wafer, the authority of God in a human pope?

Once again, my heart and head were at war.

Even so, my baptism in the Holy Spirit had planted in me the seed of a sacramental vision of the world — a vision, I believe, that most charismatics share, if they only knew it. My encounter with para-rational tongues and unexplainable miracles had suddenly introduced me to the mystery of God and chastened my tendency to rely solely on rational understanding in the search for truth.

The Pentecostal experience had also affirmed that to be human is to have a body and emotions as well as an intellect: that God's grace can be communicated through physical and emotional healing, and that worship involves not just minds, but feelings, physical postures, and pageantry as well. As a charismatic I even discovered that God could work powerfully through the spoken prayer, the anointing oil, the laying on of hands, the prayer cloth (cf. 2 Kings 13:20-21; Luke 8:43-44; Acts 19:11-12; James 5:13-15).

All these experiences convinced me that it was God's way to invest the physical with the spiritual, the human with the divine, the natural with the supernatural, the ordinary with mystery. In short, I came to see that Pentecost was a matter of spirit made flesh; a charismatic faith was inescapably a sacramental faith. But I needed more than sacramental experience, more even than that perennial longing, to take me over the intellectual mountain range that stood between me and the Catholic Church.

God knew what I needed. So he put me in a Ph.D. program in historical theology where I would find maps to help me scale those treacherous heights — maps drawn by those who had made the journey before.

The names of the mapmakers will come as no surprise: St. Augustine, John Cardinal Newman, G.K. Chesterton, Thomas Merton, many others as well. A few who never fully made it over those theological mountains themselves nevertheless stood like Moses at the peak, pointing me in the right direction — men like John Williamson Nevin and, above all, C.S. Lewis.

Lewis once wrote that, long before his reason was converted to Christian faith, his imagination had been baptized by the writings of the Scottish novelist George Macdonald. In my case, long before my reason was converted to Catholic truth, my imagination had been sacramentalized by Lewis's writings.

St. Augustine's contribution to my conversion caught me by surprise. Years ago I'd been ravished by his *Confessions*; the cries of my heart seemed like so many distant, feeble echoes of his longings from centuries before. But once he had my trust, he had me trapped: Sometime later, innocently reading his polemics against the Donatists on the evils of schism, I suddenly realized that I was a modern-day, Protestant Donatist — and he was rebuking me for remaining separated from Rome.

One by one, each question I had about the Catholic faith found an answer. Like most converts to the Church who have first had to overcome doctrinal hurdles, I found that many problems were resolved when I finally understood the truly Catholic position on a disputed matter, rather than the Protestant misconception of it. Those discoveries are familiar to former Protestants: We all had to learn, I suppose, that devotion to Mary is not worship; that the pope is not held to be infallible in every casual statement he makes.

At the same time, I began to identify and move beyond the Protestant filters through which I was reading Scripture. No longer could I insist on adhering to the "plain sense" of the biblical text yet interpret Jesus' own words about his Body and Blood "figuratively." Nor could I ignore his clear announcement that he would build his

Church on St. Peter and give him the keys of the kingdom.

Some puzzles were solved, not by the writings of great Christian teachers or a new approach to Scripture, but by the outcome of great Christian dramas of the past. Church history, I found, was theology teaching by example.

For some, the study of Christian behavior over the centuries, with all its horrors, has led to doubt, cynicism, even atheism. They see church councils bickering over petty jealousies, popes amassing wealth, bishops fathering children, monks living in dissipation; and at that dismaying sight, they lose faith. For me, however, Church history became one long confirmation of two realities: the universality of sin and the sovereignty of grace.

One stumbling block in my way had been the all-too-obvious flaws of contemporary Catholicism. Some modern "Catholic" theologians I'd read, for example, had more in common with Marx or Freud than with Augustine or Aquinas. I met monks who talked like Buddhists and nuns becoming "self-empowered" through pagan goddess worship.

But the scandal was overcome when I finally admitted that no Christian community has ever even come close to being perfect. In fact, I saw the Catholic Church's problems repeated in the history of all the groups that repudiated her, that vowed they would never be like her. They reminded me of the adolescent daughter who swears she'll never be like the mother she resents — yet ends up becoming just like her in spite of her vow.

It was simply historical proof of the Pauline judgment that my Protestant mentors had always been so fond of quoting Romans 3:23, "All have sinned, and come short of the glory of God." Each breakaway group, I learned, inexorably retraced the missteps of the Catholic tradition to one degree or another because whatever problems the

Church has, they are not exclusively Roman; they are universally human.

In taking the long view, I also came to marvel at the sovereign grace of God. Those same bickering councils that Protestants have disparaged nevertheless demonstrated the most astonishing wisdom in crafting creeds that would stand the test of time. Those avaricious popes gave their blessing to men and women of blessed poverty whose explosive holiness shamed their lax brothers and sisters and turned the Church upside down. In John Paul II, in the heroism of the Church in Eastern Europe, in the charismatic renewal and other life-giving movements, I could see signs of God's grace with us yet, despite the serious attacks on the Church both within and without.

At the same time, I saw how Rome has remained the spiritual center of gravity for the churches that have separated from her. However much they try to distance themselves, they keep finding their way back: When the arid, rigid predestinationism of Calvin grew at last intolerable, they turned to Wesley for a more human — and more Catholic — view. In the Holiness movement they recaptured something of the Catholic traditions of asceticism and works of mercy; in the Pentecostal movement they recovered a sense of sacrament and mystery.

Meanwhile, even our now-secular society — itself spawned in many ways by the logical conclusions of Protestant views — still attempts to make up for the useful Catholic traditions it has repudiated. As G. K. Chesterton once noted, whatever Catholic elements the Protestants threw out of their churches, the modern world eventually reintroduced because they couldn't live without them. But they always brought those elements back in a lower form. Instead of the confessional, for example, we now have the psychoanalyst's couch, with none of the safeguards of the confessional. Instead of a glorious communion with saints who help us on our pilgrimage to heaven, we now have spiritualists who frolic with demons that seduce us into hell.

Yet through all the confusion, I came to see, Rome remains the solid theological standard for those who have separated from her. As even the oldest denominations have succumbed to the spirit of the age on one critical issue after another, the Catholic Church has remained firm — on the sanctity of life, on the nature of sexuality, on the supernatural foundations of faith, on the essence of God and the identity of Christ. Today as yesterday, *Veritatis Splendor* — the splendor of truth, as the Holy Father has so aptly called it, blazes forth from Rome. "The light shines in the darkness, and the darkness has not overcome it."

Perhaps most importantly, my reading of Erasmus and Newman and my study of the history of liturgy helped me to see that the primitivist assumption underlying Protestant views of the Church was seriously mistaken in at least two ways. First, Erasmus and Newman taught me that the Church is a maturing organism whose life span stretches across the centuries — not an archaeological expedition always searching for fossils to help it reconstruct a primitive campsite. They challenged me to defend the Protestant notion that we should desire the embryo over the mature organism; and having studied church history, I found such a defense impossible.

Second, when I studied the history of Jewish and Christian liturgy, I found that even if we could return to the "primitive" Christian experience, that experience would not resemble most of the Protestant, especially the charismatic, churches of today. The congregations I'd been part of were for the most part assuming that they had recovered a "New Testament" model of strictly spontaneous worship, local government, and "Bible-only" teaching. But the early Church, I found, was in reality liturgical in worship; translocal and hierarchical in government; and dependent on a body of sacred Tradition that included the Scripture, yet stretched far beyond it as well.

In short, all the knotted highways and byways of Church history led at long last to the same seven-hilled city. By the time I'd finished my doctoral exams, I knew I had to enter the Church. My heart and mind were already Catholic; if I turned away from Rome, I would wander, forever thirsty, the rest of my days.

Another Baptism of Joy

The clincher came one morning when I heard about the terminal illness of an old acquaintance. I asked myself, "If you discovered that you were dying, what would you do?" The answer that leapt to mind surprised me with its suddenness and certainty: "I'd enter the Catholic Church right away." It was time to take action.

Even so, the road forward wasn't all smooth. My extended family and a number of friends found the whole matter confusing, though they were graciously supportive. I lost some important business relationships with colleagues in the evangelical publishing world who thought I'd been "deceived." I gave up my pastoral ordination and my association with a ministry network on whose board of governors I was serving.

Much more sensitive was the situation at home. Despite many conversations with me about the matter, my wife still found the notion of becoming Catholic a strange one. We finally reached an agreement: If she would come with me to RCIA (Rite of Christian Initiation for Adults) classes and support me in doing what I knew I must do, then I would exert no pressure on her, and I would respect her final decision about the Church. I entrusted her to the grace of God and the intercession of St. Ann, her patron as a homemaker and the patron of the parish where we lived.

When we went to St. Ann's Church to find out what to do next, we were met by a priest who embodied all the best of what it means to be Christian and Catholic. A Christ-centered, Christ-reflecting man of great joy and gentleness, Father Gerald Conmey won over my family immediately. His high regard for the Scripture permeated our instruction, assuring my wife that we weren't off on some dangerous theological tangent.

Not long after, my family joined me in my decision. My wife and I would be confirmed, my daughter would receive her First Communion, my son would be baptized, and all of us would be embraced at last by the Catholic Church — all on the same day. Rejoicing, I rushed out to buy them each a crucifix for the occasion.

On the afternoon before that unforgettable day, I was driving home alone from a business errand, my mind on some editing project, when suddenly a flood of joy washed over me. I threw back my head and began to laugh. It was a profound, tear-soaked laughter; a laughter of liberation and relief, the kind I hadn't experienced since that day, twenty years before, when the Holy Spirit had washed me clean inside.

"St. Augustine!" I shouted out the car window. "I'm coming home! St. Thomas! I'mcoming home! St. Catherine! I'm coming home!" And I laughed till my sides hurt, wept till my eyes ached.

Perhaps God let me undergo that new baptism at such an odd moment to spare my family the embarrassment they would have felt had I exploded in the next day's ceremony instead. In any case, when the time came to go forward for that blessed oil's anointing, I was still joyous, but composed. As I stood, I looked beyond the altar at the man on the cross.

And his open arms welcomed me.

What Is Truth?

Marcus Grodi

I AM A FORMER Protestant minister. Like so many others who have trodden the path that leads to Rome by way of that country known as Protestantism, I never imagined I would one day convert to Catholicism.

By temperament and training I'm more a pastor than a scholar, so the story of my conversion to the Catholic Church may lack the technical details in which theologians traffic and in which some readers delight. But I hope it will accurately explain why I did what I did and why I believe with all my heart that all Protestants should do likewise.

[handwritten margin note: So he hasn't studied Theology]

I won't dwell on the details of my early years, except to say that I was raised by two loving parents in a nominally Evangelical Protestant home, and I went through most of the experiences that make up the childhood and adolescence of the typical American baby-boomer. I was taught to love Jesus, to go to church on Sunday, and to salute the U.S. flag with pride. I also managed to blunder into most of the dumb mistakes that other kids in my generation made. But after a season of teenage rebellion, when I was twenty years old I experienced a radical re-conversion to Jesus Christ. I turned away from the lures of the world and became serious about prayer and Bible study.

As a young adult, I made a re-commitment to Christ, praying he would help me fulfill the mission in life he had chosen for me.

I learned tremendous lessons from my parents about perseverance and diligence. My mother had a difficult time bringing children into the world; she suffered seven miscarriages before I was born. I am grateful to my parents for their determination to keep trying to have children in the face of seemingly insurmountable odds. My parents' willingness to brave suffering and heartbreaking setbacks for the sake of their love for each other was a strong witness to me of the need for a sense of duty and persistence if one is to truly live the Christian life.

The more I sought through prayer and study to follow Jesus and conform my life to his will, the more I felt an aching sense of longing to devote my life entirely to serving him. Gradually, the way dawn's first faint rays peek over a dark horizon, the conviction that the Lord was calling me to be a minister began to grow.

That conviction grew steadily stronger while I was in college and afterward during a series of jobs in the engineering field. Eventually I couldn't ignore the call. I was convinced the Lord wanted me to become a minister, so I quit my job and enrolled in Gordon-Conwell Theological Seminary in suburban Boston. I acquired a master of divinity degree and was shortly thereafter ordained to the Protestant ministry.

My six-year old son, Jon Marc, recently memorized the Cub Scouts' oath, which goes in part: "I promise to do my best, to do my duty to God and my country." This earnest boyhood vow rather neatly sums up my own reasons for giving up a career in engineering in order to serve the Lord with complete abandon in full-time ministry. I took my new pastoral duties seriously, and I wanted to perform them correctly and faithfully, so that at the end of my life, when I stood face-to-face before God, I could hear him speak those all-important words: "Well done, good and faithful servant." As I settled down into the rather pleasant life of a Protestant minister, I felt happy and at peace with myself and God — I finally felt that I had arrived.

I had not arrived.

I soon found myself faced with a host of confusing theological and administrative questions. There were exegetical dilemmas over how to correctly interpret difficult biblical passages and also liturgical decisions that could easily divide a congregation. My seminary studies had not adequately prepared me to deal with this morass of options.

I just wanted to be a good pastor, but I couldn't find consistent answers to my questions from my fellow minister friends, nor from the "how to" books on my shelf, nor from the leaders in my Presbyterian denomination. It seemed that every pastor was expected to make up his own mind on these issues.

What about the Bible?

This "reinvent the wheel as often as you need to" mentality that is at the heart of Protestantism's pastoral ethos was deeply disturbing to me. "Why should I *have* to reinvent the wheel?" I asked myself in annoyance. "What about the Christian ministers down through the centuries who faced these same issues? What did they do?" Protestantism's emancipation from Rome's "man-made" laws and dogmas and customs that had "shackled" Christians for centuries (that, of course, was how we were taught in seminary to view the "triumph" of the Reformation over Romanism) began to look a lot more like anarchy than genuine freedom.

I didn't receive the answers I needed, even though I prayed constantly for guidance. I felt I had exhausted my resources and didn't know where to turn. Ironically, this frustrating sense of being out of answers was providential. It set me up to be open for answers offered by the Roman Catholic Church. I'm sure that if I had felt that I had all the answers I wouldn't have been able or willing to investigate things at a deeper level.

A breach in my defenses

In the ancient world, cities were built on hilltops and ringed with stout walls that protected the inhabitants against invaders. When an invading army laid siege to a city, as when Nebuchadnezzar's army surrounded Jerusalem in 2 Kings 25:1-7, the inhabitants were safe for as long as their food and water held out and for as long as their walls could withstand the onslaught of the catapult's missile and the sapper's pick. But if the wall was breached, the city was lost.

My willingness to consider the claims of the Catholic Church began as a result of a breach in the wall of the Reformed Protestant theology that encircled my soul. For nearly forty years I labored to construct that wall, stone-by-stone, to protect my Protestant convictions.

The stones were formed from personal experiences, seminary education, relationships, and my successes and failures in the ministry. The mortar that cemented the stones in place was my Protestant faith and philosophy. My wall was high and thick and, I thought, impregnable against anything that might intrude.

again what about the Word of God?

But as the mortar crumbled and the stones began to shift and slide, at first imperceptibly, but later on with an alarming rapidity, I became worried. I tried hard to discern the reason for my growing lack of confidence in the doctrines of Protestantism.

I wasn't sure what was seeking to replace my Calvinist beliefs, but I knew my theology was not invincible. I read more books and consulted with theologians in an effort to patch the wall, but I made no headway.

I reflected often on Proverbs 3:5-6: "Trust in the Lord with all your heart, and lean not unto your own understanding; in all of your ways acknowledge him and he will direct your paths." This exhortation both haunted and consoled me as I grappled with the doctrinal confusion and procedural chaos within Protestantism.

The Reformers had championed the notion of private interpretation of the Bible by the individual, a position I began to feel increasingly uncomfortable with, in light of Proverbs 3:5-6.

Bible-believing Protestants claim they *do* follow the teaching in this passage by seeking the Lord's guidance. The problem is that there are thousands of different paths of doctrine down which Protestants feel the Lord is directing them to travel. And these doctrines vary wildly according to denomination.

I struggled with the questions, "How do I know what God's will is for my life and for the people in my congregation? How can I be sure that what I'm preaching is correct? How do I *know* what truth is?" In light of the doctrinal mayhem that exists within Protestantism — each denomination staking out for itself doctrines based on the interpretations of the man who founded it — the standard Protestant boast, "I believe only what the Bible says," began to ring hollow. I professed to look to the Bible alone to determine truth, but the Reformed doctrines I inherited from John Calvin and the Puritans clashed in many respects with those held by my Lutheran, Baptist, and Anglican friends.

In the Gospels Jesus explained what it means to be a true disciple (cf. Matt. 19:16-23). It's more than reading the Bible, or having your name in a church membership roster, or regularly attending Sunday services. These things, good though they are, by themselves don't make one a true disciple of Jesus. Being a disciple of Jesus Christ means making a radical commitment to love and obey the Lord in every word, action, and attitude, and to strive to radiate his love to others. The true disciple, Jesus said, is willing to give up everything, even his own life, if necessary, to follow the Lord.

I was deeply convinced of this fact, and as I tried to put it into practice in my own life (not always with much success) I also did my best to convince my congregation that this call to discipleship is not an option — it's something all Christians are called to strive for. The irony was that my Protestant theology made me impotent to call them to radical discipleship, and it made them impotent to hear and heed the call.

One might ask, "If all it takes to be saved is to 'confess with your lips that Jesus is Lord and believe in your heart that God raised him from the dead' (Rom. 10:9), then why must I *change*? Oh, sure, I should change my sinful ways. I should strive to please God. But if I don't, what does it really matter? My salvation is assured."

There's a story about a newspaper reporter in New York City who wanted to write an article on what people consider the most amazing invention of the twentieth century. He hit the streets, interviewing people at random, and received a variety of answers: the airplane, the telephone, the automobile, computers, nuclear energy, space travel, and antibiotic medicine. The answers went on along these lines until one fellow gave an unlikely answer:

"It's obvious. The most amazing invention was the thermos."

"The *thermos*?" queried the reporter, eyebrows raised.

"Of course. It keeps hot things hot and cold things cold."

The newspaperman blinked. "So what?"

"Don't you think it's amazing that it knows which is which?"

This anecdote had meaning for me. Since it was my duty and desire to teach the truth of Jesus Christ to my congregation, my growing concern was, "How do I *know* what is truth and what isn't?"

Every Sunday I would stand in my pulpit and interpret Scripture for my flock, knowing that within a fifteen mile radius of my church there were dozens of other Protestant pastors — all of whom believed that the Bible alone is the sole authority for doctrine and practice — but each was teaching something different from what I was teaching. "Is my interpretation of Scripture the right one or not?" I'd wonder. "Maybe one of those other pastors is right, and I'm misleading these people who trust me."

There was also the knowledge — no, the gut-twisting certitude — that one day I would die and would stand before the Lord Jesus Christ, the Eternal Judge, and I would be required to answer not just for my own actions but also for how I led the people he had given me to pastor. "Am I preaching truth or error?" I asked the Lord repeatedly. "I *think* I'm right, but how can I know for sure?"

This dilemma haunted me.

I started questioning every aspect of my ministry and Reformed theology, from insignificant issues to important ones. I look back now with a certain embarrassed humor at how I fretted during those trying days of uncertainty. At one point I even wrangled with doubts over whether or not to wear a clerical collar. Since there is no mandatory clerical dress code for Presbyterian ministers some wear collars, some wear business suits, some robes, and others wear a combination of all. One minister friend kept a clerical collar in the glove compartment of his car, just in case donning it might bring some advantage to him, "Like getting out of a speeding ticket!" He once confided with a conspiratorial grin. I decided not to wear a clerical collar. At Sunday services I wore a plain black choir robe over my business suit.

When it came to the form and content of Sunday liturgy every church had its own views on how things should be done, and each pastor was free to do pretty much whatever he wanted within reason.

Without mandated denominational guidelines to steer me, I did what all the other pastors were doing: I improvised. Hymns, sermons, Scripture selections, congregational participation, and the administration of baptism, marriage, and the Lord's Supper were all fair game for experimentation. I shudder at the memory of one particular Sunday when, in an effort to make the youth service more interesting and "relevant," I spoke the Lord's words of consecration, "This is my Body, this is my Blood, do this in memory of me," over a pitcher of soda pop and a bowl of potato chips. It was the one and only time I dabbled in such silliness.

Theological questions vexed me the most. I remember standing beside the hospital bed of a man who was near death after suffering a heart attack. His distraught wife asked me, "Is my husband going to heaven?" All I could do was mouth some sort of pious but vague "we-must-trust-in-the-Lord" reassurance about her husband's salvation. She may have been comforted but I was tormented by her tearful plea. After all, as a Reformed pastor I believed John Calvin's doctrines of predestination and perseverance of the saints. This man had given his life to Christ, he had been regenerated, and was confident that he was one of God's elect. But *was* he?

I was deeply unsettled by the knowledge that no matter how earnestly he may have thought he was predestined for heaven (it's interesting that all who preach the doctrine of predestination firmly believe they themselves are one of the elect), and no matter how sincerely those around him believed he was, he may not have gone to heaven.

And what if he had secretly "backslidden" into serious sin and had been living in a state of rebellion against God at the moment his heart attack caught him by surprise? Reformed theology told me that if that were the case, then the poor fellow had simply been deluded by a false security, *thinking* he was regenerated and predestined for heaven when in fact he had been unregenerate all along and on his way to hell. Calvin taught that the Lord's elect will — *must* — persevere in grace and election. If a person dies in a state of rebellion against God he proves he never was one of the elect. What kind of absolute assurance was that? I wondered.

I found it harder to give clear, confident answers to the "will my husband go to heaven?" kinds of questions my parishioners asked me. Every Protestant pastor I knew had a different set of criteria that he listed as "necessary" for salvation. As a Calvinist I believed that if one publicly accepts Jesus as his Lord and Savior, one is saved by grace through faith. But even as I consoled others with these fine-sounding words, I was troubled by the worldly and sometimes grossly sinful lifestyles these now-de-ceased members of my congregation had lived. After just a few years of ministry I began to doubt whether I should continue.

Consider the sparrows

I rose one morning before dawn and, taking a folding chair, my journal, and a Bible, went out into a quiet field beside my church. It was the time of day I most love, when the birds are singing the world awake. I often marvel at the exuberance of birds in the early morning. What wonderfully short memories they have! They begin each day of their simple existences with a symphony of praise to the Lord who created them, utterly unconcerned with cares or plans. Sometimes, I'd "consider the sparrows" and meditate on the simplicity of their life.

Sitting quietly in the middle of the dew-covered field waiting for the sun to come up, I read Scripture and meditated on these questions that had been troubling me, placing my worries before the Lord. The Bible warned me not to "lean unto my own understanding," so I was determined to trust in God to guide me.

I was contemplating leaving the pastorate, and I saw three options. One was to become the head of youth ministry at a large Presbyterian church that had offered me the position. Another was to leave ministry altogether and go back to engineering. The other possibility was to return to school and round out my scientific education in an area that would open even more doors to me professionally. I had been accepted into a graduate program in molecular biology at Ohio State University. I mulled over these options, asking God to guide my steps. "An audible voice would be great," I smiled, as I closed my eyes and waited for the Lord's answer. I had no idea what form The Answer would take, but it was not long in coming.

My reverie ended abruptly when a merrily-chirping sparrow flew past and pooped on my head! "What are you saying to me, Lord?" I cried out with the anguish of Job. The trilling of the birds was the only response. There was no voice from heaven (not even a snicker), just the sounds of nature waking from its slumber in an Ohio cornfield. Was it a divine sign or merely Brother Bird's editorial comment on my worries? In disgust I folded up the chair, grabbed my Bible, and went home.

Later that day when I told my wife Marilyn about the three options I was considering and the messy incident with the bird, she laughed and exclaimed with her typical wisdom, "The meaning is clear, Marcus. God is saying, 'None of the above!'"

Although I'd have preferred a less humiliating method of communication, I knew nothing occurs by accident, and that neither sparrows nor their droppings fall to earth without God's knowledge. I took this as at least a comical hint from God to remain in the ministry.

But I still knew my situation was not right. Maybe what I needed was a bigger church with a bigger budget and a bigger staff. Surely, then I'd be happy. So, I struck off in the direction of the "bigger-is-better" church that I thought would satisfy my restless heart. Within six months I found one I liked and whose very large congregation seemed to like me. They offered me the post of senior pastor, complete with an office staff and a budget ten times larger than the one I had at my previous church. Best of all, this was a strong Evangelical church with many members who were actively interested in Scripture study and lay ministry. I enjoyed preaching before this large and largely-approving congregation each Sunday. At first I thought I had solved the problem, but after only one month, I realized that bigger was not better. My confusion and frustration merely grew proportionately larger.

Polite smiles beamed up at me during each sermon, but I wasn't blind to the fact that for many in the congregation my passionate exhortations to live a virtuous life merely skittered across a veneer of religiosity like water droplets on a hot skillet. Many said, "Great sermon! It really blessed me!" But I sensed that what they really thought was, "That's nice for other people, Pastor — for *sinners.* But I've already arrived. My name's already on the heavenly rolls. *I* don't need to worry about all of this stuff, but I sure do agree with you, Pastor, that we've got to tell all the sinners to get right with God."

One day I found myself standing before the local presbytery as spokesman for a group of pastors and laymen who were defending the idea that when we use parental language for God in communal prayer, we should call him "Father", not "mother" or "parent." I defended this position by appealing to Scripture and Christian tradition. To my dismay I realized that the faction I represented was in the minority and that we were fighting a losing battle. This issue would be settled not by a well-reasoned appeal to Scripture or Church history, but by a vote — the majority of the voters being pro-gender-neutral-language liberals. It was at this meeting that I first recognized the anarchistic principle that lies at the center of Protestantism.

These liberals (grievously wrong as they were in their scheme to reduce God to the mere functions of "creator," "redeemer," and "sanctifier," instead of the Persons of Father, Son, and Holy Spirit), were just being good Protestants. They were simply following the course of protest mapped out for them by their theological ancestors Martin Luther, John Calvin, and the other Reformers. The Reformation maxim of "I will not abide by a teaching unless *I* believe it is correct and biblical" was being invoked by these liberal Protestants in favor of their protest against masculine names for God. All of a sudden it hit me that I was observing Protestantism in the full solipsistic glory of its natural habitat: protest. "What kind of church am I in?" I asked myself dejectedly as the vote was taken and my side lost.

At about this time Marilyn, who had been the director of a pro-life crisis pregnancy center, began challenging me to grapple with the inconsistency of our staunch pro-life convictions and the pro-abortion stance of our Presbyterian denomination. "How can you be a minister in a denomination that sanctions the killing of unborn babies?" she asked.

The denominational leadership had bowed under the pressure from radical feminist, homosexual, pro-abortion, and other extremist pressure groups within the denomination and (though ostensibly members of individual congregations could hold pro-life views) imposed stringent liberal guidelines on the hiring process for new pastors.

When she woke me up to the fact that a portion of the donations my congregation forwarded to the Presbyterian General Assembly were going to finance abortions, and there was nothing I or my congregation could do about it, I was stunned.

Marilyn and I knew we had to leave our denomination, but where would we go? This question led to another: Where am I going to find a job as a minister? I purchased a book that listed the details of all major Christian denominations and began evaluating several of the denominations that interested me.

I'd read the doctrinal summaries and think, "This one is nice, but I don't like their view of baptism," or "This one is okay, but their view of the end times is a bit too panic-ridden," or "This one sounds exactly like what I'm looking for, but I'm not comfortable with their style of worship." After examining every possibility and not finding one that I liked, I shut the book in frustration. I knew I was leaving Presbyterianism but I had no idea what the "right" denomination was to go into. There seemed to be something wrong with each of them. "Too bad I can't customize my own 'perfect' church," I thought to myself wistfully.

Around this time a friend from Illinois called me on the phone. He too was a Presbyterian pastor and had heard through the grapevine that I was planning to leave the Presbyterian denomination.

"Marc, you *can't* leave the church!" he scolded. "You must never leave the church. You're committed to the church. It shouldn't matter that some theologians and pastors are off the wall. We've got to stick with the church, and work for renewal from within! We must preserve unity at all costs!"

"If that's true," I replied testily, "why did we Protestants break away from the Church in the first place?"

I didn't know where those words came from. I had never in my life given even a passing thought as to whether or not the Reformers where right to break away from the Catholic Church. It was the essential nature of Protestantism to attempt to bring renewal through division and fragmentation. The motto of the Presbyterian Church is "reformed, and always reforming." (It should add: "and reforming, and reforming, and reforming, and reforming, etc.")

I could leave for another denomination, knowing that eventually I might move on to another when I became dissatisfied, or I could decide to stay where I was and take my lumps. Neither option seemed right, so I decided that I would leave the ministry until I resolved the issue one way or the other. Returning to school seemed to be the easiest way to take a breather from all this, so I enrolled in a graduate program in molecular biology at Case Western Reserve University.

My goal was to combine my scientific and theological backgrounds into a career in bio-ethics. I figured that a Ph.D. in molecular biology would win me a better hearing among scientists than would a degree in theology or ethics. Besides, earning a Ph.D. in theology or ethics required learning Latin and German, and at 39 I figured my brain cells were a little too far in decline for that type of mental rigor.

The commute to the Cleveland campus took over an hour each way, and for the next eight months I had plenty of quiet time for introspection and prayer.

Soon I was deeply immersed in a genetic engineering research project, which involved the removal and reproduction of human DNA taken from homogenized male kidneys. The program was very challenging, but I loved it, although compared with the complexities of amino acids and biochemical cycles, wrestling with Latin conjugations and German declension endings suddenly seemed a lot easier.

This project fascinated and frightened me. I relished the intellectual stimulation of scientific research, but I also saw how dehumanizing the research lab can be. Genetic tissue harvested from the cadavers of deceased patients at the Cleveland Clinic were sent to our lab for DNA research. I was deeply moved by the fact that this tissue had come from *people* — moms and dads, children, and grandparents who had once lived and worked and laughed and loved, but who were now dead. In the lab these neatly-numbered vials of tissue were just tubes of "stuff," experimental "material" that was utterly dissociated from the human persons to whom it once belonged.

I wrote an essay on the ethical problems involved with fetal tissue transplantation and began speaking to Christian groups about the dangers and blessings of modern biological technology. Things seemed to be going according to plan, at least until I realized that the real reason for my return to school was not to get a degree. It was so that I might buy a copy of the local Cleveland newspaper, *The Plain Dealer.*

One Friday morning, after the long drive into Cleveland, I was eating breakfast and killing time before class, trying to stay awake. Normally I'd squeeze in a little study time, but this morning I did something unusual: I bought a copy of *The Plain Dealer.* As I slipped the quarter into the newspaper machine I had no way of knowing I had come to a momentous fork in the road and that I was about to start down the path that would lead me out of Protestantism and into the Catholic Church (and I suppose if I *had* known where it led I would have gone the other way). Skimming through, with only nominal interest, I came across a small advertisement that jumped out at me: "Catholic theologian, Scott Hahn, to speak at local Catholic parish this Sunday afternoon."

I choked on my coffee. "*Catholic* theologian, Scott Hahn?" It couldn't be the Scott Hahn I used to know. We had attended Gordon-Conwell Theological Seminary together back in the early 80s. Back then he was a staunch Calvinist anti-Catholic, the staunchest on campus! I'd been on the fringe of an intense Calvinist study group which Scott led, but while Scott and the others spent long hours scouring the Bible like detectives trying to uncover every angle of every theological implication, I played basketball.

Though I hadn't seen Scott since we graduated in 1982, I had heard the dark rumor floating around that he'd become a Catholic. I hadn't thought much of it. Either the rumor was false, contrived by someone who was offended by (or jealous of) the intensity of Scott's convictions, or else Scott had flipped. I decided to make the hour and a half trip to find out. I was totally unprepared for what I discovered.

Much learning hath made you mad!

I was nervous as I pulled into the parking lot of the huge gothic structure. I had never been inside a Catholic church, and I didn't know what to expect.

I entered the church quickly, skirting the holy water fonts, and scuttled down the aisle, unsure of the correct protocol for getting into a pew. I knew Catholics bowed, or curtsied, or did some sort of jig-like obeisance toward the altar before entering the pew, but I just slipped in and scrunched down, happy not to have been recognized as a Protestant.

After a few minutes of no grim-faced usher tapping me on the shoulder and jerking his thumb back toward the door — "Come on, pal, hit the road. We all know you're not Catholic" — I began to relax and gape at the strange but undeniably beautiful interior of the church.

A few moments later Scott strode to the podium and began his talk with a prayer. When he made the sign of the Cross, I knew he had truly jumped ship. My heart sank. "Poor Scott." I groaned inwardly. "The Catholics got to him with their clever arguments." I listened intently to his talk on the Last Supper entitled "The Fourth Cup," trying hard to detect the errors in his thinking. But I couldn't find any. (Scott's talk was so good I plagiarized most of it at my next communion service sermon.)

As he spoke, using Scripture at each step to support Catholic teaching on the Mass and the Eucharist, I found myself mesmerized by what I heard. Catholicism was being explained in a way I had never imagined possible — from the Bible! As he explained them, the Mass and the Eucharist were not offensive or foreign to me. At the end of his talk, when Scott issued a stirring call to a radical conversion to Christ, I wondered if maybe he had only feigned conversion so he could infiltrate the Catholic Church to bring about renewal and conversion of spiritually-dead Catholics.

It didn't take long before I found out.

After the audience's applause subsided I went up front to see if he would recognize me. He was surrounded by a throng of people with questions. I stood a few feet away and studied his face as he spoke with his typical charm and conviction to the large knot of people. Yes, this was the same Scott I had palled around with in seminary. He now sported a mustache, and I had a full beard (quite a change from our "clean-cut" seminary days), but when he turned in my direction his eyes sparkled as he grinned a silent hello.

In a moment we stood together, clasped in a warm handshake, he apologizing if he had offended me in any way. "No. Of course not!" I assured him, as we laughed with the sheer delight of seeing each other again. After a few moments of obligatory "How's-your-wife-and-family?" chit-chat, I blurted out the one thought on my mind. "I guess it's true what I've heard. Why did you jump ship and become Catholic?" Scott gave me a brief explanation of his struggle to find the truth about Catholicism (the throng of people listened intently as he gave a mini-conversion story), and suggested I pick up a copy of his conversion story tape, copies of which were being snapped up briskly at the literature table in the vestibule.

We exchanged phone numbers and shook hands again, and I headed for the back of the church where I found a table covered with tapes on the Catholic faith done by Scott and his wife Kimberly, as well as tapes by Steve Wood, another convert to Catholicism who had studied at Gordon-Conwell Seminary. I bought a copy of each tape and a copy of a book Scott had recommended, Karl Keating's *Catholicism and Fundamentalism*.

Before I left, I stood in the back of the church, taking in for a moment the strange yet attractive hallmarks of Catholicism that surrounded me: icons and statues, ornate altar, candles, and dark confessional booths. I stood there for a moment wondering why God had called me to this place, then I stepped out into the cold night air, my head dizzy with thoughts and my heart flooded with a confusing jumble of emotions.

I went to a fast food restaurant, got a burger for the long drive home, and slipped Scott's conversion tape into the player, planning to discover where he had gone wrong. I didn't get half way home before I was so overwhelmed with emotion that I had to pull the car to the side of the highway so I could clear my head.

Even though Scott's journey to the Catholic Church was very different from mine, the questions he and I had grappled with were essentially the same. And the answers he found which had so drastically changed his life were very compelling to me. His testimony convinced me that the reasons for my growing dissatisfaction with Protestantism couldn't be ignored. The answers to my questions, he claimed, were found in the Catholic Church. This idea pierced me to the core.

I was at once frightened and exhilarated by the thought that God might be calling me into the Catholic Church. I prayed for awhile, my head resting on the steering wheel, collecting my thoughts before I started the car again and drove home.

The next day, I opened *Catholicism and Fundamentalism*, and read straight through, finishing the final chapter that night. As I prepared to retire for the night, I knew I was in trouble! It was clear to me now that the two central dogmas of the Protestant Reformation, *sola scriptura* (Scripture alone) and *sola fide* (justification by faith alone), were on very shaky biblical ground, and therefore so was I.

My appetite thus whetted, I began reading Catholic books, especially the early Church Fathers, whose writings helped me understand the truth about Church history prior to the Reformation. I spent countless hours debating with Catholics and Protestants, doing my best to subject Catholic claims to the toughest biblical arguments I could find. Marilyn, as you might guess, was not pleased when I told her about my struggle with the claims of the Catholic Church. Although at first she told me, "This too will pass," eventually she too became intrigued with the things I was learning, and she began to study for herself.

As I waded through book after book, I shared with her the clear and common-sense teachings of the Catholic Church I was discovering. More often than not we would conclude together how much more sense and how much truer to Scripture the views of the Catholic Church seemed than anything we had found in the wide range of Protestant opinions. There was a depth, an historical strength, a philosophical consistency to the Catholic positions we encountered. The Lord worked an amazing transformation in both our lives, coaxing us along, side by side, step by step, together all the way.

But, with all these good things we were finding in the Catholic Church, we were also confronted by some confusing and disturbing issues. I encountered priests who thought me strange for considering the Catholic Church. They felt conversion was unnecessary. We met Catholics who knew little about their faith, and whose life-styles conflicted with the moral teachings of their Church. When we attended Masses we found ourselves unwelcome and unassisted by anyone. But in spite of these obstacles blocking our path to the Church, we kept studying and praying for the Lord's guidance.

After listening to dozens of tapes and digesting several dozen books, I knew I could no longer remain a Protestant. It had become clear that the Protestant answer to Church renewal was, of all things, unscriptural. Jesus had prayed for unity amongst his followers, and Paul and John both challenged their followers to hold fast to the truth they had received, not letting opinions divide them. As Protestants we had become infatuated by our freedom, placing personal opinion over the teaching authority of the Church. We believed that the guidance of the Holy Spirit is enough to lead any sincere seeker to the true meaning of Scripture.

The Catholic response to this view is that it is the mission of the Church to teach with infallible certitude. The apostles and their successors were promised by Christ, "He who listens to you listens to me. And he who rejects you rejects me and rejects the one who sent me" (Luke 10:16). The early Church believed this too. A very compelling passage leaped out at me one day while I was studying Church history:

"The Apostles received the gospel for us from the Lord Jesus Christ; and Jesus Christ was sent from God. Christ, therefore, is from God, and the Apostles are from Christ. Both of these orderly arrangements, then, are by God's will. Receiving their instructions and being full of confidence on account of the Resurrection of our Lord Jesus Christ, and confirmed in faith by the Word of God, they went forth in the complete assurance of the Holy Spirit, preaching the Good News that the kingdom of God is coming. Through countryside and city they preached; and they appointed their earliest converts, testing them by the spirit, to be the bishops and deacons of future believers. Nor was this a novelty: for bishops and deacons had been written about a long time earlier. Indeed, Scripture somewhere says: 'I will set up their bishops in righteousness and their deacons in faith'" (Clement of Rome, *Epistle to the Corinthians* 42:1-5 [ca. A.D. 80]). [1]

Another patristic quote that helped breach the wall of my Protestant presuppositions was this one from Irenaeus, bishop of Lyons:

"When, therefore, we have such proofs, it is not necessary to seek among others the truth which is easily obtained from the Church. For the apostles, like a rich man in a bank, deposited with her most copiously everything which pertains to the truth; and everyone whosoever wishes draws from her the drink of life. For she is the entrance to life, while all the rest are thieves and robbers. That is why it is surely necessary to avoid them, while cherishing with the utmost diligence the things pertaining to the Church, and to lay hold of the tradition of truth. What then? If there should be a dispute over some kind of question, ought we not have recourse to the most ancient churches in which the apostles were familiar, and draw from them what is clear and certain in regard to that question? What if the apostles had not in fact left writings to us? Would it not be necessary to

---

[1] Some patristics scholars (e.g. W.A. Jurgens and J.A.T. Robinson) date this epistle as early as A.D. 80, though the traditional dating favors A.D. 96. A concise treatment of the arguments for the earlier dating is found in William Jurgens, *The Faith of the Early Fathers* (Collegeville: Liturgical Press, 1970) vol. 1, 6-7.

follow the order of tradition, which was handed down to those to whom they entrusted the Churches?" (*Against Heresies* 3,4,1 [ca. A.D. 180]).

I studied the causes of the Reformation. The Roman Catholic Church of that day was desperately in need of renewal but Martin Luther and the other Reformers chose the wrong, the *unbiblical,* method of dealing with the problems they saw in the Church. The correct route was and still is just what my Presbyterian friend had told me: Don't leave the Church; don't break the unity of faith. Work for a genuine reform based on God's plan, not man's, achieving it through prayer, penance, and good example.

I could no longer remain a Protestant. To do so meant I must deny Christ's promises to guide and protect his Church and to send the Holy Spirit to lead it into all truth (cf. Matt. 16:18-19, 18:18, 28:20; John 14:16, 25, 16:13). But I couldn't bear the thought of becoming a Catholic. I'd been taught for so long to despise "Romanism" that, even though intellectually I had discovered Catholicism to be true, I had a hard time shaking my emotional prejudice against the Church.

One key difficulty was the psychological adjustment to the complexity of Catholic theology. By contrast Protestantism is simple: Admit you're a sinner, repent of your sins, accept Jesus as your personal Savior, trust in him to forgive you, and you're saved.

I continued studying Scripture and Catholic books and spent many hours debating with Protestant friends and colleagues over difficult issues like Mary, praying to the saints, indulgences, purgatory, priestly celibacy, and the Eucharist. Eventually I realized that the single most important issue was authority. All of this wrangling of how to interpret Scripture gets one nowhere if there is no way to know with infallible certitude that one's interpretation is the right one. The teaching authority of the Church in the magisterium centered around the seat of

Peter. If I could accept this doctrine, I knew I could trust the Church on everything else.

I read Fr. Stanley Jaki's *The Keys of the Kingdom* and *Upon This Rock*, and the Documents of Vatican II and earlier councils, especially Trent. I carefully studied Scripture and the writings of Calvin, Luther, and the other Reformers to test the Catholic arguments. Time after time I found that the Protestant arguments against the primacy of Peter simply weren't biblical or historical. It became clear that the Catholic position was the biblical one.

The Holy Spirit delivered a literal *coup de grace* to my remaining anti-Catholic biases when I read John Henry Newman's landmark book, *An Essay on the Development of Christian Doctrine.* In fact, my objections evaporated when I read 12 pages in the middle of the book in which Newman explains the gradual development of papal authority. "It is a less difficulty that the papal supremacy was not formally acknowledged in the second century, than that there was no formal acknowledgment on the part of the Church of the doctrine of the Holy Trinity till the fourth. No doctrine is defined till violated."

My study of Catholic claims took about a year and a half. During this period, Marilyn and I studied together, sharing together as a couple the fears and hopes and challenges that accompanied us along the path to Rome. We attended Mass together weekly, making the drive to a parish far enough away from our home town (my former Presbyterian Church was less than a mile from our home) to avoid the controversy and confusion that would undoubtedly arise if my former parishioners knew I was investigating Rome.

We gradually began to feel comfortable doing all the things Catholics did at Mass (except receiving Communion, of course). Doctrinally, emotionally, and spiritually, we felt ready to formally enter the Church, but there remained one barrier for us to surmount.

Before Marilyn and I had met and fallen in love, she had been divorced after a brief marriage. Since we were Protestants when we met and married, this posed no problem, as far as we and our denomination were concerned. It wasn't until we felt we were ready to enter the Catholic Church that we were informed that we couldn't do so unless Marilyn could receive an annulment of her first marriage. At first, we felt like God was playing a joke on us! Then we moved from shock to anger. It seemed so unfair and ridiculously hypocritical: that we could have committed almost any other sin, no matter how heinous, and with one confession been adequately cleansed for Church admission, yet because of this one mistake our entry into the Catholic Church had been stopped dead in the water.

But then we remembered what had brought us to this point in our spiritual pilgrimage: We were to trust God with all our heart and lean not on our own understanding. We were to acknowledge him and trust that he would direct our paths. It became evident to us that this was a final test of perseverance sent by God.

So Marilyn began the difficult annulment investigation process, and we waited. We continued attending Mass, remaining seated in the pew, our hearts aching while those around us went forward to receive our Lord in the Holy Eucharist and we could not. It was by not being able to receive the Eucharist that we learned to appreciate the awesome privilege that Jesus bestows on his beloved of receiving him Body and Blood, Soul and Divinity in the Blessed Sacrament. The Lord's promise in Scripture became real to us during those Masses: "The Lord chastises the son whom he loves" (Heb. 12:6).

After an eight-month wait, we learned that Marilyn's annulment had been granted. Without further delay our marriage was blessed, and we were received with great excitement and celebration into the Catholic Church. It felt so incredibly good to finally be home where we belonged. I wept quiet tears of joy and gratitude that first

Mass when I was able to walk forward with the rest of my Catholic brothers and sisters and receive Jesus in Holy Communion.

I asked the Lord many times in prayer, "What is truth?" He answered me in Scripture by saying, "I am the way and the truth and the life." I rejoice that now as a Catholic I can not only know the Truth but receive him in the Eucharist.

Apologia pro a final few words sua

I think it's important that I mention in closing one more of John Henry Newman's insights that made a crucial difference in the process of my conversion to the Catholic Church. He wrote that "To be deep in history is to cease to be a Protestant." This one line summarizes a key reason why I abandoned Protestantism, bypassed the Orthodox Church, and became a Catholic.

Newman was right. The more I read Church history and Scripture the less I could comfortably remain a Protestant. I saw that it was the Catholic Church — the Roman Catholic Church — that was established by Jesus Christ, and all other claimants to the title "true Church" had to step aside. It was the Bible and Church history that made a Catholic out of me, against my will (at least at first) and to my immense surprise. I also learned that the flip side of Newman's adage is equally true: To cease to be deep in history is to *become* a Protestant.

That's why we Catholics must know *why* we believe what the Church teaches as well as the history behind these truths of our salvation. We must prepare ourselves and our children to "Always be ready to give an explanation to anyone who asks for a reason for your hope" (1 Peter 3:15). By boldly living and proclaiming our faith many will hear Christ speaking through us and will be brought to a knowledge of the truth in all its fullness in the Catholic Church. God bless you!

A Triumph and a Tragedy

James Akin

I BROKE OFF a piece of the popsicle in my hand and placed it carefully in the mouth of my dying wife. Renée lay on her back, restless in the hospital bed, suffering from an advanced case of colon cancer which we had discovered a little more than a month before. She ate several more pieces of popsicle as I broke them off for her, then said she could eat no more, so I let her rest.

When our parish priest arrived he and I went into a conference room down the hall to talk. The news about my wife's condition was not good. Renée's caretakers had outlined three things which could kill her in the short term: one of them instantly, one in a week or so, and one in a few weeks. The doctor said she still had a chance of responding to the chemotherapy and might conceivably live for a few months, possibly even six or more, but that a year would be miraculous. In light of the urgent state of Renée's condition, we talked about accelerating my entrance into the Catholic Church. It didn't look like there was much time.

I was born in 1965 in Corpus Christi, Texas, and grew up in Fayetteville, Arkansas. My mom and dad took me to a local Church of Christ until I was five or six, but then quit going. After that I was raised outside any church. This did not mean I was uninterested in religion — I was. When I was thirteen or fourteen, I started reading the Bible, but only those parts I thought dealt with the "end times." As a result of what I read in the Bible, I got scared, seeing terrifying visions of God's wrath and judgment without having them balanced by the message of his wondrous grace and mercy. This helped drive me into the next phase of my religious development: the New Age movement. The reason I moved in that direction was that New Age philosophy holds that there is no hell. New Agers believe we reincarnate through many lives until we become perfect. This made the New Age attractive to me, not only because it presented reincarnation as a bold adventure where you get to go to exotic places and be exotic people, but because believing in reincarnation allowed me to escape having to believe in hell.

I was a New Ager for about five years. But in my first year of college I broke with the New Age movement and began to drift into a no man's land between religions. During this time I did believe in God, but I didn't believe anyone knew anything about him or what he wanted. The only stable thing in my personal religion at this time was an intense dislike of Christians, whom I had learned to detest in high school. The mere sight of a person with Christian mannerisms aggravated me. It was not until some time later that I found a preacher who acted enough like a non-Christian for me to be able to listen to him.

He was a hum-dinger. Dr. Gene Scott was a late night TV preacher and end-times guru based in Southern California. I discovered him on my television late one evening after work and was entranced. He looked less like a typical, three-piece suit, Southern Baptist preacher than anyone I had ever seen. He talked about God, but wore leather jackets and cowboy hats. He had long white hair and a beard, smoked cigars, and felt no compunction about cursing on the air. He wasn't *anything* like a typical televangelist. After listening to him for about six months, I called up and joined his church — the first one of which I had ever been a member.

My fascination with Gene Scott lasted for some time, but when his organization fell on hard times and his program was taken almost completely off the air in my area, I decided to find some other religious affiliation. Eventually I settled on the conservative denomination, the Presbyterian Church in America (PCA). After becoming a Gene Scott devotee, I voraciously read books on theology. My greatest desire was to enter full-time Christian ministry, either as a pastor or as a seminary professor, but something intervened: my marriage.

Renée

I met my future wife, Renée Humphrey, at a party shortly after I became a Christian. Although she was a Catholic who held many New Age beliefs, I dated her anyway. If we had met a year later, I would have been a much stronger Evangelical and would not have done so. She caught me early enough, though, so I went ahead.

Renée was a small woman with dark hair and dark eyes. She too was a voracious reader, but her passion was for history and literature instead of the theology and philosophy I craved. Although she was self-educated in these areas, she knew more about history than many people with college degrees in that discipline. Sometimes it was difficult to watch movies with her. She would point at the screen and say, "That style of dress was not introduced until thirty years *after* this story is set."

Renée also had a melancholy side, in large part due to suffering from poor health. Since high school she had been plagued by health problems. When they first appeared she received what she viewed as incompetent medical care, with the result that she developed a strong phobia about doctors and needles, a phobia which regularly prevented her from seeking proper treatment. Her principal medical problem was ulcerative colitis, a condition which caused perpetual irritation of her colon. This condition weakened the muscles supporting her spine, causing her vertebrae to pinch her nerves, sending sharp, shooting pains down her legs. Even when she was not having leg pains, she always walked with a limp. When her nerves would flare up, she often could not walk at all.

One of the first things we bought after we were married was an aluminum walker, the kind used by the elderly, which Renée needed at the age of twenty-three.

Before we could be married, there were a couple of issues I had to get settled with Renée: her New Age beliefs and her Catholicism. Because she was such an avid reader, I gave her a Christian book on reincarnation, and it convinced her the doctrine was false. "Great!" I thought. "One problem down and one to go."

I was pleased at having convinced her not to be a New Ager; now all I had to do was to convince her to not be a Catholic. This was something I knew I had to do. There was no way I could allow myself to marry a Roman Catholic while I was planning on being a Protestant pastor or seminary professor. Even if I could have found someone willing to ordain me in spite of the fact that I had a Catholic wife, I felt I couldn't in good conscience accept the ordination. I recognized that New Testament ministers were required to have religious solidarity with their families. For example, Titus 1:6 says the children of elders must be raised in the Christian faith.

Because of the success I had obtained by loaning Renée the book criticizing reincarnation, I decided to try this strategy again and loaned her a book which tried to put the Vatican in a bad light. After reading it she quit identifying herself as a Catholic and began to speak of herself as an Anglican. Although I hadn't achieved her complete alienation from Catholicism, this was okay with me. I wanted her in the same denomination I was in, but I could settle for her being an Anglican, at least for the time being. I assumed her stint in Anglicanism would be just an intermediate stage before she entered mainstream Evangelicalism. I was wrong.

During Renée's Anglican period, she and I were married, and shortly after our wedding Renée reverted to Catholicism. Now that we were married and the pressure of losing me was off, she could become Catholic again. This threw a formidable monkey-wrench in my plans. I had to abandon my hope of a career as a minister, the only thing I wanted to do with my life, and I had to abandon my self-image as a teacher of God's Word. This put stress on our otherwise happy marriage.

Things went from bad to worse when Renée discovered something I already knew, but never mentioned: Our marriage was not valid in the eyes of the Catholic Church. As a result, Renée was barred from the sacraments. This revelation caused her a great deal of pain and put still more tension between us. She was unwilling to leave me, and I was unwilling to be remarried in the Catholic Church. The situation was complicated by the fact that Renée had no driver's license, and I refused to take her to Mass. This meant she could almost never attend.

But things began to change.

Since becoming a Christian I had read theology intensively, but I started making discoveries in the Bible which troubled me. For example, the shocking "Catholicity" of certain verses leaped out at me. I was bothered by Christ's statements about the apostles having the power to bind and loose (Matt. 16:18 and 18:18) and about their having the power to forgive sins (John 20:21-23). I didn't know what to make of these passages, so I simply put them aside, planning to deal with them later. Eventually, when the time came to deal with them, I had to conclude that Jesus had meant exactly what he had said: His ministers really do have the power to forgive and retain sins. I had to admit to myself that the Catholics were right about the sacrament of confession, and Presbyterianism was simply out of synch with Scripture on this point.

One of the things that helped me to arrive at this conclusion was a paper written by Leon Holmes. Leon used to attend the Protestant church where I worshipped, but some time before I started attending there he and his family had moved away. Eventually they became Catholic and settled in Little Rock. Leon wrote a paper on Mary and sent it to friends in Fayetteville; I was one of the people who read it. Even though at the time I thought I could refute most of what he said, there was one passage in the paper that made me squirm.

Leon wrote, "Most of the Catholic distinctives that are criticized by our Evangelical brothers are rooted in taking Scripture at face value." This claim shocked my Protestant sensibilities. "What does he mean? *Catholics* take the Bible at face value on the points where Protestants criticize them?" I asked, flabbergasted at the thought. "How can he possible say that? Everyone knows it's Protestants, not Catholics, who are taking the Bible at face value!"

Leon backed up his shocking statement by citing the following verses: "Jesus said to them, 'I tell you the truth, unless you eat the flesh of the Son of Man and drink his blood, you have no life in you' " (John 6:53); "This is my body . . . " (Luke 22:19); "I tell you the truth, unless a man is born of water and the Spirit, he cannot enter the kingdom of God" (John 3:5); "[D]on't you know that all of us who were baptized into Christ Jesus were baptized into his death?" (Rom. 6:3); "baptism . . . now saves you . . . " (1 Peter 3:21); "If you forgive anyone his sins, they are forgiven; if you do not forgive them, they are not forgiven" (John 20:23); "And I tell you that you are Peter, and on this rock I will build my church . . . " (Matt. 16:18).

I thought I could deal with most of these verses, but I had no idea how to refute the Catholic interpretation of 1 Peter 3:21 and John 20:23. Most startling was the very suggestion that Catholic theology rested on the literal interpretation of the Bible. This thought stayed with me and kept bugging me. Eventually it played a significant role in my conversion to the Catholic Church.

I also began to have problems with the two fundamental doctrines of Protestantism: *sola fide*, the claim that we are saved by faith alone, and *sola scriptura*, the claim that Christians are to use only the Bible in matters of doctrine and practice.

The first began to be problematic for me because I started noticing certain passages in Scripture which contradicted the doctrine. In Romans 2:7, for example, the Apostle Paul tells his readers that God will give the reward of eternal life to those who "seek after glory, honor, and immortality by perseverance in good works." In Galatians 6:6-10, Paul tells his readers that those who "sow to the Spirit" by "doing good to all" will from the Spirit reap a harvest of eternal life. It was especially noteworthy that I was finding these verses in Romans and Galatians, the very epistles on which Protestants claim to base the doctrine of justification by faith alone.

These verses do not mean we earn our salvation by good works, a doctrine many Protestants mistakenly attribute to the Catholic Church, but they do mean that the simple "faith alone" formula is not an accurate description of what the Bible teaches about salvation. These and other passages reveal that, as a result of God's grace, we are capable of doing acts of love which please God and which he freely chooses to reward. One of the rewards, in fact the primary reward, is the *gift* of eternal life.

There was still the matter of how to explain passages such as Romans 3:28, where Paul says that a man is justified by faith apart from works of the law, but this did not trouble me much since I had recognized from my earliest days of Bible reading that Paul was talking about the Mosaic Law in Romans and Galatians, which is why he spent so much time hammering home the fact that it is not necessary to be circumcised to be saved — circumcision being one of the key rituals of the Mosaic Law. What Paul is saying is absolutely true: We are justified by faith apart from works of the Mosaic Law.

This would be more obvious to English-speaking Bible readers if translators used the Hebrew word for law, *Torah,* which is also the name of the first five books of the Bible which contain the law of Moses. Paul said, "We hold that a man is justified by faith apart from works of the *Torah*" (Rom. 3:28). We can prove this by looking at the very next verse: "Or is God the God of Jews only? Is he not the God of Gentiles also? Yes, of Gentiles also" (Rom.

3:29). If Paul did not mean "works of the *Torah*," then this question and its answer would be meaningless. By the phrase "works of the Law" Paul refers to something Jews have but Gentiles don't: the Mosaic Law. He makes this point in the next verse: "Since God is one; and he will justify the circumcised [Jews] on the ground of their faith and the uncircumcised [Gentiles] through their faith" (Rom. 3:30). So the "works of the Law" Paul talks about in verse 28 are those works which characterize Jews, not Gentiles, the chief work being circumcision (cf. 3:29-30).

This means that the Jewish laws of circumcision, ritual purity, kosher dietary prescriptions, and the Jewish festal calendar are, now that we are under the New Covenant in Christ, entirely irrelevant to our salvation. Keeping the ceremonial Law of Moses is not necessary for Christians. What is important is keeping "the law of *Christ* "(Gal. 6:2) which is summarized as "faith *working* through love" (also translated as "faith made effective through love" [Gal. 5:6]).

One passage that highlighted the sacramental manner in which God gives us his grace was 1 Peter 3:20-21, where we're told that "God waited patiently in the days of Noah while the ark was being built. In it only a few people, eight in all, were saved through water, and this water symbolizes baptism that now saves you also; not the removal of dirt from the body but the pledge of a good conscience toward God. It saves you by the resurrection of Jesus Christ." The meaning of Peter's statement, "Baptism now saves you," is clear from the context of the passage. He's referring to the sacrament of water baptism, because he says eight people were saved through water. Baptism does not save us by removing dirt from our bodies. The merely physical effects of pouring water in baptism are unimportant. What counts is the action of the Holy Spirit though baptism, for in it we "pledge . . . a good conscience toward God," (that is, we make a baptismal pledge of repentance) and are saved "by the resurrection of Jesus Christ."

I began to discover this sacramental principle throughout the Bible. In both the Old and the New Testament there are incidents where God uses physical means to convey grace. One striking example is the case of the woman with a hemorrhage: "When she heard about Jesus, she came up behind him in the crowd and touched his cloak, because she thought, 'If I just touch his clothes, I will be healed.' Immediately her bleeding stopped and she felt in her body that she was freed from her suffering. At once Jesus realized that power had gone out from him. He turned around in the crowd and asked, 'Who touched my clothes?' 'You see the people crowding against you,' his disciples answered, 'and yet you can ask, "Who touched me?"' But Jesus kept looking around to see who had done it. Then the woman, knowing what had happened to her, came and fell at his feet and, trembling with fear, told him the whole truth. He said to her, 'Daughter, your faith has healed you. Go in peace and be freed from your suffering'" (Mark 5:27-34, NIV).

This passage contains all the elements of the sacramental principle: the woman's faith, the physical means (touching Jesus' clothes), and the supernatural power that went out from Jesus. When the woman came up to him and, with faith, touched his garment, the power of God was sent forth, and she was healed. This is how the sacraments work; God uses physical signs (water, oil, bread, wine, the laying on of hands) as vehicles for his grace, which we receive in faith.

Thomas Aquinas pointed out that, since we are not simply spiritual beings, but physical creatures also, it is fitting for God to give us his spiritual gift of grace through physical means. I later discovered that even Martin Luther recognized this. In his *Short Catechism* he stated that baptism "works the forgiveness of sins, delivers from death and the devil, and grants eternal salvation to all who believe." Sadly, he ignored the Biblical evidence for five of the seven sacraments (retaining only baptism and the Lord's Supper), and most Protestants lost even Luther's view of the sacraments as means of grace, departing from the Biblical teaching that "baptism now saves you."

God sometimes gives saving grace apart from baptism (cf. Acts 10:44-48), but he ordained baptism to be the normative means through which we first come to him and become members of his Church. Peter told the crowd on the day of Pentecost, "Repent and be baptized, every one of you, in the name of Jesus Christ for the forgiveness of your sins. And you will receive the gift of the Holy Spirit" (Acts 2:38). Paul was told at his baptism, "And now what are you waiting for? Get up, be baptized and wash your sins away, calling on his name" (Acts 22:16).

The Protestant doctrine of *sola scriptura* also began to trouble me as I wondered how it is that we can know for certain which books belong in the Bible. Certain books of the New Testament, such as the synoptic gospels, we can show to be reliable historical accounts of Jesus' life, but there were a number of New Testament books (e.g., Hebrews, James, 2 Peter, 2 and 3 John, Jude, and Revelation) whose authorship and canonical status were debated in the early Church. Eventually the Church decided in their favor and included them in the canon of inspired books, but I saw that I, a person two thousand years removed from their writing, had no possibility of *proving* these works were genuinely apostolic. I simply had to take the Catholic Church's word on it.

This meant that for one very foundational doctrine — the doctrine of what Scripture is — I had to trust the Church since there was no way to show from within Scripture itself exactly what the books of the Bible should be. But I realized that by looking to the Church as an authentic and reliable Witness to the canon, I was violating the principle of *sola scriptura*. The "Bible only" theory turned out to be self-refuting, since it cannot tell us which books belong in it and which don't!

What was more, my studies in Church history showed that the canon of the Bible was not finally settled until about three hundred years after the last apostle died. If I was going to claim that the Church had done its job and picked exactly the right books for the Bible, this meant that the Church had made an infallible decision three hundred years *after* the apostolic age, a realization which made it believable that the Church could make even later infallible decisions, and that the Church could make such decisions even today.

A year or two after reading Leon's paper on Mary, I read a book by a Catholic author who gave a long quote from Matthew 16 in his section on the pope. In this passage Christ says, "You are Peter and on this rock I will build my Church." Up to this time I had always thought the rock on which the church was built is the *revelation* that Jesus is the Christ, and I could argue this position well. As my eyes scanned the passage, I noticed for the first time a structural feature in the text which *required* that Peter be the rock.

In Matthew 16:17-19 Jesus makes three statements to Peter: (a) "Blessed are you Simon Bar-Jonah," (b) "You are Peter," and (c) "I will give you the keys to the kingdom." The first of these is clearly a blessing, something which builds Peter up and magnifies him. Christ declares him blessed because he has had a special revelation from God. The third statement is also a blessing: Christ declares that he will give Peter the keys to the kingdom of heaven. This is clearly a beatitude, something that magnifies and builds Peter up. And if Christ's first and third statements to Peter are blessings, the middle statement in its immediate context must also be a blessing.

This was a problem, because in order to defend the view that Peter is *not* the rock on which the Church is built, I had to appeal to a minor difference in the Greek text between the word used for Peter (*Petros*) and the word used for rock (*petra*).

According to standard anti-Catholic interpretation, *Petros* means "a small stone" while *petra* means "a large mass of rock," and the statement "You are Peter [*Petros*]," should be interpreted as something that stresses Peter's insignificance. Evangelicals picture Christ as having meant, "You are a small stone, Peter, but I will build my Church on this great mass of rock which is the revelation of my identity."

One problem with this interpretation, which many Protestant Bible scholars admit,[1] is that while *Petros* and *petra* did have these meanings in some ancient Greek poetry, the distinction was gone by the first century, when Matthew's Gospel was written. At that time the two words meant the same thing: a rock. Another problem is that when he addressed Peter, Jesus was not speaking Greek, but Aramaic, a cousin language of Hebrew. In Aramaic there is no difference between the two words which in Greek are rendered as *petros* and *petra*. They are both *kepha;* that's why Paul often refers to Peter as *Cephas*[2] (cf. 1 Cor. 15:5, Gal. 2:9). What Christ actually said was, "You are *Kepha* and on this *kepha* I will build my Church." But even if the words *Petros* and *petra* did have different meanings, the Protestant reading of two different "rocks" would not fit the context.

The second statement to Peter would be something which minimized or diminished him, pointing out his

---

[1] For example, D.A. Carson admits this in his commentary on Matthew in *The Expositor's Bible Commentary*, Frank Gaeblin, ed. (Grand Rapids: Zondervan, first edition).

[2] *Cephas* is the Greek transliteration of the Aramaic *Kephas* (sometimes rendered *Kepha* or *Kêpa*). The Gospels contain a number of Hebrew and Aramaic words and phrases which were transliterated into Greek for the benefit of non-Jewish readers. See, for example, John's usage of the Hebrew and Aramaic terms *messiah* and *Kephas* in John 1:41-42. This passage sheds light on the apparent difference in meaning of *Petros* and *petra* in Matthew 16:18. John 1:41 says Simon Bar-Jonah's new name would be *Kephas* (a massive rock) "which is translated Peter" (*Petros*).

insignificance, with the result that Jesus would be saying, "*Blessed* are you, Simon Bar-Jonah! You are an *insignificant* little pebble. Here are the *keys* to the kingdom of heaven!" Such an incongruous sequence of statements would have been not merely odd, but inexplicable. (Many Protestant commentators recognize this and do their best to deny the obvious sense of this passage, however implausible their explanations may be.)

I also noticed that the Lord's three statements to Peter had two parts, and the second parts explain the first. The reason Peter was "blessed" was because "flesh and blood has not revealed this to you, but my Father who is in heaven" (v.17). The meaning of the name change, "You are Rock," is explained by the promise, "On this rock I will build my church, and the powers of death shall not prevail against it" (v. 18). The purpose of the keys is explained by Jesus' commission, "Whatever you bind on earth shall be bound in heaven, and whatever you loose on earth shall be loosed in heaven" (v.19). A careful reading of these three statements, paying attention to their immediate context and interrelatedness, clearly shows that Peter was the rock about which Jesus spoke.

These and other considerations showed me that the standard anti-Catholic interpretations of this text could not stand up to careful biblical scrutiny. They were forced to wrench the middle statement to Peter out of its context. I reversed my interpretation, conclude that Peter was indeed the rock on which Jesus built his Church. This is, I believe, what an unbiased reader looking at the grammar and literary structure of the text would conclude.

If Peter in fact was the rock Jesus was talking about, that meant he was the head apostle (The Greek text reveals that Peter alone was singled out for this praise, and he alone was given the special authority symbolized by the keys of the kingdom of heaven, though other disciples shared in a more general sense Peter's authority of binding and loosing [cf. Matt. 18:18]). If he was the head apostle, then once Christ had ascended into heaven,

Peter would have been the earthly head of the Church, subordinate to Christ's heavenly headship.

And if Peter was the earthly head of the Church, he fit the most basic definition of the office of the pope. As a result, I had to conclude that the Catholics were right in saying that Peter was the first pope. Whether Christ intended there to be any other popes was a question I still had to settle, but already I had seen enough to know that I would have to re-investigate Catholic theology. If Catholics could be right on this issue, they could be right on other issues as well. It unsettled me to know they were right on the sacrament of confession.

I relent

I knew I had a lot of theological re-investigation to do, so over the next year I began reading Catholic doctrine intensively. During this time I softened my stance on Catholicism. I began taking my wife to Mass and also became willing to be married in the Church. On December 1, 1991, she and I were married by Fr. Mark Wood, the priest of the parish Renée attended. The service was extremely simple (we had two witnesses, my wife's sister and nephew), and it took only five minutes. The shortest wedding I have ever been to was my own, but it was still very meaningful to both of us.

As far as Renée knew, my view of Catholicism had softened but I still remained opposed to the Church on theological grounds. I decided to keep hidden from her the fact I was actually thinking about converting. After all we had been through, I could not cruelly get her hopes up and then disappoint her if I discovered some fatal flaw in Catholic teaching. In January 1992 I let Renée in on the secret I had been keeping and told her I might be joining the Catholic Church. This made her happy, though, ironically, I seemed more excited about it than she did.

As Lent approached, I began to make plans to enter the Church at Easter Vigil. This did not work out, but in the process of getting ready I notified my Protestant friends of the direction in which I was heading. They took the news pretty well; after all, some of the groundwork had been laid when Leon's family and a number of other people from my church had become Catholics.

One thing I was concerned about was that since my wife was a Catholic people might think I was converting to please her. This was not the case. On a human level, if my interaction with her over Catholicism would have done anything, it would have made me resent the Church. Catholic apologist Scott Hahn once told me he was surprised I did not give up theology altogether after I suffered the disappointment of giving up my career because of Renée's Catholicism. Fortunately my Protestant friends knew me well enough to know this was not a conversion for the sake of my marriage.

Then something happened that would change my life forever. In late June 1992, shortly after her twenty-seventh birthday, Renée became ill. At first we thought it was a flare-up of her ulcerative colitis, since the symptoms were the same: loss of appetite, periodic intestinal pain, and general weakness. Whatever it was, it also triggered a reflex in her body which brought on severe muscular back pain and headaches.

Via Dolorosa
Almost from the time the intestinal pain began Renée was bedridden, unable to eat and too weak to move. When the back and head pains started, all she could do was lie still and moan. I remember days when I would lie on the bed beside her, as she cried from the pain while I whispered words to help her vent her frustration and distress at what was happening to her.

We had trouble getting doctors to treat her for the pain. Her chiropractor helped some, as did a massage therapist. Then one day when Renée was having a massage for the back pain, her therapist discovered a large lump at the base of her neck, just above her left collarbone. We had never seen this lump before and figured that it must have come up very quickly.

The next day we took Renée to the first in a series of doctors who performed x-rays, CAT scans, ultrasounds, biopsies, and a colonoscopy. They didn't find just one lump in her body; there were dozens everywhere — in her lymph nodes, her lungs, her liver, and in her colon. One tumor in her colon was the size of a baseball. It turned out that she had an advanced case of malignant colon cancer, which would certainly kill her.

The surgeon who broke this news to us did not have much of a bedside manner. Because Renée was now unable to walk, I had rented a wheel chair and wheeled her into the surgeon's office, where she had sat slumped, unable to sit up straight due to exhaustion. When the doctor finally arrived, he spent only a few minutes with us. Renée was forced to sit upright as the doctor checked the dressing on her shoulder where a biopsy on her neck mass had been done. Weakened from lack of food and sleep, Renée cried as the doctor peeled back the adhesive tape on the dressing. I remember her long, brown hair, normally her most beautiful feature, matting on her skin from the tears. While examining the wound, the doctor curtly informed us, "I am afraid we have a malignant process going on here."

After this brief and graceless encounter with the surgeon, Renée again slumped forward in her chair, trying to regain her composure and absorb the shock of his terse sentence. In a daze I wheeled her across the courtyard to the first of several meetings with her cancer specialist. Although we had to wait interminably for him to arrive, we were relieved to find he had a much more sensitive way of dealing with his patients. Before he entered the room to see Renée, I stepped outside and privately told him it would be better not to discuss possible time frames regarding how long she might live. She was not ready for that subject yet. The doctor said that would be no problem since he as yet had little idea how long she might be expected to live. One particular memory of that conversation was my mention of Pope John Paul II's successful operation to remove an orange-sized benign tumor in his intestines which had been discovered that very week. Renée was not as lucky as the pope.

We put her in the hospital for a week of chemotherapy, then took her home for a couple of days before having to return her to the hospital. This was necessary because a device they had used to give her the chemotherapy had caused a blood clot to form in one of her arms. Once Renée was back in the hospital, the nurses became concerned she might get pneumonia from being unable to sit up. Pneumonia would be particularly dangerous because the chemotherapy from the previous week was killing off her white blood cells, which she would need to fight the disease.

It was hard not knowing how long Renée had to live. According to her doctor, she could have gone instantly from a blood clot, or in a week from pneumonia, or in a few weeks or months from the cancer. I realized that things were moving too quickly, and so I called my parish and left a message for the priest, who came to our hospital room that night. He and I talked about Renée's condition and about my coming into the Church.

A week or so earlier I had told him I was virtually ready to join. I had been more or less ready intellectually for some time, but when we discovered Renée had terminal colon cancer, I began to feel that God was telling me I had delayed long enough and that it was time to make a commitment. The fact that my wife was dying did not determine *that* I would join the Catholic Church, but it did help answer the question of *when* I would join: soon. I very much wanted to give her the present of the two of us being united in one Church and one faith before she died.

It was a Friday night when he and I talked, and we planned on my entering the Church the next Sunday. But Saturday morning Renée's condition had grown critical, and I was told she could stop breathing at any moment. A doctor had already been summoned, and he was expected to put Renée in the intensive care unit.

I called Fr. Wood and told him we had to move our schedule up. I needed to come into the Church *now*. It could not wait until the next day. He said he would be right there. But before he arrived, the doctor came and informed me that he had examined Renée's chest x-ray, and that the pneumonia the nurses feared was not the problem. Her breathing problems were caused by numerous, small tumors in her lungs.

While her long-term prognosis was no better, she was not in the kind of immediate danger we thought. The doctor estimated she probably still had a few weeks left to live. This was very heartening news. I had worried she would die immediately or within the next few days. At least this way, she and I had a little more time to prepare ourselves for the parting we knew would come.

Shortly afterward, Renée received her first morphine shot. Then our priest arrived. In private, he gave me the sacrament of confession. Then, in Renée's hospital room, using the emergency, shortened form of the rites, he brought me into the Church. He gave me conditional baptism, and then confirmed me. After giving Renée the anointing of the sick, he gave us the Eucharist, which he had brought from the tabernacle in our parish. My wife and I communicated together for the first and last time, sharing pieces from the same host. Although Renée was able to receive communion the next day, I was not present for that. This was the only time the two of us would share the Lord Jesus in this way.

Because of the morphine injection Renée had received immediately before Fr. Wood arrived, she was very sleepy during my reception into the Church. But she knew what was going on and tried to participate as best she could, such as when she managed to eat a small fragment of the host when we received communion. When my reception into the Catholic Church was completed, I hugged her and told her I was inside the Church. There was a beautiful, peaceful smile on her face — a smile which lasted a long time.

One night Renée paid me what is probably the greatest compliment I will ever receive in this life. I was in the hospital waiting area when Renée's mother came and told me that Renée was demanding to see me. I went to her room and discovered she had awakened and, though groggy, wanted me to arrange for her to get another morphine shot. This was something her mother or anyone could have done for her. All it required was pushing the call button for the nurse to come. But even in her semi-conscious state, Renée relied on *me* to get it for her. Many in her situation might have retreated into a childlike state, clinging to their mothers for help, but Renée had clung to me. Though groggy and in pain, the thought stood out in her mind: "James is here. James will take care of me. He will see that I get what I need." As I realized this my heart ached anew with the pain of losing her.

After she had been on morphine for a few days, I began to worry that Renée was sleeping too much. She was only waking up long enough to ask for another morphine shot and then would go right back to sleep. I feared she would sleep away the rest of her life and I would not have a chance to talk seriously with her before she died. I prayed desperately to God that I could have just twenty minutes of lucid time with her to tell her some things before she died.

God gave me those twenty minutes, and between two morphine naps I was able to have the conversation with Renée that I needed. I told her softly how much I loved her and how much everyone else did as well. I said that, once she was on the other side, she would be able to look into my mind and see how much I loved her. I began to cry. At her behest I put my head down on the bed beside her, and she put her arm clumsily around the back of my head, to comfort me as best she could. Afterwards I felt much better, and sensed that Renée and I were as prepared for her departure as we could be.

The next morning I spoke to Scott Hahn on the phone about 10:30 a.m. The two of us had become phone friends during my conversion process. He was going to pray in front of the Holy Eucharist at 11:00, so I asked him to pray that Renée would respond spiritually to the things I was telling her, that she would die quickly, and that the doctors would be unable to resuscitate her. Scott went to pray in front of the Eucharist at 11:00, and Renée died at about 11:10. As I later realized, Scott was in front of Jesus praying for exactly the things that happened at exactly the time they happened —a divine coincidence which has been of enormous comfort to me. At the end Renée looked me straight in the eyes. I told her that everything would be okay, to trust God, and that I loved her. Then I kissed her on the lips. With that, Renée and I parted.

I believe that God brought us together to give each other gifts. I gave her the gift of freedom from the New Age movement, and in the end I helped give her the gift of eternal life. Renée helped give me the gift of Catholicism because as a result of my marriage to her I studied Catholic theology harder than I otherwise would have. Even though I was studying it so I could try to pull her out of the Church, it was that very study which led me to recognize that the Catholic faith is the faith of the Bible.

Renée is still giving me gifts. One of the things I did in my conversation with her the day before she died was give her a list of things to pray for when she was on the other side. Now that she has gone to be with Christ, even if she is not yet fully united with him, she can pray for me in a more powerful way than she ever could have while on earth.

I am comforted that Renée is praying for me, an intercessor I can still talk to in times of need, who is even now asking God to show me how I can best serve him in his Holy, Catholic Church during the remainder of *my* life.

A Prodigal's Journey

Steve Wood

W E SAT on metal folding chairs, shivering under wool blankets as we peered into the windows of the building. Although I had arrived early for the mid-week service, this little church on the edge of Costa Mesa, California was already filled to capacity. "How strange!" I thought to myself. "At my home church in Florida I could come late to the Sunday service and easily get a front row seat." Here I was at a mid-week service and the best I could get was a seat *outside* the building and a loud speaker that brought me the voice of the preacher I watched through the side windows.

This church was packed with young people who bore the identifying marks of the youth counter-culture: Levi's, tee-shirts, and long hair. I found it hard to believe what I was seeing. This church was filled with hippies singing praises to Jesus and studying the Bible!

Something very different from what I was used to was going on here, and I was thrilled to be part of it. I had no inkling that day I first visited Calvary Chapel that I was witnessing the cultural surprise of the early 1970s. A worldwide phenomenon was about to explode from Calvary Chapel, making it one of the "mother churches" of what would soon become known as the "Jesus Movement."

I took the prodigal's route to Calvary Chapel. During the late 60s I was caught up by the rebellious winds of the

the counter-culture that blew across college campuses. In high school I pursued the "wild and crazy" scene — a pursuit that went into high gear while I attended the University of Florida. I joined the wildest, hardest-drinking fraternity on campus. But this didn't seem to be enough to sate my appetite for thrills, so a few of us formed a sub-fraternity, within our fraternity, called the "berserkers."

After a while, I began to sense that hedonism and carousing couldn't deliver the satisfaction I and my generation were desperately searching for. I was in college to prepare myself to land a great job and achieve the financial success at the heart of the American dream, yet this didn't seem to offer much of an incentive for me. Something was missing. I had no idea where I was headed in life or what meaning my existence had beyond my limited universe of daily classes, sporadic studying, and the moral squalor of our fraternity beer parties. But since I was aware enough to realize, however dimly, that I wasn't finding answers to any of life's big questions at the University of Florida, I decided to drop out of college.

The Vietnam War was in full swing, and as a college dropout I had two alternatives — enlist in the military (and get the branch of my choice) or be drafted. So I enlisted in the Naval Reserves. During my active duty the counter-culture was exploding, even in the military. On my ship marijuana was almost as common as Marlboros. Many of us looked to the Woodstock rock festival as the dawn of a new era. We saw ourselves as the "Woodstock Generation," and we wanted freedom from vain materialism, war, the strictures of conservative politics, and Christian moral taboos — the legacy, we naïvely supposed, of our parents' decidedly un-hip generation. These counter-culture yearnings awakened in me deeper desires for meaning and purpose in life. I began to reflect on the question: "Is there a spiritual meaning to my life?" I felt I had to find out.

My discovery of the answer began when my ship was home-ported in Norfolk, Virginia. During my free time I began studying various Eastern religions and enlightenment practices at Edgar Cayce's Institute in Virginia Beach. I earned the nickname "Cosmic Man" as word of my new interests spread to my shipmates. I became convinced that fulfillment would come with a freeing of my karma and moving to a higher form of consciousness.

A friend who served as my personal guru told me I needed to investigate Christianity before I could move on to a higher plane of consciousness. I protested, sneering, "I went to Sunday school." He assured me that it was with a purpose that I was born into a Christian family. I needed to study Christianity so I could then move on to some "weightier" religion. Overcoming my initial reluctance, I decided to study the Bible.

Immediately, I was faced with a decision: which Bible? There were so many different translations to choose from. Some were just New Testaments. Some were New and Old Testaments. At the Cayce Institute there were even editions that claimed to include lost and hidden books of the Bible. Which one was the right one? Faced with this bewildering choice I decided to meditate in front of the various Bibles at the Cayce Institute bookstore and would purchase the one that gave me the best "vibes."

I ended up with a *New English Version* of the Old and New Testaments. As I was paying the cashier, she asked me to pray before I read the Bible. "Okay," I said politely, but without really meaning it. Amazingly, she withheld the Bible from me until I promised her I'd ask God to help me understand the Bible. Somewhat sheepish at her insistence, I promised, but it was a promise I kept. When I got home I said a heartfelt prayer before starting to read.

To my astonishment, the Scriptures seemed to be opened to my understanding. I felt as though God were speaking to me personally through the pages of Scripture. My appreciation for Christianity soared. I came to believe that Jesus was the one through whom true enlightenment was found. He claimed to be "the light of the world." To his followers he promised "the light of life." I wanted to follow Jesus Christ, but I wasn't sure how.

It didn't take much Bible reading to discover that I was a sinner and needed Christ's forgiveness. I went through two rounds of repenting of my sins and privately confessing them to God, but I felt no different. About this time a shipmate gave me a little, red Penny Bible that someone had lost or thrown away. It contained Scripture passages showing our sinfulness and how Christ promises to cleanse us whiter than snow from our sins. It also contained a short prayer of repentance and belief.

I said the prayer earnestly and was enveloped in a wave of conviction for my past sins. The reality and gravity of my years of rebellion, stubborn will, and ingratitude toward God loomed before me. I recoiled in horror from this realization of my sinfulness and wondered if a person like me could ever be forgiven by God. I pled for forgiveness and cast myself on his mercy. I went to bed wondering if I could ever find acceptance with God.

Awakened by pre-dawn reveille, I rolled out of my bunk a new man. I felt lighter; the weight of my guilt was gone. A tremendous joy and a burst of new life filled my heart. I *knew* my sins were forgiven! God had accepted me!

At breakfast in the mess hall, my best friend, Jack, noticed my unusual behavior. He gawked at the broad smile on my face. "Steve, for the sake of our friendship, I am going to ask you to dump whatever drugs you're on over the side of the ship." "I'm not 'on' anything," I said. Then in a rush of words, I excitedly told him about my encounter with Jesus, my repentance and prayer for forgiveness, and the incredible feeling of joy and freedom that I had as a result. Jack started choking, and spat out his scrambled eggs, looking at me with amazement.

Once out to sea, other shipmates noticed the change in me. Thinking I was hoarding some drugs that were responsible for the "super-high" they thought I was on, a group of sailors surrounded me, demanding that I share my secret stash with them. They didn't believe me when I explained that it was Jesus who was causing this effect in me; one even threatened me with his fist in my face. This group watched me closely to see where my hiding place was for my supply of drugs.

My shipmates wondered what had happened to me until *Time* magazine featured "The Jesus Revolution" emblazoned on the cover. I (and as I soon learned, most of my shipmates) scrutinized the article, looking carefully at the faces of those who were "finding Jesus." The article told of hundreds of hippies in California who were having conversion experiences similar to mine. Word spread quickly around the ship: "Wood is a Jesus freak!" Most of the guys thought my new-found belief in Jesus amusing, and some derisively gave me the "One Way" sign (an upraised index finger) when I'd pass by. But I wasn't bothered by their mocking; it actually made me more convinced I had made the right choice.

It took me twenty-one years to realize that Jesus was what I had been looking for in life. Now I faced another question. Where do I find Jesus' church? I never imagined that it would be another two decades of searching for the answer to this question. I started visiting churches in the Norfolk and Virginia Beach area in my search for the "real" church. Since I had been raised a Presbyterian, I first attended a Presbyterian church . What I found was a church that differed little from contemporary culture in its attempt to be trendy and open-minded. But I was looking for something different, something truly "counter-cultural."

I visited other mainline Protestant churches, even a Pentecostal "holy roller" church. I didn't have a sufficient knowledge of Christianity to evaluate the various churches I was visiting, so all I could do was observe the worshipers during the service. I reasoned that if Jesus was really present in a particular congregation, he would have a profound effect on the peoples' lives. I was disappointed with what I found. I remember waiting for the service to begin in one particular church and hearing two women discussing another woman's new hairdo. It didn't seem like Jesus was having much of an impact on the people there.

My guru friend who had suggested I read the Bible told me about St. Francis of Assisi. He said St. Francis really *lived* his Christianity, and that he still had some followers who lived in monasteries. About to be released from the Navy, I headed for a phone booth with a pocket full of quarters. I made a lot of calls before I finally reached a Franciscan monastery. I blurted out that I was a newly-dedicated follower of Jesus, and that I wanted to join the monastery upon my discharge from the Navy. I could sense the puzzlement on the other end of the phone. The man explained that I had to be a Catholic before I could join the monastery. Since denomination labels had little meaning for me, I said, "Okay, I am a Catholic. Now can I come?" Now he was really puzzled. He responded by saying that I had to be a Catholic for at least one year. I was deflated. I thought I was so close to finding a group of committed Christians. I thanked him but said I couldn't wait a year to follow Jesus.

The path to Rome via Costa Mesa

I went back to Florida not knowing what to do about finding a good church. In Florida I ran into one of my friends from the University of Florida. We had both gotten caught up in the counter-culture craze and had grown disillusioned with our career track at the university. We both dropped out of college and joined the Navy Reserves. He had been stationed in California and had a spiritual experience very similar to mine, with one exception. He had found a really dynamic church. He told me what was happening at Calvary Chapel in Costa Mesa. With his encouragement, I moved 3,000 miles to be near this church. I arrived in Costa Mesa in 1971 and quickly enrolled in an Assembly of God college down the street from Calvary Chapel, so I could begin religious studies. I felt as though I had reached the promised land.

Calvary Chapel attracted me and so many others because it offered a style of worship dramatically different from what was available in mainline Protestant churches. The most immediately noticeable difference was that Calvary Chapel was *exciting*. It was experiencing explosive growth as it evangelized the counter-culture in non-threatening ways.

Through Calvary Chapel's aggressive evangelization programs, young people were being challenged by the gospel, and hundreds responded, finding new meaning in life by deciding to follow Jesus. The church had to move into a large circus tent while a new sanctuary was constructed. Unlike other churches I had visited, at Calvary Chapel the seats in the front row seats filled up *first*. Also, the vibrant praise and singing at Calvary Chapel were so different from the lifeless singing in many mainline Protestant churches.

For many, the singing at Calvary Chapel is what caused the deepest impression. I remember the Sunday morning I brought my mother and uncle to a Sunday service. They were reluctant and somewhat uncomfortable to attend a church that met in a circus tent. But seeing the joyful faces and hearing the heart-felt singing during the worship service deeply moved both of them.

Another reason Calvary Chapel was such a magnet to young people was its many Bible studies. At Calvary Chapel you could attend a Bible study on almost every night of the week. To this day, though I strongly disagree with much of his theology, I am deeply indebted to Pastor Chuck Smith for his systematic Bible teaching. To a large extent, he was responsible for imparting to me a deep love for Scripture and a strong desire to study it. Every Sunday evening he would teach from several chapters of Scripture, covering the entire Bible in a two-year period. I have never lost my deep appreciation for Pastor Smith's down-to-earth, heartfelt, and understandable Bible teaching.

At Calvary Chapel I was given my first ministry experience, working in the children's church. Within a few months I found myself in charge of the fastest growing Sunday school and children's ministry in Southern California. A few months later I also started a junior high ministry. It was a rewarding time, and the experience was invaluable. Within a couple of years I was invited to teach for a semester in Calvary Chapel's Bible school for ministry training.

It was during my stint at Bible school that I realized with sadness that I couldn't remain at Calvary Chapel. My differences with the pastor's views on prophecy were simply irreconcilable. Chuck Smith and the other leaders at Calvary Chapel championed the doctrine of the "secret rapture," a special resurrection and assumption into heaven reserved only for born-again Christians. The "secret rapture," Smith taught, would occur 1007 years before the end of human history. After I had learned New Testament Greek I saw that the biblical text did not support Smith's teachings about a "secret rapture." Also, my study of early Church history showed that the Calvary Chapel idea of a "secret rapture," was not held by early Christians. This bothered me.

Calvary Chapel prides itself in being "non-denominational" and in its avoidance of the restrictions of a written creed. Yet I learned that non-denominational churches can be far more rigid and denominational than the mainline creed-oriented churches. I now call non-denominational churches "non-denominational denominations." The unwritten creed in non-denominational churches is whatever the pastor happens to believe. Woe to the member who crosses the line and disagree with the pastor.

I decided to leave Calvary Chapel and went back to Florida to begin sharing the Jesus Movement there. I started beach and campus Bible studies, worked in youth evangelism projects, led prison ministries, organized an adult institute of biblical studies. I became a youth pastor at an inter-denominational charismatic church, and in 1978 I was ordained a minister by this church.

That same year I both met and married my wife, Karen. Around the time of our marriage the church I was serving in went through a terrible split. It was one of the most unpleasant experiences of my life. It opened my eyes to see that church splits were a regular feature of independent churches and of Protestantism in general. A desire for church stability and unity was planted like a seed in my heart.

I felt ready to pursue additional theological studies, so Karen and I moved to Massachusetts so I could enroll in Gordon-Conwell Theological Seminary. During my seminary studies there, I had a burning compulsion to find the answer to a theological question: infant baptism. Karen was pregnant with our first child, and we wanted to decide whether or not we should baptize the baby. Calvary Chapel had taught me to renounce infant baptism as "unbiblical." So I rejected it even though I had been baptized as an infant. I was under the impression that some Protestant groups baptized babies merely because they had leftover trappings of Roman Catholicism that should have been abandoned at the Reformation. But in seminary I was studying under Protestant theologians who had a deep personal devotion to Christ and who believed in infant baptism.

With our baby's birth almost upon us, what had been a question of no importance was now a question of supreme importance. I was about to become a father and I wanted to do the right thing regarding baptism.

Around this time, some Reformed-Presbyterian friends introduced me to a covenantal perspective of Scripture. A covenant is the special relationship God establishes with his people. From this perspective I saw the various Old Testament covenants — such as those with Adam, Noah, Abraham, and David — along with the New Covenant explained in the New Testament, form a unified theme running from Genesis through Revelation. I also saw that just as both the Old and the New Testaments shed light on each other, so too, the Old Covenants help us understand the New Covenant.

The Old Testament was clear about the necessity of giving the covenant sign of circumcision to children of believers. The New Testament said baptism replaced circumcision as the sign of membership and entrance into the New Covenant. If children received the covenant sign in the Old Testament, I reasoned, then they certainly should in the New Covenant as well.

After graduating from seminary, I returned to Florida to start my own church. I continued to wrestle with the infant baptism question, but after several months I became convinced that infant baptism was not only permissible, but important. So, I baptized my baby girl when she was thirteen months old. Seeing that the anti-infant-baptism teaching was incorrect and that the more historic forms of the church, both Protestant and Catholic, were right on this issue was a turning point for me. I was humbled by this historic Christian teaching that I had previously scorned. This led me to embrace a new attitude towards more "established" forms of the Church. One of the fruits of this shift in perspective was that my new congregation sought affiliation with an evangelical Presbyterian denomination.

My life was busy with a growing family and pastoring a new congregation. As pastor of my own church I had the liberty to try some innovations that would never fly in a more established, denominational setting. I introduced my congregation to something that had transformed my conception of the church and Christian worship: the weekly celebration of the Lord's Supper.

Most Presbyterians celebrate the Lord's Supper every three months, or at most, monthly. I was convinced from New Testament and historical studies that the pattern in the early Church was a weekly Lord's Supper. I saw the Protestant reluctance to regularly practice the Lord's

Supper as an unfortunate fruit of the Protestant Reformation that smacked of an overreaction to the "errors" of Catholicism. It struck me as ironic that on the front of our communion table were engraved Jesus' words, "Do this," and yet we were not regularly doing it. So we changed our worship practice. I'm convinced the Lord used this small liturgical change to prepare me for the greater theological changes he had planned for me.

During my Calvary Chapel days I had a very low view of the sacraments; I was almost anti-sacramental. But when I discovered the true role of baptism and the Lord's Supper in Christian worship and living, a corresponding appreciation for the role of the Church began to blossom. That's when I did something really dangerous. I started reading the early Church Fathers firsthand. I had studied some early Church history, but too much of it was from perspectives limited by Protestant history textbooks. I was shocked to discover in the writings of the first-, second-, and third-century Christians a very high view of the Church and liturgy, very much unlike the views of the typical Evangelical Protestant. The worship and government of the early Church didn't look anything like the things I saw at Calvary Chapel or my own congregation. It looked a lot more, well, Catholic.

The testimony of history

Studying the Apostolic Fathers, the earliest of the Church Fathers, terribly upset my Presbyterian convictions. You see the word "Presbyterian" comes from *presbuteros*, the Greek word meaning elder. The name of the Presbyterian Church reflects the belief that the Church is to be ruled by elders, not by bishops. My studies showed, however, that the early Church was ruled by bishops. Early Church history attested that the apostles had laid hands on men and installed them as bishops. Once I became a Presbyterian minister I thought my search for the Church was over. But now Church history was forcing me on.

Pastoral necessity prohibited me from speaking openly of my pilgrimage towards a fuller expression of the Church. Thankfully, I had Karen with whom to share my growing convictions. We were on this pilgrimage as a couple, though we weren't sure of our destination.

We thought we had two options for a more historic and scriptural expression of the Church, the Episcopal Church, or an Evangelical wing of the Orthodox Church. The Roman Catholic Church, although ruled by bishops, was an unthinkable option.

Our anti-Catholicism was still strong enough to rule *that* choice out entirely. For one thing, Roman Catholicism was abhorrent to my Evangelical spiritual sensitivities. My chief opposition to Catholicism stemmed from my belief that the Catholic Church was leading millions of people to hell because of its teachings on salvation. I thought, as I had been told by countless Protestants from Calvary Chapel to seminary, that the Catholic Church denied that salvation was by grace alone. Since the Bible is clear that salvation is by grace, not by works, and since I thought the Catholic Church taught salvation by works, as far as I was concerned, Catholicism was fatally wrong. What I didn't realize was that the Catholic Church has consistently condemned the idea of salvation by works, teaching that salvation comes solely by God's free gift of grace. Later, when the Catholic position was explained to me, I was amazed at how often it is misrepresented and caricatured by Protestant critics.

But before I investigated the issue of salvation, I first had to answer a more fundamental theological question that had troubled me for a long time. It came to a head in 1986 when I realized I simply couldn't reconcile two pieces in the biblical puzzle.

The first piece of the puzzle was Christ's high priestly prayer recorded in John 17:1-26, specifically the phrase, "I pray not only for them, but also for those who will believe in me through their word, so that they may be one, as you, Father, are in me and I in you, that they may also be in us, . . . so that they may be one, as we are one, I in them and you in me, that they may be brought to perfection as one . . . " (v. 20-23). In this prayer, offered to the Father the night before the crucifixion, Jesus prayed for a visible supernatural unity in his Church. I was struck by the Lord's strong emphasis on the unity of his Church, as illustrated by his repetition of the phrase, "so that they may be one."

The second piece to the puzzle was in James 5:16, "The prayer of a righteous man has great power in its effects." Here was the problem: Jesus is *perfectly* righteous. Why, I asked myself over and over again, was his prayer for the unity of his Church not realized? How could Protestantism be his "church" when Protestant was nothing but disintegration, splintered, not unified, a frightening proliferation of squabbling, competing denominations, many masquerading under the title "non-denominational." The disunity and doctrinal chaos with Protestantism became deeply unsettling to me. I found I couldn't recite the Nicene Creed without the words "I believe in the one, holy, catholic, and apostolic church" raising afresh this troublesome question.

A Catholic reading this will say that the answer to the puzzle is easy. There is one, unified, and visible Church. It is the Catholic Church. It has been in existence since Christ established it 2000 years ago. Yet, as an Evangelical Protestant, I found it *unthinkable* that the Catholic Church could be the missing piece to the puzzle. As far as I was concerned, the Catholic Church was not a real Christian church at all. Calvary Chapel had taught me that the Catholic Church had completely departed from the Christian gospel long ago, when it stopped teaching that one is saved by grace alone. I had seen no reason to dispute this conviction.

My stubborn refusal to even consider the Catholic Church was obliterated in 1986 when something unthinkable occurred. Scott Hahn and Gerry Matatics, two of the brightest and most zealously anti-Catholic of my seminary friends were thinking about becoming Catholics! When I heard this through the grapevine I was stunned. I couldn't believe it! I quickly got in touch with Gerry and, to my shock, was informed that Scott was a lost cause to Catholicism. He was very close to becoming a Catholic. I was relieved that Gerry seemed to have slipped less far down the slippery slope to Rome, and I hoped he might still be willing to listen to reason. We'd been friends in seminary, so I felt it was my Christian duty to rescue him from the clutches of Rome. With grim determination I set out to expose for him all the Romanist errors he had somehow missed.

Gerry and I rekindled our friendship by telephone. In seminary he had helped me to develop my covenantal understanding of Scripture and the case for infant baptism. It was time for me to return the favor. During our long conversations I found myself secretly agreeing with many of his reasons for wanting to move to a "higher" church setting. But I still urged Gerry to consider an option other than Catholicism. He didn't listen to my advice. He too converted to the Catholic Church that spring.

I was nonplused at these two defections from "biblical Christianity." I had been able to view abstractly the biblical arguments for Catholicism that Scott and Gerry had shared with me, keeping them at arms-length. But when these two hard-core anti-Catholic Evangelicals actually *converted* to Catholicism, I knew I had to confront honestly the possibility that Rome might be right. This opened up for me a whole new area of investigation, and I began to read scores of books on the issue. Over and over again, the Catholic Church had the answers to all of my biblical objections. The clues I had been searching for began to fall into place.

The Catholic Church has bishops who claim apostolic succession, and can back it up biblically and historically; the Catholic Church, unlike Protestantism, possesses visible doctrinal unity; and like the early Church I had read about so wistfully, the Catholic Church had the Eucharist at the center of its worship. These truths intrigued me, but other questions arose. What about Mary? What about salvation by works? What about the Mass and purgatory and praying to the saints? — doctrines which I thought denied the finished work of Christ on the Cross? A huge misunderstanding of these Catholic beliefs still kept me at a distance from Catholicism. Yet there was one aspect of Catholicism that deeply attracted me.

In the midst of this period of searching for the true Church I was intensely involved in the pro-life movement. Anyone immersed in the pro-life movement will find Catholics everywhere! Through my involvement with Operation Rescue I saw exceptional Christian piety in the lives of the Catholics I met and worked with. This impressed me as no doctrinal arguments ever could have. Sharing a prison cell with Catholics helped me to recognize them as my spiritual friends. I knew that we are living through the greatest holocaust of innocent human lives, the bloodiest assault upon the kingdom of God in human history, and Catholics were standing shoulder-to-shoulder with me and other Evangelicals fighting this horror. Catholics, I began to see, were certainly not God's enemies.

By 1986 I had been fighting the pro-abortion extremists for more than a decade, with not much visible success. I was open for answers that got to the root causes of the abortion holocaust. Catholic pro-life leaders were providing clear and convincing answers. The abortion holocaust, they explained, is the direct result of the sexual revolution.

The sexual revolution was the direct result of the contraceptive revolution. They pointed out to me the tragic "coincidence" that both the advent of the pill and the sexual revolution came in the sixties.

I was also shocked when they showed me that until 1930, *every* branch of Protestant Christianity gave a resounding condemnation of artificial birth control. Since then, all Protestant denominations have capitulated and now allow it, and some even promote it. Why, I wondered, was the Catholic Church alone in holding the line in this vital area? Why did the Protestant churches cave in to the Planned Parenthood philosophy?

A few years before joining the Catholic Church, I heard a warning about the abortifacient nature of the pill from a minister friend. The potential for destruction on a vast scale of innocent human life shortly after conception was incomprehensible to me at first. It took a year or so to sink into my mind that the pill causes an incalculable number of in utero deaths.

My first visit to the Catholic Diocese of Venice, Florida, was to talk with the Respect Life director about the abortifacient nature of the pill. I went to see her for a reality check. I wanted to know if it was true that tiny developing babies were being chemically aborted by the thousands, even by sincere pro-life Christians who unwittingly used the pill.

After meeting this Catholic pro-lifer I knew that the future of the abortion battle would not be over clinics, but over chemicals. In the late 1980's, the notorious abortifacient drug, RU-486, was being promoted as "a second generation birth control pill."

Many forms of the pill serve as a pre-implantation abortifacient (i.e., through a chemical action that prevents the baby from implanting in its mother's uterine lining after conception. The child is therefore denied nourishment and dies). RU-486 is simply a post-implantation abortifacient — it dislodges the baby after it has implanted in its mother's uterus. If one accepts the pill, there is no logical, moral, or medical reason not to accept RU-486.

I saw in the Catholic teaching on birth control and contraception the solution for getting at the root of the abortion holocaust and for achieving victory in the abortion battle. I say I "saw" the answer because I couldn't bring myself to embrace it, since it came from the Catholic

Church. I needed another shove to get over my anti-Catholic prejudices. The "shove" came in the form of a theological crisis in my pastorate.

As a pastor, I was witnessing the pain and devastation that the breakdown of marriages was causing couples, and especially their children. After considerable study and reflection, I saw that Scripture taught the indissolubility of the marriage bond.

An examination of history revealed that the teaching of the ancient Church was the same. I saw firsthand that an exception made to Christ's norm on the indissolubility of marriage would grow into a thousand exceptions, resulting in a "norm" that ultimately vanished.

This crisis came to a head during a sermon I was preaching on the Old Testament book of Hosea. Through his unfaithful wife and broken marriage, Hosea was a prophetic picture of the apostasy of Israel. The clearest picture God could give to his apostate people depicting their true spiritual condition was the image of an adulterous spouse. Christian teaching about marriage is not a side issue as many people imagine. From Genesis through Revelation, God uses marriage as an image of his covenant relation with the Church. That's why many of the prophets described the apostasy of the Covenant People as "adultery."

I have to choose

I became very anxious as I was preparing my sermon on the book of Hosea. In this book, the Lord speaks forcefully against unfaithful marriage partners. All of my growing convictions about the indissolubility of marriage came to the front of my consciousness, and I knew I would have to speak frankly on this subject, a subject that was bound to offend people.

Previously, I had been able to ignore these convictions — acting upon them would have enormous implications for my life and for those to whom I was ministering. Many in my congregation were unbiblically divorced and remarried. Some, I am sad to say, had done so with my counsel and approval.

To my surprise, the sermon seemed to go quite well. Nobody walked out. I felt my sermon was faithful to my convictions without unraveling situations in my congregation that would be impossible to repair in my denominational setting. Thinking that the pressure was off, I sat down during the offertory to prepare my thoughts for the Lord's Supper. What followed were five of the most intense minutes of my life.

Suddenly a warning bell went off regarding the Lord's Supper. Paul said, "Whoever eats the bread or drinks the cup of the Lord unworthily will be guilty of the body and blood of the Lord. A person should examine himself, and so eat the bread and drink the cup. For anyone who eats and drinks without discerning the body, eats and drinks damnation unto himself."

My heart was flooded with conviction and sorrow. I felt God was telling me I had no right to administer the Lord's Supper in this situation. I realized that as a pastor, I couldn't continue to overlook the unbiblical marriages in my congregation. The Holy Spirit was prompting me in the strongest possible way to cease, then and there, administering the Lord's Supper. I thought to myself, "Well, I can take some time over the next few weeks to think this over." Yet I sensed deep down that I had reached a critical cross-roads in my spiritual life. I knew that God was passing by, and he was saying to me, "Come now or never."

The implications of obeying raced through my mind. "I have a wife and five children to support. If I do this now, publicly, I will not only be unemployed, but unemployable as a Protestant minister. This isn't just my job, this is my *career*, my calling. I have invested over two decades of my life preparing to be a Protestant minister. How can I throw all of that time and effort away and walk away from my ministry?" I wished I could talk it over with Karen first, but God didn't let up. His call was very direct. "Do it *now* !" He seemed to be saying.

I stood up and walked to the communion table. I apologized to my congregation and said that I was unprepared to administer the Lord's Supper that day. The reaction from the congregation was shocked silence and confused looks. Everyone was wondering why their pastor was "unprepared" to serve them communion. What had he done?

I pronounced a benediction, walked out of the sanctuary, and went into my office. Without looking behind me, I knew I was followed by the elders of the church. It didn't take long to explain my actions to them. A few months before, I had requested that I not be required to assist in the ordination of any man who had been divorced and remarried, sharing with them my beliefs regarding the indissolubility of marriage. I now explained that these beliefs had seized my conscience and my ministry. I knew I couldn't proceed on a course that would permit divorced and remarried individuals to function in the church as though nothing were amiss. I told them that I couldn't continue kidding myself and them that it was all okay. They agreed with me that my ministry in that church was over. But I knew it was over for me as a Protestant minister.

I went home that day in a state of great sadness and worry. I was now not only without a pastorate and a means of supporting my family, I was a man without a church home. When I explained to Karen what had happened, I was deeply thankful for the wonderful wife God had given me. Fully aware that we had a very bumpy road in front of us, she gave me her unconditional support. Unlike the pilgrim in *Pilgrim's Progress*, I was privileged to travel towards the Celestial City with my wife.

A few days later I pulled off my bookshelf a copy of Vatican II and post-Vatican II documents. I said to myself, "I wonder what the Catholic Church has to say about the marriage bond." I opened to *Familiaris Consortio* (*The Christian Declaration on the Family*) by Pope John Paul II. I was astounded by its wisdom, its fidelity to Christ's teaching, and its pastoral graciousness. I was instantly hooked. It was so good that I began to wonder what else the Catholic Church had to say. I was now open for an honest investigation of Catholic teaching. Between Gerry Matatics, Scott Hahn, and Catholic Answers, a well-known apologetics organization, I was amply supplied with books and tapes which explained and defended Catholic teaching.

A few months before this occurred, I had called Gerry to ask for some Catholic materials on marriage, divorce, and remarriage. He responded to my request with a prophetic remark. "It is only a question of time until your views on marriage are going to affect your ecclesiology." This is exactly what happened. I struggled with trying to figure out why such sincere Protestant theologians, Scripture scholars, and pastors could miss what Christ taught about the indissolubility of marriage.

Then it hit me. Protestants are blind to the fact that divorce and remarriage is unlawful because Protestantism itself is an unlawful divorce from the Church. As in Hosea's case, the true spiritual condition of the Covenant People with God is reflected in marriage. There may have been several areas within the Catholic Church that needed change at the time of the Reformation, yet problems within the Church, like problems within a marriage, do not merit a divorce.

A few weeks after I left my pastorate, I was faced with a 60 day jail sentence on the county road gang stemming from my participation in a rescue at an abortion clinic. I told Karen that my secret prayer during the jail time was for an answer in finding the true Church. By special permission, my attorney brought Catholic theology books to the jail. I thought my answer would come in the form of an idea. To my great surprise, we received a visit from the Catholic Bishop of the Diocese of Venice, Most

Rev. John J. Nevins. During his visit he invited my rescue friends and me to be his special guests at a Respect Life Mass at Epiphany Cathedral after our release. I joyfully accepted his invitation. In hindsight, I can see that his visit was a dramatic answer to my prayer in search of the Church.

The diocese arranged for a priest to meet with Karen and me privately as we explored the Catholic Church. I went to the first meeting without Karen to make an initial inquiry. In opening small talk Father Schevers asked where I went to seminary. "You probably never heard of it," I said. "I went to Gordon-Conwell in Massachusetts." He smiled and said he knew the place well. He had taught there for years.

He explained that what is now Gordon-Conwell seminary used to be a Catholic boys school operated by the Carmelite fathers. The Carmelites prayed for vocations to come from the young men at their school. Eventually, though, enrollment dwindled, and they were forced to sell the campus. The new owners were the Protestant founders of Gordon-Conwell seminary.

God often answers prayers with a sense of humor. I picture him as an old-fashioned switchboard operator hearing all those prayers for vocations. The good Carmelite fathers had intended certain connections, but with a smile, God unplugged the wires and put them into other sockets. Presto! He arranged for that Evangelical seminary to provide some if its most anti-Catholic students as converts to Catholicism who are now serving as apologists, theology professors, and pro-life leaders.

Evangelicals around the country are bewildered as to why Gordon-Conwell graduates are converting to Catholicism. Was something deficient in the curriculum? Many ask. No. In substantial measure, we converts from Evangelicalism are the fruit of the prayers of those faithful Carmelite priests.

By mid-1990, Karen and I had spent a tremendous amount of time studying the Catholic Church and praying for the Lord's guidance. We and our five children (with number six in the womb) were ready to enter the Church. On July 1st, in Epiphany Cathedral, we were formally received into the Catholic Church by Bishop John Nevins. We had made it! After two decades of searching for the Church established by Jesus Christ, I found it. Our hearts were filled with joy and tension. Although the Catholic community welcomed us with open arms, many of our Evangelical friends and family did not understand or like our decision to become Catholic. Yet *we* knew we had taken the right step.

Since that day, we have hoped and prayed that other Protestants would follow us into the Church; some already have. One of the former elders in my church, along with his entire family, converted a few months after we did. In the ensuing years, other friends have also converted, and many more are open and still searching. One thing we found was that Catholicism is not given much first-hand consideration. Most of my Evangelical friends who tried to get me to change my mind had not read even one book written by a Catholic explaining Catholicism. There are many Protestants who have read dozens, even hundreds, of books on theology, Church history, and Scripture, but have never read a single book on Catholicism written by a Catholic. They assume Catholicism is wrong without any serious investigation.

There was one surprising step left in my pilgrimage from Costa Mesa. I would receive an invitation literally to go to Rome and meet with the Pope! After I left my pastorate I entered a full-time pro-life ministry in Florida with the encouragement of Randall Terry, founder of Operation Rescue. Thirty days before my family converted I received an "out-of-the-blue" offer from a businessman to pay my expenses to go to Rome with Randy and meet with the Pope. I was happily shocked by the offer, and immediately took him up on it.

Just over a year later, Randy Terry and I were on an airplane bound for Rome where we would attend an international pro-life summit sponsored by the Vatican's Pontifical Council on the Family. The pro-life leaders in attendance were blessed with a special audience with Pope John Paul II.

He reminded us that "the family is the sanctuary of life," and warned that our world has embraced a "culture of death" that "is causing a number of deaths without precedent in human history." This culture of death, he said, must be changed. "The first essential structure capable of doing this is definitely the family." The family must become the center of our pro-life activity.

I was impressed and inspired by the simplicity and wisdom of the pope's words. Afterward each of us was able to greet the pope personally. I approached the Holy Father with great joy in my heart, and asked him to bless some rosaries for my family. He did that and also pronounced his apostolic blessing upon me and my family. That meeting made a profound impact on me.

I returned from Rome reflecting on the Holy Father's blessing upon my family, his exhortations about the need for family apostolates, and my marriage and family convictions prompting me towards the Catholic Church. I sensed a call to strengthen the fragile modern family with a rock-solid foundation from the practical application of Catholic truths. In response, I am launching a new apostolate named the Family Life Center, International. Our purposes are to promote and strengthen the family, the marriage covenant, the sanctity of all innocent human life, and the historic Christian faith. Our handbook is *Familiaris Consortio.*

Was my pilgrimage from Costa Mesa to Rome just a quirk, or was I just early in discovering Catholicism? Although the press stopped reporting on the Jesus Movement over a decade ago, the movement has continued. Thousands in my generation have experienced the fruits of dramatically changed lives: repentance, a deep love for God, freedom from addictions and sinful lifestyles, and extraordinary graces. Some of the purposes of this outpouring of the Holy Spirit on my generation have not yet been fully realized.

As we enter the new millennium, Christianity faces one of its greatest challenges in history. The modern media have already composed Christianity's epitaph, so certain they are that the Church will soon be dead. In the mid-sixties the cover of *Time* magazine announced that "God is Dead." But a few years later *Time* reported his surprising resurrection in the Jesus Movement.

The intense longings and searchings of the sixties and seventies were only partially fulfilled by the first stage of the Jesus Movement. I and thousands of others in the movement found fulfillment through a deeply personal relationship with Christ. Yet there is an additional dimension to our relationship with Christ that is discovered only in a relationship with the Church he founded 2000 years ago. The fullness of the riches of Christ are found in having a personal relationship with him and in a corporate relationship with his Body, the Catholic Church.

I pray that my fellow prodigals of that turbulent era will launch phase two of the Jesus Movement as they come all the way home to Rome.

From Controversy to Consolation

Bob Sungenis

MY CONVERSION to the Catholic Church started with a wrong phone number. Gerry Hoffman, a friend of mine, was making a routine call to Bob Swenson, another friend. Bob's name was listed right after mine in Gerry's address book, and he accidentally dialed my number. I used to work with Gerry and Bob at Family Radio, an Evangelical radio network based in Oakland, California. Since leaving Family Radio, I hadn't talked to Gerry in a long time, so he took the opportunity to tell me what was going on in his life.

I was stunned when he told me he was thinking seriously about becoming Catholic. "*Catholic*?" I thought to myself angrily. "Gerry's a born-again, Bible-believing Christian. How could he possibly consider joining the Catholic Church — a Church which is so unbiblical?" I remembered, unhappily, that Bob had already converted to the Catholic Church, so I listened to Gerry uneasily.

Gerry explained with enthusiasm the things he was learning about the Catholic Church. My dismay at hearing him extol Catholicism made me want to try to convince him he would be committing a horrible, possibly damnable, mistake if he continued down the path to Rome. But since Gerry was my friend, I resolved to give him ten minutes and then make a polite excuse to end the conversation. But within a few minutes I'd forgotten entirely about this plan.

As an Evangelical Protestant, I had been in plenty of conversations with Catholics in which I showed them from the Bible why their beliefs were "unbiblical." Usually it took only a few well-placed challenges on issues such as "Mary worship," or purgatory, or the Mass, before the Catholic's arguments would be in tatters. Like many Evangelicals, I was adept at using the Bible to "disprove" Catholic beliefs. And if I didn't have a handy Bible verse to sling I could always fall back on the show-stopper question: "Where does it say *that* in the Bible?" I'd grin triumphantly as the Catholic would flail around, trying in vain to explain why the words "purgatory" or "Immaculate Conception" appeared nowhere in the Bible. But my conversation with Gerry was different. Even though I gave him a few of the standard objections to Catholic doctrines, for some reason his answers did not make me feel combative. In fact, his explanations made me feel like listening instead of attacking.

As those who knew me at that time would have attested, this was not my normal response to a conversation about politics or religion — especially religion. For the next hour, Gerry and I discussed Catholic doctrines, and he consistently used Scripture to show why he believed they were true. I was amazed at the strength of his biblical explanations.

Gerry must have filled Bob in on the details of our conversation because within a few days I received boxes of Catholic materials from each of them with their request that I read and consider the case for Catholicism. This was a spiritual "one-two" punch. I was only trying to be polite when I told them I'd read the books — I actually had no intention of doing so, though I was intrigued by what they were telling me. (But the Lord had different plans for me.)

At first I just skimmed through the books, mildly curious as to what the Catholic Church could possibly say in defense of its doctrines. But soon I was reading carefully, and after a while I simply couldn't put the books down. I found myself saying, "It makes so much sense" or, "I can't believe I couldn't see this before." I soon found myself poring through a stack of these books at one time because I literally couldn't wait to see how the next author would explain the Catholic faith. And then there were the cassette tapes. I was surprised to encounter conversion testimonies that told of situations similar to mine: militantly anti-Catholic Evangelicals who were being swept off their feet by the compelling biblical case for the claims of the Catholic Church. But what I found most unnerving was that these Evangelicals were actually *converting* to Catholicism.

Scott Hahn, a former Presbyterian minister who converted to the Catholic faith, was particularly helpful. His conversion story, as many have discovered, is one of the most fascinating and challenging testimonies ever heard. He found that the notion of *sola scriptura* (the formal principle of the Reformation: The Bible is the sole infallible authority for Christians) is so ingrained in Protestant thinking that most take it for granted without any solid proofs. Hahn's study of Scripture led him to the conclusion that *sola scriptura* is not only unhistorical and unworkable, it was unbiblical. He argued very persuasively that, far from being merely a concept with obscure or minimal scriptural support, *sola scriptura* is simply not taught anywhere in the Bible, either explicitly or implicitly.

If Protestantism's fundamental doctrine was nowhere to be found in Scripture the implications are devastating to Protestantism: If *sola scriptura* is not taught in the Bible then it is a self-refuting proposition. As Martin Luther, John Calvin, and other Reformers claimed, if *sola scriptura* is false, Protestantism, as a theological response to the Catholic Church, is likewise false, since Protestantism was founded upon the idea of the Bible as the sole infallible rule of faith for the Church.

This realization staggered me. I began my own study of Scripture, scouring the Old and New Testaments in an effort to discover where it taught *sola scriptura*. After a period of diligent study, including a careful search of numerous Evangelical commentaries and works on biblical authority, I was horrified to find that there was absolutely no Scriptural warrant for the Protestant claim that the Bible is the sole infallible guide for Christian doctrine and practice.

I had made a life out of studying the Bible and proclaiming Evangelical Protestantism as the "truth" the world so badly needed to hear. In many Protestant circles I was known — to my great private satisfaction — as "Bible Bob." When someone had a doctrinal question or wanted to find something in the Bible, I usually had the answer. This time I didn't.

Growing up, I never really excelled at any one thing. I was a "jack-of-all-trades, master-at-none" kind of guy. This changed in college when I had an intense spiritual experience after reading the Bible. Sometimes, when I'm out with a friend and we drive past the building where I lived on the campus of George Washington University, I point to the window of my room where I was "saved." That was the day I surrendered my life to Christ and decided to devote my life to studying Scripture, making it my area of expertise.

My Early Years

I was raised in the Catholic religion from the cradle, but like so many others, I never took the time or had the motivation to really understand Catholicism. I went through Catholic grade school and high school, was confirmed by my bishop, and even thought about being a priest for a while. But by the time I was a freshman in college and was away from the constraints of a nominally-Catholic home, I did what so many in my situation have done: I made friends with the wrong crowd and promptly fell away from the Church. I soon found myself floundering with no sense of direction, and for a pre-med major hoping to follow his father's footsteps and become a doctor, this was not a promising start.

One day, a college friend and I were having an unusual conversation about Jesus — I say unusual because at this time in my life I rarely gave Jesus and his claims on me a second thought. Somehow we got on to the subject of the Second Coming, and my friend made the claim (which struck me as outlandish even then) that Jesus was going to "get married" when he came back to earth. Being quite theologically ignorant at this time, I pondered this exotic idea with interest. When I shared this theory with my roommate, Bill Bryan, who had been raised in a Christian family, he snorted at the idea and snapped back that if I insisted on spreading such a fantastic claim about Jesus, I should first be able to prove it from the Bible. Pulling his New Testament off the shelf, he challenged me to show where the Bible taught this novel idea. Accepting the challenge, I took his Bible and began to read it. I started with the Gospels, moving swiftly from one parable to another. For reasons I didn't then understand, I became deeply attracted to this spiritual book, fascinated by the story of Jesus. And though I never did find the passage which said Jesus would take a wife at his second coming, the Lord used this quirky episode to kindle in me a love for his written Word that has never diminished.

That summer of 1974 I devoured the New Testament. I was fascinated by Jesus. His wisdom and wry wit was especially attractive. When seemingly trapped by his adversaries, Jesus would retort with sayings like, "Give to Caesar what is Caesar's, and to God what is God's," or, "He who is without sin, let him cast the first stone." Only an extraordinary person could think up such astounding answers like these on the spur of the moment. But it was the love and compassion of Jesus that finally pierced my heart. I was moved as I read of the love he showed others, even as he was dying. I saw that he cared for others more than he cared for himself. Though before I thought that such altruistic relationships existed only in fairy tales, I knew in my heart that the Jesus of the Bible was no fairy tale. I began to see that Jesus was a real person, and that he made claims on my life that I couldn't ignore. I knew that if I accepted his lordship over my life I would have to change my life and live for him, not for myself. This knowledge both frightened and exhilarated me.

Several months later, one Sunday night in January 1975, I sat alone in my dorm room reading the Bible. I pondered Jesus' words in Matthew 11:28, "Come to me, all of you who are tired from carrying heavy loads, and I will give you rest. Take my yoke and put it on you, and learn from me, because I am gentle and humble in spirit; and you will find rest. For the yoke I will give you is easy, and the load I will put on you is light." As I read this passage, I suddenly felt as if Jesus were talking directly to me, beckoning me to come to him. I later learned that St. Augustine's conversion began along similar lines. Daydreaming one afternoon about spiritual things, Augustine overheard a boy's voice saying, "*Tolle et lege*" (Latin: "Pick it up and read it"). He felt he was being exhorted to pick up the Bible his mother Monica had given him, so he read a few lines of Scripture, and for the first time in his life was filled with an awareness of the awesome presence of God. He embraced Christ, was baptized a Catholic, and went on to become one of the Church's greatest bishops and theologians. Similar to Augustine's experience, I went to sleep that night feeling Jesus beckoning me through his words in Matthew 11:28.

At that moment I surrendered my life to Christ. Drained by the emotional impact of this encounter with Jesus, I fell into a deep sleep. When I woke up the next morning I knew something wonderful had happened to me. The Spirit of God had entered my life. The change of status that I felt was dramatic and decisive. I still can't find the right words to describe the intense spiritual and emotional experience this was for me.

My college friends and others I had known could not believe how I had changed. Wanting to imitate the early Christians I read about in the New Testament, I began to give away my belongings, striving for the holy perfection Jesus spoke of in Matt. 19:21, "If you wish to be perfect, go, sell what you have and give to the poor, and you will have treasure in heaven." My college buddies were happily astonished as they became recipients of much of my meager belongings. I wasn't sure of all that was happening but one thing I knew positively: Jesus had made his presence known to me. I loved him, and I loved the Bible that taught me about him.

For a few months I continued to attended the Catholic church in my neighborhood in Washington D.C. At this point I wasn't trying to figure out whether the Catholic Church was the true Church. I just wanted to know Jesus as I well as I could. I fasted and prayed frequently and read the Bible voraciously. I also began searching the radio bands for a Christian station. One Saturday evening I found a call-in radio program in which the host was answering Bible-related questions. I was enthralled. I wanted to soak up any information about the Bible and Christianity that I could find.

At one point in the show, a particular doctrine of the Catholic Church was the topic of discussion. The host informed his audience that this particular Catholic belief was "unbiblical," and offered a few verses to support his claim. I naively agreed with his arguments and, without realizing it just then, took my first step away from the Catholic Church. I found myself wanting to do what this teacher was doing — be on the radio and answer people's questions about the Bible. (Little did I know that in seven years I would be working for this same man, and would even have my own call-in radio program.)

Not long after this, I met with some well-intentioned Protestants who, once they found out I was Catholic, persuaded me that the Catholic Church was too steeped in meaningless ritual and corrupt traditions and had strayed far from the Bible. They convinced me that what I really wanted was a simple faith, a "biblical" faith that I couldn't enjoy within the strictures of Catholicism — just me, Jesus, and the Bible. My newfound love for Jesus and the Bible coincided with a rejection of the Catholic Church, which I thought had "hidden" Jesus from me — a notion my Protestant friends egged me on to believe. My weak moorings to the Catholic Church were easily cut under the sharp knife of their anti-Catholic arguments, and I soon found myself no longer a Catholic.

I had accepted the Protestant recipe for eternal happiness and began to grope my way toward what I hoped would be a vibrant relationship with Jesus, not realizing that each step was leading me away from his Church. But as so often happens, I didn't merely drift away from the Church. Without the influence of any informed Catholics, and under the zealous tutelage of my new-found Protestant friends, I developed a robust hatred for Catholicism. I embraced their view of the Catholic Church, seeing it as a deception, a diabolical detour which led souls away from Christ by entangling them in a morass of ritual, legalism, and unbiblical traditions of men. I'm ashamed now at the memory of how I so effortlessly allowed myself to be talked into leaving the Church. I saw Catholicism as something not simply to be rejected but as something to be actively opposed since, I thought, it gave people a false understanding of Jesus and of salvation.

I abandoned the Catholic Church, and for the next seventeen years, as a staunch Evangelical Protestant, I fancied myself (as so many Protestants do) a David, courageously defying the towering Catholic Goliath. In the face of centuries of Catholic councils and papal statements and traditions, I would do battle armed only with the Bible, the weapon which would, I firmly believed, lay waste to the deceptions of the Catholic Church.

But God was keeping his eye on me, waiting for precisely the right moment to quell my rebellion, correct my misunderstandings, and bring me back to his Church.

What Bishop Fulton Sheen once said about anti-Catholics was also true for me: "There are not a hundred people in the world who hate the Catholic Church, but there are thousands who hate what they mistakenly believe the Catholic Church to be."

I went through the school of hard knocks in being introduced to Protestantism. Right away I encountered the sorry legacy of division left behind by the Protestant Reformers. With each denomination I visited I found a host of different doctrines that one was required to believe. Being true to the name "Protestant," I eventually left one denomination after another, due to disagreements in doctrine.

My self-guided study of the Bible — a study which lasted several hours a day, most days of the week, for the next seven years — helped me become something of a scriptural know-it-all. This didn't make my search for the truth any easier. In my smugness, every time I ran into a doctrine I didn't think was "biblical," I moved on to the next denomination.

Being away from home at college meant I was separated from my family and friends. When I did see them now and then we didn't relate very well; they couldn't understand my new-found spiritual life. I took a job as a desk clerk at small hotels where there was little traffic on the graveyard shift, just so I could study the Bible without interruption.

Later, even after I had married and settled into a successful sales career, I continued to study the Bible. I accumulated eighteen Bibles, most of which are marked with voluminous notes and cross references from my tedious work to organize what I studied. I developed a system of over one hundred symbols that I used to mark verses to help me remember the interpretation.

During my time as a Protestant I wrote a book entitled *Rewards in Heaven?* that critiqued the Catholic, and sometimes Protestant, concept of heavenly merit for works done on earth. I had recently sent the manuscript out to various publishers waiting for a favorable response when Gerry mistakenly dialed my number. I believed the Bible was my ultimate authority, and I believed, as most Protestants do, that God had especially blessed me to understand its meaning.

I first went to Washington Bible College outside of Washington, D.C. and there learned what it meant to be a "Fundamentalist." Everyone seemed so happy and spiritual. I felt like I had found heaven on earth, at least until I began to question some of the doctrines unique to this particular strain of Fundamentalism.

These people claimed that the prophetic portions of the Bible should be interpreted from a contemporary perspective. They ended up with all kinds of fanciful and sensational interpretations of future world events. I frequently saw that their methods of interpreting the Bible were inconsistent; they interpreted literally only those passages that supported their peculiar ideas. My habit of pointing out these anomalies in a rather pugnacious way created a strain between me and the faculty, which forced me to leave the institution after only one year.

I went back to my original choice for college, George Washington University in Washington D.C., and changed my major from pre-med to religion. Still indignant over the theological short-sightedness of the Fundamentalists, I re-entered school with a tempered enthusiasm.

I quickly found myself at odds with most of my professors who espoused "liberal" Protestant theology — the exact opposite of the Fundamentalist party line, though even more unsatisfying. In liberal Protestantism, hardly anything in the Bible was taken literally. Rather, it was relegated to the realm of myth and legend. I persevered, though, and eventually received my B.A. in religion.

I give much credit to the late Evangelical theologian, Francis Schaeffer, with whom I corresponded, for helping me navigate safely past the shoals of liberalism. I didn't see it then, but Schaeffer was very close to Catholicism without realizing it. He once confided that he loved and admired Mother Teresa and even worked with her on occasion.[1]

I next pursued graduate studies at Westminster Theological Seminary in Philadelphia, a bastion of conservative Reformed theology and, as would be expected, a bastion of anti-Catholicism. Not being totally convinced that the militant Calvinistic theology espoused at Westminster was correct, I continued to find myself in theological debates with professors and fellow students.

One thing we all agreed on, though, was that the Catholic Church was a counterfeit form of Christianity. I read many works written by Westminster's most lauded professor, the late Dutch theologian, Cornelius Van Til, and constantly came across his references to the "Romanists," a pejorative term for Catholics. Of course, I accepted this with glee and admiration.

During my time at Westminster something happened at the seminary that still reverberates unpleasantly in the minds of many reformed Protestants, known as "the Shepherd Issue." Professor Norman Shepherd, a tenured professor of twenty-years with the seminary teaching systematic theology, began to voice his opinion that good works were "necessary" for salvation. These "Romanist" statements alarmed faculty and students alike and resulted in something akin to a heresy trial being initiated to deal with this wayward professor. Shepherd had become convinced that, beginning with the Reformers, Protestants had misinterpreted the many clear references to the necessity of good works in the epistle of James and in the Gospels. In class, Professor Shepherd and I had engaged in some heated discussions on this issue. I attacked his view as "compromising" the gospel and the

---

[1] His son Frank has said as much (cf. *Christianity Today*, "Franky Schaeffer Chides Evangelicals," October 1993).

heart of the Reformation. I saw him as having sold out to the Romanists. Many others shared my view, and Shepherd was eventually fired from his teaching post and sent off to academic oblivion. I was amazed, however, at the support he received from a small but noticeable proportion of the faculty and students. There was an undercurrent of "Catholic" sentiment at Westminster that was most unsettling. Although I was able to dismiss Shepherd's ideas, I still wasn't totally satisfied with the classical Protestant view of salvation, either. I graduated from Westminster with a nagging feeling of uncertainty about this issue.

After receiving my masters degree in theology, I accepted a position as a Bible instructor with Family Radio in Oakland, California. Here I found my dream come true — my own call-in radio program answering callers' questions about the Bible. In addition, I was teaching over a thousand students through correspondence courses and in our local adult education classes. (One student, Brigitte, eventually became my wife). I created my own course called "Contemporary Issues," in which I dealt with the major controversies within Protestantism, such as "speaking in tongues," miracles, divorce and remarriage, the role of women in church, contraception, predestination and free will, and biblical interpretation. I also wrote several 50-75 page booklets for Family Radio explaining the biblical truth, as I saw it, on these topics. But I didn't make much money, and I didn't care. I was having the time of my life doing the "Lord's work."

After two years of enjoyable and challenging work at Family Radio, something happened that shattered my life-long dream of being a Bible teacher: another doctrinal controversy. As I delved deeper into the Bible, I noticed that some of the things that were taught at Family Radio were not "biblical." I voiced my concerns to the president and chief theologian of Family Radio, Harold Camping. My ideas were not well-received. This was the first of several clashes we had over what I saw as his erroneous and sometimes downright bizarre ways of interpreting Scripture. The strain between us increased, and I sensed that my days at Family Radio were numbered. My disagreements with Camping resulted in my dismissal a few months later.

Although I had been expecting to leave Family Radio for some time, having to abandon my own radio program and the writing of books — two jobs I enjoyed immensely — was quite a shock. Teaching Scripture was something I had dreamed of doing for many years, and after only two years of doing it at Family Radio, it had vanished. I chafed at having no formal outlet for my interest in the Bible, but I see now that God had a better plan in store for me. Leaving Family Radio was symbolic of my gradual escape from the solipsism and doctrinal confusion of Protestantism, and was the first step in my long and trying journey back to the Catholic Church.

When I left Family Radio I decided to take a break from employment in the field of theology, deciding to do secular work. But I still had to find a church for my family to attend. My wife, Brigitte, had grown up in a strict Dutch Calvinist home, and her family and I got along well since we shared Reformed theology in common. We tried to make our home in the Presbyterian Church but doctrinal controversy continued to follow us.

Presbyterians are known in Protestant circles as the "split P's" because of all the factions created over their divergent interpretations of the Bible. When I joined the fray, things didn't get any better. We were in and out of five different Presbyterian churches within the next five years, each move being due to disagreements on the pastor's interpretation of the Bible. I found that many Protestants wonder when the next split will occur in their church. It's not uncommon for Protestant churches to split two or three times within a generation.

In one church we attended I was elected an elder, and my wife was appointed to the pastor-seeking committee. We got to see the inner workings of the politics and

intrigue that took place in the decision making body of
the typical Protestant church. It was an eye-opening experience. Everyone had his own agenda and a litany of
Bible verses to back up his views. With no clear authority
in this independent Bible church, everything was up for
grabs.

The final straw came as the church was making the
decision on a new pastor. Most of the elders favored the
new breed of Protestant minister who concentrates on
"felt needs" and on accruing the marks of temporal success rather than on the rigors of authentic Christian living. This kind of "Madison Avenue Christianity" has
taken over many Evangelical churches. I was part of the
dissenting minority, arguing that the new pastor should
be concerned with helping his flock deal with sin and
suffering, not with simply how to make people feel good
about themselves. As a result of this clash, Brigitte and I
left that church, disgusted with the superficial sort of
Evangelical Christianity we saw all around us.

Still searching for truth, we entered a small, vibrant
denomination, the Boston Crossroads Movement of the
Church of Christ. Like those I met in Bible college, these
Church of Christ people with whom we fellowshipped
were young, happy, and spiritual. Brigitte and I fit in very
well and were being groomed for leadership. As I look
back on this experience, I can see that God had used our
time spent in the Boston Church of Christ as another
stepping-stone to Rome.

The Church of Christ is one of the few Protestant
denominations that teaches the doctrine of baptismal
regeneration. Coming from a Reformed Presbyterian
background, however, I was convinced that baptism was
merely symbolic, and I could never see myself accepting
any other view. But these people challenged me to study
the issue again and encouraged me to take the Bible "at
face-value." Well, I did study the issue, and quite intensely.

As a result of the biblical evidence, I not only changed my mind and embraced the doctrine of baptismal regeneration, I ended up writing a lengthy paper defending it — a work, I'm somewhat chagrined to say, that is still used by the Church of Christ. This experience had a monumental effect on my faith. I was haunted by the realization that even though I knew the Bible well, I could be dead wrong in my understanding of what it teaches. "If I've been completely wrong on the doctrine of baptism for so long," I asked myself, "what other errors have I been reading into the Bible all these years?"

Although I capitulated on the doctrine of baptismal regeneration, one point I assured myself I wouldn't budge on was infant baptism. I believed in it firmly — it was deeply rooted in my biblical psyche. The Church of Christ tried their best to convince me that infant baptism was "unbiblical," but without success. Since I was being groomed to take over a position of leadership in the Church of Christ, my unflinching belief in infant baptism became a serious problem. The leadership of the local church we attended began to pressure me to reject a doctrine I knew to be true. This led to tension and a series of arguments on other related issues. Once again, I found myself having to leave another church over doctrinal controversy.

Next, at the invitation of some long-time Protestant friends who had been pleading with us to leave the Church of Christ, we briefly attended their independent Bible church. Here, though, I found the same sanctimonious attitudes and doctrinal inconsistencies that I had seen in many other Fundamentalist groups. Ironically, this particular church was home to one of Catholicism's most ardent critics, James G. McCarthy. He has recently produced a video entitled "Catholicism: Crisis of Faith," in which he purports to expose all the evils in the Catholic Church for the purpose of "saving" Catholics. Brigitte and I were members of his church for only two months, but I now see why God had us make this "pit stop" before coming home to Rome. (My acquaintance with Jim McCarthy has allowed me to open up lines of communication with him now that I am a Catholic. I am presently corresponding with him, pointing out the errors and distortions in his video.)

When I had my Augustine-like experience in college at the age of nineteen, I began praying for a wife. For eight years I prayed three times a day for this intention. I told God all the special qualities I wanted in a wife. I remember praying specifically for someone beautiful on the inside and out, and one who loved God more than anything, including me. I'm overjoyed that God answered my prayers beyond my dreams.

Brigitte is everything I had ever hoped to have in a wife. One of her great qualities is loyalty — it knows no definition better than my wife. Through each of my "protests" against Protestantism she was at my side. Even though I made her spiritual life topsy-turvy by making us go through the revolving door of Protestant denominationalism, she trusted me to the very depths of her being. She didn't follow me blindly, though. At each of our theological crossroads, Brigitte examined the issues for herself, listening carefully to both sides of the story before she made up her mind. Catholicism was an especially difficult step for Brigitte because there were so many doctrinal questions to be studied through and answered.

Once the basic questions were worked through (*sola scriptura*, the authority of the Church, Marian doctrines, and the Church's prohibition of contraception) she began to relax. Though there was still much to learn about the Catholic faith, she felt she was finally "home." Her countenance radiates each day with the love of God and a renewed appreciation and love for his Church. Right before our conversion to Catholicism we were contemplating using birth control for the first time in our marriage. Thanks to our discovery of the wisdom of Catholic teaching on this subject, we were blessed with our fourth child, Augustine Joseph.

It was at this point in my life that the Lord guided Gerry Hoffman to make his "accidental" phone call. I see now it was no accident. Although still firmly entrenched in the smugness of my Protestant anti-Catholicism, I was dejected and frustrated by the experience of "church hopping" for so many years. Evangelicalism had turned out to be merely a mirage of the shining theological Camelot I had envisioned it to be all those years ago when I became "born again."

I still loved Jesus, but I was ready to give up trying to find his Church. After searching for so long and being disappointed time after time, I had lost hope in finding the Church he promised would never be overcome (Matt. 16:18), the Church he promised he would be with until the end of the world (Matt. 28:20).

But the Lord rescued me from my wanderings. What heavenly irony that he chose to use former Evangelical anti-Catholics —Gerry Hoffman, Bob and Julie Swenson, Scott and Kimberly Hahn, Thomas Howard, John Henry Newman, and others — to show me the way back home to Rome.

As I sifted through the pile of Catholic books Bob and Gerry had sent me, the first thing I reexamined was the Protestant concept of *sola scriptura*, the notion that the Bible alone is our authority. It was like a slap in the face to realize the truth of the Catholic claim that *sola scriptura* is a false doctrine, a tradition of men. The Bible (and by extension *sola scriptura*) was the very thing to which I dedicated my life. As I studied the Catholic case against *sola scriptura* I knew instinctively that the whole debate between Catholicism and Protestantism could be boiled down to authority. Every doctrine one believes is based on the authority one accepts. I decided to test this pet theory of the Reformers by asking numerous Protestant scholars and pastors to help me find *sola scriptura* in the

Bible. By this point, I wasn't too surprised to find that none was able to provide a convincing answer.

They pointed to verses that spoke of the veracity and inerrancy of the Bible, but could show none that explicitly taught that Scripture is our sole, formally sufficient authority. Interestingly, some of these Protestants were candid enough to admit that the Bible nowhere taught *sola scriptura*, but they compensated for this curious lacuna by saying the Bible doesn't have to teach *sola scriptura* in order for the doctrine to be true. But I could see that this position was utterly untenable. For if *sola scriptura* — the idea that the Bible is formally sufficient for Christians — is not taught in the Bible, *sola scriptura* is a false and self-refuting proposition.

As I studied Scripture in the light of the Catholic materials I had been sent, I began to see that the Bible in fact points to the Church as being the final arbiter of truth in all spiritual matters (cf. 1 Timothy 3:15; Matthew 16:18-19; 18:18; Luke 10:16).

This made sense, especially on a practical level. Since only an entity with the ability to observe and correctly interpret information can act as an authority, I saw that the Bible, though it contains God-breathed revelation, cannot act as a final "authority" since it is dependent on thinking personalities to observe what is says and, more importantly, interpret what it means. I also saw that the Bible warns us that it contains difficult and confusing information which is capable (if not prone) to being twisted into all sorts of fanciful and false interpretations (2 Peter 3:16).

During my years of wandering through the theological wilderness of Protestantism, I always knew that something was wrong with it, but I just couldn't put my finger on it. Now I was beginning to put the pieces of the puzzle together. The more I thought about it the more I began to see that the theory of *sola scriptura* had done untold damage to Christendom. The most obvious evidence of this damage was Protestantism itself: a huge mass of conflicting, bickering denominations, causing, by its very nature of "protest" and "defiance," an endless proliferation of chaos and controversy.

My seventeen-year experience with Protestant biblical scholars had made one thing very clear to me: *Sola scriptura* is a euphemism for "sola ego." What I mean is that every Protestant has his own interpretation of what Scripture says and, of course, he believes that his interpretation is superior to everyone else's. Each advances his own view, assuming (if not actually claiming) that the Holy Spirit has personally led him to that interpretation.

As a Protestant I greatly admired Martin Luther and John Calvin for their boldness to interpret the Bible for themselves. Now I was faced with the probability that these heroes of mine were very intelligent but also very prideful and rebellious men. After I had read a few scholarly biographies of these two reformers I realized that much about their personal lives was never told to us in seminary. These insights caused me to take an even more skeptical look at the Reformers and the Reformation as a whole.

I realize that there are problems within the Catholic Church. In every age, the Church has had to endure the blight of worldly, sinful, and heretical members. At present, the Church is fighting the destructive forces of liberalism which have influenced a portion of the Church, especially in the United States. But one must realize that aberrations among its members does not negate the Catholic Church's authenticity as Christ's true Church. One must distinguish between what is done in the name of Catholicism from what is officially taught by the Catholic Church. Rebellious members should not surprise us. The Bible warns that many in the Church will sin and become corrupt, although maintaining the appearance of spirituality. As Jesus said himself, the wheat will grow up with the tares until he comes back to judge the world.

Many Protestants are amazed that despite these grave challenges, the Catholic Church has an uncanny ability to weather the storms of controversy, heresy, and schism. There have been countless predictions of Rome's imminent demise, but it still stands. As I studied Church history I saw that of all the churches (dioceses) mentioned in the New Testament, with the exception of Jerusalem, only the church at Rome still exists. Besides the major sees of Corinth, Ephesus, Philippi, Thessalonica, Colossae, and the region of Galatia, the New Testament reminds us of less prominent churches which today are extinct (cf. Rev. 2 and 3). The longevity and universality of the Catholic Church is indicative of its divine origin.

There is no purely natural explanation for the fact that the Catholic Church still exists after all these centuries — but there is a supernatural explanation. Jesus promised he would lead his Church into all truth and would protect it from all forces aimed at its destruction, without or within, including even the gates of hell. In light of Jesus' clear promises of the doctrinal integrity and temporal perpetuity of the Church (cf. Matt. 7:24-25; 16:18-19; 18:18; 28:20; Luke 10:16; John 14:16-18; 14:26; 16:13), the Protestant claim that for fifteen hundred years the Church was corrupt and did not know the way of salvation, is absurd and unbiblical.

Sensing the logic of these Catholic arguments, some Protestants try to get around Jesus' statements by claiming that the church he protects is a "spiritual," invisible church, not a particular visible church. This notion is refuted by Jesus' teaching that the Church is a "city set on a mountain [that] cannot be hidden" (Matt. 5:14). This is an example of the error of "spiritualizing" biblical passages that don't fit with one's pre-fabricated theology. The word "church" (Greek: *ekklesia*) appears over one hundred times in the New Testament, not once with the meaning of a "spiritual" church. The thought of a merely spiritual and invisible church composed of some sort of amorphous collection of "true believers" from every denomination, as many Protestants conceive of it, is completely unbiblical. Jesus established only one Church, not a group of squabbling rival denominations. ✳

My Protestant friends were so proud of the "Bible churches" they attended, claiming that the majority of their members are sincere "Christians," but denying that Catholics are. Interestingly, many of today's so-called "Bible churches" are barely two or three generations old. Many were formed when a group of people rallied around a prominent figure who introduced a new and "brilliant" interpretation of the Bible.

Imbued with fervor, they left their former church which no longer held to "biblical truth," and formed a new and supposedly better church. But eventually the initial enthusiasm wanes, the doctrines begin to change, and once again, people fall away, some going on to start up yet another sect. Often the church of the third or fourth generation hardly resembles the church of the first generation. This scenario has happened thousands of times in the few hundred years Protestantism has existed. This syndrome of fragmentation is the Reformation's tragic legacy of confusion and disunity. ✳

Some Protestants respond to this criticism by saying that the Catholic Church has changed its doctrines, but this is not true. Practices and disciplines can and do change in the Catholic Church but dogma does not change. Practices such as celebrating Mass in Latin (in the Roman Rite), abstinence from eating meat on Friday, priestly celibacy, and other ancient practices are good and helpful to the life of the Church, but they are not dogmas, and so can be modified or dispensed with as the need arises. Catholic dogmas include such things as the Trinity, the Incarnation, the inspiration and inerrancy of Scripture, purgatory, the Immaculate Conception, and the Real Presence of Jesus in the Eucharist. The Catholic Church rests secure in Jesus' promise that he would send the Holy Spirit to lead his Church into all truth (John 16:12), that he would bind and loose in heaven whatever it bound and loosed on earth (Matt. 18:18), and that he would protect it from destruction (Matt. 16:18).

Jesus established a Church through which he intended to make himself known to the world (Matt. 5:14-15, 28:18-20, Eph. 3:10). Through the authoritative Scripture, oral preaching, and infallible decisions that came from Jesus through his Church (Luke 10:16, Acts 15), the Lord began the slow but steady process of working through the instrumentality of his Body the Church (cf. Rom. 12:1-5; 1 Cor. 12:12-27; Eph. 3:4-6; 5:21-23; Col. 1:18) to bring all things captive in obedience to himself (2 Cor. 10:5).

In order to accomplish this mission of God's mercy, the Church must be able to teach the truth all the time. If the Church is not protected from teaching error, God's people would have absolutely no trustworthy foundation upon which to build their faith. Protestants disagree, claiming that their doctrinal certitude is based on Scripture alone. But Scripture nowhere claims to be sufficient for this task. It warns that it can be misinterpreted (2 Pet. 1:20, 3:15-16).

One passage that helped me see the infalliblity of the Church was Matthew 16:18-19. I had read this passage hundreds of times but never understood its meaning. I knew Catholics say Peter is the "rock" (something which many conservative Evangelical scholars now admit is true, based on the context and linguistic evidence in the text), but I saw that the dynamic relationship between the binding and loosing on earth and in heaven clearly implies the Church's infallibility.

I understood that if God reciprocated with an identical binding or loosing in heaven, then the binding and loosing done on earth must of necessity be free from all error. If this were not so, God would have put himself in the impossible situation of affirming that which is not true. How does the Church exercise this prerogative of binding and loosing? She is guided by the Holy Spirit to make decisions without error (John 16:13), so Jesus Christ can ratify those decisions. I was awestruck by this realization. The Catholic claim of infallibility was not simply brash human conceit; it was foretold in Scripture itself.

I found an indisputable example of the infallibility of the Catholic Church when I began to reflect on the question of the canon of Scripture — how the books of the Bible were determined, an issue often ignored by Protestants. There is no "inspired table of contents" anywhere in Scripture. The decision as to which books should be included in the Bible and which books should not, was made by the Catholic Church in the councils of Hippo (A.D. 393), and Carthage (A.D. 397, and 419). These decisions were later ratified and solemnly defined by the ecumenical councils of Second Nicea (787), Florence (1440), and Trent (1525-46). One of the books that really helped me see this was Henry G. Graham's compact book, *Where We Got the Bible* (Rockford, IL: TAN Books). Since the Bible does not indicate which books belong within it, and since Protestants do not believe the Church has any authority to infallibly determine which books belong and which books don't, Protestants are left in an epistemological dilemma. Hence they are forced to the logical but heretical conclusion that there may be inspired books that should be in the Bible but were left out in error, and that there may be uninspired books in the Bible that have no business being there, but were added in error.

Martin Luther, for example, wanted to delete the books of James, Hebrews, 2 Peter, and Revelation, since he believed they were added in error. If it had not been for the persuasion of his contemporaries, these books may well have been deleted from Protestant Bibles.

In holding to the "fallible canon" theory, Protestants cannot be infallibly certain that the Bible they hold in their hands is in fact the Bible. The issue of the canon is an unsolvable epistemological problem for Protestants. For if one cannot be certain which books belong in the Bible, how can one presume to use it "alone" as a reliable guide to saving faith in God? The irony is that while Protestants use the theory of *sola scriptura* to advance their attacks on the Catholic Church, they have no infallible way of knowing what comprises Scripture in the first place.[2] Furthermore, if the canon is indeed fallible, there is no reason why future generations of Protestants could not remove certain books now in the Protestant canon or add new ones. This is not as far-fetched as it may seem, since many liberal Protestant theologians and Scripture scholars have already recommended the removal of several New Testament books (some have gone so far as to call into question the entire canon). Nor could one be absolutely sure that the very words of Scripture are inspired.

In seminary we were taught a variation on the "fallible canon" theory. The Bible was said to be "self-authenticating," in other words, the Bible, by its very nature, simply compelled one to accept its books as inspired. That may be a comforting thought for Protestants, but it is no different from the Mormon's claim that he just knows the Book of Mormon is the inspired word of God, because the Book of Mormon feels true to him. This is hardly a reliable way of ascertaining which books belong in the Bible. And don't forget, there are a number of books in the Bible, such as Philemon, 3 John, and others, that don't jump out

---

[2] A glaring example of the utter absence of biblical evidence for *sola scriptura* and of the inability of Protestant apologists to deal with the epistemological problem of the canon as it relates to *sola scriptura*, is seen in a debate on *sola scriptura* between Catholic apologist Patrick Madrid and Fundamentalist apologist James White. Cassette tapes of this debate, "Does the Bible Teach *Sola Scriptura*?", are available from Catholic Answers, P.O. Box 17490, San Diego, CA 92177, (619) 541-1131. See also Madrid's follow-up article on the debate, "The White Man's Burden" (*This Rock*, October 1993, 11-16).

at the reader as being particularly inspired (read them sometime, and see what you think).

But even if a book claimed to be inspired, how would we know it is in fact inspired? There were many books circulating in the early centuries of the Church that either claimed to be inspired or seemed to be inspired but never made it into the canon (e.g. The Gospel of Peter, The Epistle of Barnabas, The Acts of Paul, The Epistle of Clement to the Corinthians). In addition, there are many apparent inconsistencies and contradictions between the canonical books of the Bible, that if one were not predisposed to accept them as canonical, would certainly seem to be spurious.

The truth is, Protestants are living off the borrowed capital of the Catholic Church, for it was the Catholic Church that infallibly recognized, under the divine guidance of the Holy Spirit, the canon of Scripture. Each time Protestants quote from the Bible they unwittingly acknowledge their trust in the infallible divine guidance given to the Catholic Church by Christ. Many Evangelicals and Fundamentalists argue that the Catholic Church did not give us the canon, the Holy Spirit did. But there is no argument between Catholics and Protestants here. Of course the Holy Spirit gave the canon of the Bible, say Catholics. The real question is how he gave it. How did the Holy Spirit communicate the knowledge of the canon to the Church? By asserting that the Holy Spirit gave the canon to the Church, the Protestant must admit that the Holy Spirit guided the Church into an infallible decision. The only way out of this dilemma is the so-called "fallible canon" theory which some have already begun to promote. R.C. Sproul, a prominent Evangelical theologian, is a good example of those who hold to the "fallible collection of infallible books" theory.

Luther tried to solve the problem of the canon by accepting only those books which in some measure dealt with his favorite theme of "justification by faith" (Romans and Galatians were shoo-ins under this test). Conversely, he rejected books that did not seem to contain that notion. But the facts of history forced me to see that the Catholic Church made the decision on the canon. And if the Catholic Church's decision was infallible, it had to have been guided by the Holy Spirit.

I realized that if the Holy Spirit did inspire the Church to write infallible Scripture, preach infallible doctrine, and infallibly determine the biblical canon, there was absolutely no rational basis to claim that the Church was not infallibly guided down through the ages until the present day. Jesus promised to guide his Church into *all* truth (John 16:13) and to be with it till the end of the world (Matt. 28:19-20).

Protestants who honestly examine this issue are faced with a crisis of truth. If they admit that God guided the Catholic Church to infallibly recognize and codify the canon, they must also admit that there is no rational or biblical basis for denying that the Catholic Church continued to be infallibly guided by the Holy Spirit. That conclusion, of course, would demand that they become Catholic. For many, such a capitulation is unthinkable. After nearly five centuries of prejudice it is extremely difficult for some to see things any differently. Many prefer uncertainty than to acknowledge that the Catholic Church is Christ's Church.

After all the anti-Catholic propaganda to which I had been exposed in my Protestant years, what I found in the Catholic Church were the most reasonable and trustworthy interpretations of Scripture I had ever seen. It was this faithfulness to Scripture that sealed my decision to enter the Catholic Church.

I had struggled all my adult life with how to correctly interpret the Bible. I had read countless books on biblical interpretation written by Evangelical theologians and biblical scholars, and discussed this issue with numerous mentors and friends. While at Family Radio, I wrote a 200-page book on biblical interpretation. But because of the staggering variety of Protestant interpretations, each interpreter trying to make his exegesis sound the most convincing while condemning as "unbiblical" the interpretations of others, I knew the understanding of any given passage would always be up for grabs.

My study of the Fathers of the Church and the Bible commentaries of subsequent Catholic theologians and exegetes taught me that the most faithful way to interpret the Scripture was to take it at face value. In Protestant exegesis I was used to twisting and spiritualizing many passages since interpreting them otherwise would destroy the theological infrastructure that we so desperately needed to maintain.

Each denomination has its particular set of verses that it emphasizes, and these form the base from which it interprets the rest of Scripture. The problem is that each denomination emphasizes a different set of Scriptures, and holds to its own peculiar interpretation of that set. Catholic exegesis interprets Scripture according to the living Tradition of the Church, often called the "analogy of faith" by the early Church Fathers.

There are many examples of passages that, when interpreted at their face value are easily understood and are harmonious with the rest of Scripture. In John 3:5 the word "water" in the clause, "unless a man is born of water and Spirit" refers to water baptism, at which time the Spirit enters our life and our sins are forgiven. (Protestant interpretations of this verse are quite diverse and self-serving. Most do their best to spiritualize the water into being a metaphor for the Word of God. Similar interpretations are given to such clear passages as 1 Peter 3:21; Ephesians 5:26; 4:5; Acts 2:38; and Romans 6:1-4. Some even hold that the water refers to the amniotic fluid in the womb.)

Jesus' statement, "Whose sins you shall forgive they are forgiven," (John 20:23) refers to the forgiveness granted by Christ through his ministers (cf. 2 Corinthians 5:18-20). Jesus' statement, "This is my body" (Luke 22:19), is interpreted literally to mean that the Passover bread became Jesus' actual body. The statement in James 5:14 regarding the anointing of the sick with oil so that sins would be forgiven is taken literally. Genesis 1:28 is interpreted literally as an argument against birth control. (Before the 1930's all Protestant denominations, without exception, viewed birth control as a sin. The Episcopal church was the first to relax sanctions against it. Today, all Protestant denominations allow it.)

Jesus' words in Matthew 19:1-9 prohibiting the dissolution of marriage are strictly heeded in the Catholic Church which has never sanctioned divorce or remarriage.[3] James 2:24 says that Abraham was not justified by

---

[3] The Pope's refusal to grant Henry VIII a divorce is probably the best example of this resolve. Ever since the Reformation, Protestant interpretations have allowed fornication and desertion as valid reasons for divorce and remarriage. This has further developed into a multitude of excuses that are now practiced without the slightest impunity. Catholic interpretations have allowed separation based on fornication but maintain that the couple is still married in the eyes of God and thus cannot remarry. This is also supported by Paul's teaching in Romans 7:1-3 and 1 Corinthians 7:10-11. As for the exception clause in Matthew 19:9, Catholic exegesis states that because the exception clause appears in between "whosoever divorces his wife" and "marries another commits adultery," rather than before both clauses or after both clauses, then the exception only applies to the divorce, not the remarriage. Moreover, since Jesus specifically prohibited remarriage, calling it the sin of adultery, then the "putting away" does not refer to a legitimate and legal divorce but only to an indefinite separation (See Paul's statement in 1 Corinthians 7:11, "But if she departs, she must remain unmarried, or else be reconciled to her husband." Even after her departing, Paul still recognizes the man as her "husband.") Though some accuse the Catholic Church of granting annulments, when two people are illegitimately married, then there simply is no marriage. Divorce, on the other hand, seeks to dissolve the bond between two validly married people.

faith alone but also by his works. This means that works of loving obedience, the fruit of God's free gift of grace working in each Christian,[4] are an integral part of our justification before God.[5] Though Protestants often claim these passages are either symbolic or culturally outdated, I came to see that it is the Catholic interpretations which are in harmony with the rest of Scripture, whereas Protestant interpretations often are not.

Another compelling factor that convinced me of the truth of the Catholic Church was the realization that since Christ had given the Church the mission to teach the truth (Matt. 28:18-20), mere men could not take away either the mission or the authority to carry it out. The Protestant Reformers claimed that the Catholic Church had become

---

[4] Cf. Matt. 6:46; 7:21-23; 19:16-21; 25:31-46; Acts 10:34-35; Rom. 2:5-6, 13; Gal. 5:4-6; Phil. 2:12-13; James 1:22-25; 2:4-26; 1 John 3:7; 3:19-24; 4:17-21; 5:2-4.

[5] In order to substantiate his claims that man was justified by faith alone, Luther deliberately added the word "alone" to his German translation of Romans 3:28. In reality, the only time "alone" appears with the word "faith" in the Greek text is in James 2:24 where it says we are "not saved by faith alone." Luther defended his novel addition bragging, "You tell me what a great fuss the Papists are making because the word 'alone' is not in the text of Paul. If your Papist makes such an unnecessary row about the word 'alone,' say right out to him: 'Dr. Martin Luther will have it so,' and say: 'Papists and asses are one and the same thing.' I will have it so, and I order it to be so, and my will is reason enough. I know very well that the word 'alone' is not in the Latin or the Greek text, and it was not necessary for the Papists to teach me that. It is true those letters are not in it, which letters the jackasses look at, as a cow stares at a new gate ... It shall remain in my New Testament, and if all the Popish donkeys were to get mad and beside themselves, they will not get it out." Cited in John Stoddard, *Rebuilding a Lost Faith*, (Rockford, IL: TAN Books), 136-137.

hopelessly corrupted and had lost its identity as Christ's true Church. To reinforce this claim they called the Catholic Church the "Whore of Babylon" and pointed to certain scandalously sinful popes as "antichrists."

Many Protestants claim that the Church of the first three centuries was a "pure" church, and only after the legalization of the Christian faith by the Roman emperor Constantine (in A.D. 312) did the church become "Catholic" and corrupt. But upon studying this issue I found that the doctrines of post-Constantine Catholicism are the same doctrines, some in more primitive form, that were held by Christians for the preceding three centuries.

My study of the writings of the Church Fathers revealed that the early Church believed in the Real Presence of Christ in the Eucharist, confession of sins to a priest, baptismal regeneration, salvation by faith and good works done through grace, that one could reject God's grace and forfeit salvation, that the bishop of Rome is the head of the Church, that Mary is the Mother of God and was perpetually a virgin, that intercessory prayer can be made to the saints in heaven, that purgatory is a state of temporary purification which some Christians undergo before entering heaven. Except for the perpetual virginity and divine motherhood of Mary, all of these doctrines were repudiated by the Protestant Reformers. If the Catholic Church is in error to hold these beliefs, then it was in error long before Constantine legalized Christianity. This would mean that the Church apostatized before the end of the first century, when the apostles were still alive! An absurd theory which even the most anti-Catholic of Protestants can't quite bring themselves to accept.

What I discovered by reading the Church Fathers was that present day Catholic interpretations of Scripture were held by the earliest Christians. They were passed down by Sacred Tradition and preserved and disseminated just as carefully as the Scripture was preserved and copied. Verses I had read hundreds of times concerning "tradition" now took on a whole new meaning. I finally understood the value and necessity of Sacred Tradition. Tradition did not contradict the Bible, rather, it supported it and made it clearer.

The most important of these verses was 2 Thessalonians 2:15 where Paul specified that oral tradition was to be preserved and obeyed the same as the written tradition. Because of my inherited Protestant aversion to "tradition" (In Matt. 15:3-9, Mark 7:1-15, and Col. 2:22 traditions of men are condemned), I had never really appreciated the value of good and wholesome traditions, especially those Sacred Traditions that were given by God and are preserved by the infallible guidance of the Holy Spirit in the Church. I also learned that in places where the Scripture was ambiguous (e.g. infant baptism), Sacred Tradition helped us to understand the intent of the apostles.

How God Deals With Rebellion

As I pondered the phenomenon of the Protestant Reformation, I wondered why God would allow such rebellion to arise and flourish. So I looked to see what Scripture said about such rebellion. I saw that rather than sending immediate destruction upon the rebellious, as in the case of Korah (cf. Num. 16:1ff), God sometimes gave those who rebelled exactly what they asked for, but with a punitive twist.

For example, when the Jews complained to God that they were tired of eating manna and wanted meat, God dealt with their rebellion, saying, "You want meat? I'll give you meat; in fact I'll give you so much meat it will come out of your nostrils until you are sick of it." God caused a great plague, probably due to spoiled meat, that killed many in the wilderness (Num. 11:18-20). The people recognized this punishment for their ingratitude and rebellion and repented, but within a few years they were once again straying from God.

One of the signs of a deteriorating society is a high divorce rate; this was certainly true in ancient Israel.

Rather than continually pleading with them to stop, God allowed Israel to have their divorces as a sign of their hard-heartedness against him (Matt. 19:8; John 12:39-40). They wanted their own way so God allowed them to have their own way, allowing them to sink into apostasy. In the end, God gave Israel a taste of their own medicine, using the very same divorce law for which they had clamored, to "divorce" himself from that spiritually adulterous nation (cf. Is. 50:1; Jer. 3:8).

When the Israelites didn't want God to be their king, asking instead for an earthly king, God knew they were rejecting him so he turned them over to wicked earthly kings (1 Sam. 8:1f). Only later did they realize that when God was their king he had been sparing them the treachery of earthly rulers. Most of Israel's kings were very wicked, leading many people into idolatry and destruction. God allowed these rebellions to run their courses, but worked out his secret plan, nonetheless.

I believe God has dealt similarly with the Protestant rebellion against the Catholic Church. If God spoke now as he spoke in Numbers 11, he might say: "You want a different church? I'll give you a different church. In fact, I'll give you so many different churches you won't be able to count them all." Isn't this exactly what has happened? God has given the protesters what they wanted — and much more: one long, continuous line of protesters: protesters protesting against the Catholic Church and protesters protesting against their fellow protesters. This plague of "protestantism" has spawned thousands of quarreling sects. Time itself has shown that Protestantism is not God's plan for his Church, but rather, is a dismal failure.

As a Catholic, I am now at peace, away from the roiling controversies of Protestantism, secure in the consolation of the truth. I have taken my place in the army of Christ the King in this great battle for souls which has raged from ancient times. I must help others, especially my former Protestant brethren, to see, as I did, that the

Catholic Church is not just the true Church, it's home — it's where we all belong.[6]

After so many wrong turns and blind alleys, I now see and love the Catholic Church for what it is: the ancient, indestructible Church that Jesus established 2000 years ago. So often we are blind to the many good things God has planned for us in life. They're usually placed right in front of us, though we don't (and sometimes *won't*) see them. As an anti-Catholic Protestant, I was like the blind man Jesus healed by rubbing mud on his eyes (John 9:1-17). I rejoice in God's free gift of grace that opened my eyes to see the truth that had always been plainly evident, though I had missed it all those years.

My heavenly Father waited patiently for me, his prodigal son, to wend my way home after I had run away. The day I came home to the Catholic Church I know he smiled down on me and said, "Let us celebrate with a feast, because this son of mine was dead, and has come back to life again; he was lost and has been found!"

[6] I am inspired by the holy example of the Counter-Reformation apologist, St. Francis de Sales (1567-1622). His sermons and apologetics writings converted over *60,000* Reformed Protestants back to the Catholic Church as a result of his bold proclamation of biblical truth. The story of his ministry among the Calvinists, as well as the scriptural and patristic arguments he employed to combat the heresies of Calvin and Luther, can be found in *The Catholic Controversies* (Rockford, IL: TAN Books).

This I Seek: to Dwell in the House of the Lord

Julie Swenson

WITH NOSTALGIC reverence I write the account of my conversion on All Saints' Day. On this day, November 1, 1992, my family and I entered the Catholic Church. It's with gratitude for our Lord's mercy in opening my eyes to the truth of his Church, that I recount the journey that brought me into the Bark of Peter.

I feel a sense of bittersweet irony as I write this testimony of my love for the Catholic Church on the anniversary of the start of the Protestant Reformation. I pray that my conversion story may act as a reparation for my intentional and unintentional sins of slander against the Church when I was a Protestant. I also hope to repair in some small measure the damage done by my Protestant forefathers who broke the unity of the Church. They chose to deal with the problems in the 16th-century Church, not by following the way of prayer and humility and the Cross, but by following the path of rebellion.

It feels good to write down the story of my conversion. Doing so provides a merciful release for the many emotions that accumulate over the course of such a rigorous journey. But it's not easy to convey all the reasons why a complacent, staunchly anti-Catholic, reformed Calvinist would one day find herself outside the doors of the Catholic Church on her knees, begging to be let in.

I'll do my best to describe the series of divine actions that led me from Geneva to Rome.

Like so many other Protestants who wake up one day to find themselves Catholic, converting was the last thing on earth I ever considered. Peter Kreeft, the well-known author and convert from Calvinism, once observed that "No one reads the Bible as an extraterrestrial or as an angel; our church community provides the colored glasses through which we read, the framework or horizon, or limits within which we understand. My 'glasses' were of Dutch Reformed Calvinist construction with a theological framework that stopped very far short of anything 'Catholic.'" Kreeft's observation was certainly true in my case.

Because my Calvinistic framework was so limited, it made the Holy Spirit's work of grace in my life even more remarkable. I had always seen the Catholic Church through glasses not merely colored, but scratched by countless misconceptions about Catholic beliefs and the scandal of the unholy lives of many Catholics who were members of a Church which claims it is the "one, holy, catholic, and apostolic church" of the Nicene Creed.

One thing you must know at the outset is that my conversion journey was not a solo flight — I did not become a Catholic on my own (thank the Lord), but made the journey with my family: my husband Bob, and our children, Holly, Joel, Heather, and Hannah. Although I'm the one who will relate it to you, please bear in mind that this is not my story; it's ours.

A daughter of the Reformation

I was born into a fundamental baptistic family and grew to adulthood utterly contented with the Evangelical piety and theology of my upbringing. My parents imparted to me a strong conviction and knowledge of my Evangelical faith, and neither they nor I ever dreamed that we might not know the whole story of the Christian Church. My mother and father were good and loving parents who nurtured me in a solid Christian environment, inculcating in me a deep love for Jesus and for the Bible. Later, as an adult, I moved away from baptistic theology and embraced Calvinism. But I didn't just switch denominations, I embraced John Calvin's system of theology with gusto and thought of myself Reformed with a capital "R."

Looking back on my Protestant upbringing, I am grateful to God for all the good teaching I received: the Trinity, the divinity of Christ, the reality of heaven and hell and sin, the virgin birth, salvation by grace alone, and my personal need for Christ as my savior. The only real problem I had, though I could not articulate it at the time, was in understanding the role of Church in my life. "What exactly is the Church?" I often wondered to myself. "What is its purpose? And if there is such thing as the 'true' Church, which Protestant denomination is it?"

In 1988, while attending an Orthodox Presbyterian church in Berkeley, I was studying what Scripture says about the importance of the home and family and the role of women in the home. I became fascinated with Scripture's numerous references to the "house of God." What and where was the "house of God?" I asked myself.

I believe this question grew out of my love of Psalm 27:4 (which in my youth I had chosen as my life verse): "One thing have I desired of the Lord and that will I seek after, to dwell in the house of the Lord all the days of my life." I had always imagined the "house of the Lord" to be a physical place, most probably heaven, but it never occurred to me, until now, that it might refer to the Church. As an Evangelical, I had been taught that the Church is an invisible, spiritual body of believers. The notion that Christ's Church was visible and tangible had always seemed far too "Catholic" for me to consider seriously.

One Sunday morning I was listening to a Protestant radio program while I prepared for church. The radio preacher mentioned the "house of God," citing 1 Timothy 3:15. I made a mental note of this, and when I got to church I opened my Bible and looked up the verse, hoping excitedly that it would explain what the Lord's "house" is. What I discovered unsettled me.

The context of the passage is Paul giving pastoral advice to the young bishop Timothy with the proviso, "If I am delayed, you will know how people ought to conduct themselves in God's household, which is the church of the living God, the pillar and foundation of the truth." I was struck by Paul's description of the Church as the "household" of God (cf. Heb. 10:21), and I asked myself how Protestantism could fit that description.

This passage jangled a warning bell deep within me. My instincts told me that the Lord's household must be one of harmony and unity. And even though I was a committed Evangelical, I couldn't deny the fact that the collection of denominations that is corporately known as "Protestantism" is fraught with division and doctrinal disagreements.

"Is Protestantism the pillar and foundation of truth?" A simple question, to be sure, perhaps one easily dismissed without a second thought by countless Evangelicals, but for me it was unnerving. How could it be that the thousands of competing and conflicting Protestant denominations were somehow corporately a stable "pillar and foundation" for the truth? After all, no one of them agreed totally with any of the others as to what the truth is. Which one had the truth?

I closed the Bible in disappointment, unable to accept the implications of this verse, which protrayed a unified, stable, and visible Church. My Protestant concept of the Church was an invisible, fragmented entity composed of individualistic members, bound together by the common cord of Protestant precept that teaching authority comes through the individual Christian's search of the Bible, aided directly by the Holy Spirit.

1 Timothy 3:15 threatened my secure, independent spirit. I was my own authority and determined truth using Scripture as my sole guide. When I shut the Bible in dissappointment I also shut out 1 Timothy 3:15 from my mind. The lack of a final interpretive authority in

Protestantism's theory of an "invisble church" made any consideration of the authority of the Catholic Church remote. I reminded myself that the Roman Catholic Church was the "whore of Babylon"; it taught a false gospel propagated by Satan to deceive and damn. Besides, I reassured myself, it did not really matter whether or not I found *the* denomination, as long as I had a personal relationship with Jesus. As long as I trusted in him for my salvation and read the Bible, I was okay. I reassured myself that I was "saved," and that despite its imperfections, Reformed Christianity was plenty big enough to fill my mind and satisfy my heart. As the service started I did my best to put the whole issue out of my mind and lost myself in the singing of the opening hymn.

That small voice quieted down a bit, but it never went away.

The view of Rome from Geneva

I had embraced Calvinism and its "doctrine of grace" precisely because it offered a satisfying, closed system of theology that gave me all the answers I needed as well as the security of knowing that I was right and everyone else wrong. My smugness was reinforced by Martin Luther, whose pugnacious writings I so enjoyed, who wrote volumes about the horrors of the apostate Catholic Church. I especially relished his anti-Catholic polemics.

I was anti-Catholic, not because I was against Catholics, but because I was against their doctrines. I believed Catholicism was anti-biblical; it did not know the way of salvation; it had added its man-made traditions to the Bible; it could offer no assurance of salvation; its adherents felt they had to earn their salvation, and they lived in constant fear of damnation. My view of Catholicism was no different from that of most Evangelicals and Fundamentalist Protestants.

In the Spring of 1990, Bob and I began attending an Orthodox Presbyterian Church in San Francisco. During that time I experienced a physical and spiritual crisis. I see now that God used this trial to peel away the layers of complacency and smugness in which I had insulated myself for so many years of my Christian life. God led me into a desert of emotional, physical, and spiritual suffering that began when I was confined to bed due to pregnancy complications, and stretched into the miscarriage of my unborn child whom I loved and in whom I had placed so much hope. Having to undergo major surgery following the miscarriage was the wreath of thorns that crowned my suffering.

God used this painful time to reveal much to me about myself. During my pre-miscarriage bed rest and my later convalescence from surgery, I had limitless time for introspection. I began to reexamine my relationship with Christ, and even my motives for being a Christian. The Lord began to show me what a spiritual Pharisee I had become — how prideful and smug I was. I recoiled in shame when the Lord held up a mirror to my soul and I caught a glimpse of myself. For the first time I realized how superior I felt in the armor of my Calvinism, and how pathetic all non-Reformed Christians seemed to me, precisely because they didn't hold to my beliefs.

This confrontation with myself caused me to wrestle with my deeply-held belief in the Calvinist dogma of total depravity. As a staunch spiritual daughter of Calvin, I believed that the unregenerate man is ever in a state of rebellion against God, incapable of doing anything right and good in God's sight. Christians are not themselves righteous, but are merely clothed in the robe of Christ's righteousness — a righteousness that is merely imputed to them; they are not intrinsically made righteous by God's sovereign grace.

I believed Luther's bleak dictum that "We are dunghills covered over with snow." No matter how pure we might appear on the outside, we're not really pure — we remain wretched sinners. I never realized until this point how much this view had distorted my self-image and my view of others. It was easy to see others (especially non-Evangelicals) as pathetic and lost and wretched.

After all, weren't even the best of us merely snow-capped dunghills? And ironically, in spite of my smugness, I was really no different fromthe rest. Everything I did seemed a failure because, as Luther taught, everything I did was polluted by pride, selfishness, or some other sin. But the one difference between me and the "unregenerate" masses was that I trusted Christ; I believed that his grace would vouchsafe my salvation, regardless of the enormity of my sins.

As I lay on my bed of pain the Lord began to show me that this view was a twisted combination of truth and error. It is true that I desperately need the grace of Christ to buoy me up above the inclination to sin that threatens to draw us all downward into ruin, but I also realized that God's grace is not to be presumed upon. God had created me a responsible, rational person who must continually reach out for his grace and, aided by that grace, turn away from sin in order to be saved.

During this desert experience I was further discouraged by my inability to pick up the Scriptures and raise myself out of depression. This inability to find solace in the Bible caused another crisis for me. I had been raised to believe that the written Word of God alone was my sure guide to salvation. Yet for the first time in my life, reading Scripture was insufficient to get out of this spiritual desert. It had never before occurred to me to wonder what Christians did before they had the Bible, though I was always curious to understand how those persecuted for their faith under Communism could be so strong in faith and holiness without Bibles.

Now I began to ponder that question.

God offered me graces during that gloomy summer and fall of my recovery. I begged him to reveal to me the roots of my depression and self-doubt. He answered me in, of all things, the music of a Catholic singer. One Sunday as I lay in bed listening to Christian music on the radio program produced by the Evangelical station where my husband Bob worked, I received an introduction to the Catholic view of the dignity of man and the infinite worth God places on each individual. All my Christian life I had unconsciously avoided cultivating the gifts God had given me in the field of art because they conflicted with my fundamentalist scheme of holiness and service to God. It was difficult to see myself as a unique individual created by God with great potential for using the talents he had placed within me. Although I had the love and support of my husband and children, I still felt alone in my grief and depression.

I found myself calmed and refreshed by the dulcet melodies of John Michael Talbot's music as it came over the radio. His music caught my attention immediately; it was different from anything I had heard before. I was soothed by the music and began to concentrate on the lyrics. I had heard about him, and it amazed me that this Roman Catholic seemed to know Scripture so well that he could write such beautiful songs and sing them as if he really knew who Christ was. The more I listened the more I suspected he did know Christ in a way I did not. He wasn't merely singing about Christ, he seemed to be singing *to* Christ — to be worshipping him in song.

As I lay there listening to the music, I glanced at the Bible lying beside me on the bed. I picked it up but put it down again, unable to read it. I was too spiritually dry to find comfort in its words. I found myself jealous of Talbot's burning love for Christ, and I began to long for the same kind of relationship with Jesus.

At that time, my idea of worshipping Jesus amounted to reading about him in Scripture, singing about him in church, and listening to others preach about him. But none of that was really him. Little by little, the realization began to dawn on me that for so many years I had had a relationship with an idea, a concept called "Jesus," not the real person.

Long ago I had been born again "the Bible way" — as Protestants term the act of surrendering one's life to Jesus Christ, accepting him as one's personal Lord and savior, and trusting in him alone for salvation — but now saw I lacked a relationship with the living Christ. I had worked hard at cultivating a knowledge of Scripture at the expense of cultivating a deeper relationship with the author of Scripture. (I sensed I might even be mildly guilty of worshipping the Bible.)

John Michael Talbot continued to sing to my soul. He sang about bowing in humility before the Lord, about worshipping and calling upon him for mercy and forgiveness, about the value of holy poverty and simplicity, and about the sheer joy of being in the presence of the Lord. As I listened I began to pray along with the music.

A scriptural passage came to mind: Christ's command to die to self by taking up one's cross and suffering with him. I began to see that by his passion and crucifixion Jesus had given me himself as the example I should follow in my suffering. 2 Timothy 2:11-12 says: "If we have died with him we shall also live with him. If we persevere, we shall also reign with him. But if we deny him, he will deny us."

This realization of the profound role of suffering in the life of a Christian was something about which I knew little. As a secure, "don't worry, I have it all worked out" Calvinist, I never felt the need to embrace suffering. Sure, I would put up with it as best I could when it happened to come my way, but that was mere toleration of suffering, a sort of Christian stoicism. I never felt I had to do anything to persevere toward final salvation.

Mine was a Christian mentality that said God did everything for my salvation, and there is nothing for me to do. The idea of embracing suffering as a redemptive act of love and union with Christ crucified was utterly new to me. But in my heart I sensed I had discovered an important truth.

John Michael Talbot's music was so scriptural, and its message seemed to apply much better in the practical outworking of Christian life than much of the typical Christian music to which I was accustomed. When I later learned that he was himself a convert from Fundamentalist Christianity I was shocked.

My ascent through purgatory

It was during this convalescence that I had my first glimpse into the doctrine of purgatory. In fact, I began to believe in it intuitively, though I would not gain a solid scriptural and theological understanding of the doctrine until months later. A turning point in my desert experience came when I began to contemplate the nature and purpose of suffering and pain instead of simply trying to endure or ignore it.

Paul's admonition took on a whole new meaning: "You have been purchased at a price. Therefore, glorify God in your body" (1 Cor. 6:20). This instruction isn't restricted just to those times when one's body is healthy and feels great; I realized that the duty to glorify God in our bodies is perpetual, regardless of the condition of the body. In fact, the more I read Paul's letters, gleaning from them anything I could find on the theme of suffering, the more I realized that Christians are called to glorify God *especially* when enduring physical suffering. This scriptural truth struck me with a force I can't adequately convey in words. I saw that suffering is a gift, not a curse, if only it is accepted as a gift and used to glorify the Lord. The emotional ratification of this truth soon followed the intellectual.

One day while I was praying, I became aware that the offering of my pain to the Lord actually caused me to feel joyful. I didn't just know, I felt the truth that my act of offering my suffering to the Lord was a precious gift that made him happy. Only the fire of God's love can truly purge away sin with its crippling effects and also heal the soul. This process of purification involves suffering, but I understood that suffering was not to be feared as long as it was lovingly returned to the Lord as a gift. And as a loving Father who delights in giving gifts to his children, the Lord isn't satisfied with merely purifying us — he is eager to imbue that purification process with joy, if only we'll let him. Once I was willing to let him, God used my sufferings to burn away the years of spiritual pride and smugness and the stunting effects of a poor self-image that was rooted in the arid soil of Calvin's total depravity doctrine.

The Lord's refining fire began to consume my selfishness and replaced it with humility and gratitude for his love, mercy and compassion. The Lord wanted me to offer him even my desolation, so he could purify it as well. In the months that followed that summer of 1990, the Lord used my emotional and physical purgatory to prepare me for the theological purging he had planned for me. I know I wouldn't have been disposed to consider the case for Catholicism if I hadn't first been chastened through suffering.

John Michael Talbot's Catholicism had become an issue of concern for me. I had to find out if he knew something I didn't. I decided to get hold of some books with which to investigate the Catholic Church. I did so, and God promptly tore the roof off of my neatly-arranged theological house, and started moving out the furniture. The whole Calvinist decor had to go.

It was painful. It was humbling to admit that I had been taught wrongly about certain doctrines. More painful yet, all my years of sneering at Catholics and their beliefs came back to haunt me now. And yet I felt purified and clean as I studied Catholic beliefs in the clear light of a willingness to know the truth. The experience was difficult but joyful. I felt free to believe as the Church has believed for two thousand years. As painful as it was to redefine my doctrines, my desire to love and be loved by the living Christ was stronger, and I was not afraid. I wanted to know the truth about Jesus and his Church, whatever the cost.

In the words of Leonie Caldecott, another convert to Catholicism, "How does one find the truth? In my case it was not an intellectual matter. I had to undergo a conversion of the heart, a reorientation of the will before I could shift my perspective to the Church. In order for this to happen, my heart had to be broken, my will crushed by events beyond my control, events I was not able to rationalize while they were happening. My need

of God and his Church had to be overwhelmingly demonstrated to me." And it certainly was! I no longer saw
myself as merely an individual, mystically united with
Christ in some obscure, indefinite way; I was really one
with Christ, united to his Body the Church.

This internal change of direction became external in
October 1990 when my brother Doug returned to California after a visit to the East Coast. For fifteen years he
had been wrestling with his desire to live a life of dedicated prayer while working as a youth minister. He was
restless, wanting to live totally by faith, but continually
hindered by the practical realities of making a living and
conforming to the sometimes rigid confines of the Evangelical congregations in which he ministered. Upon his
return, he was determined to obey God in his calling of
a life of faith and prayer no matter how others objected
or disapproved.

The Sunday after Doug returned we attended services as usual at the Orthodox Presbyterian Church in San
Francisco. That particular day a visiting elder preached
a sermon entitled, "What is Worship?" In his sermon he
posed the question: Why do you come to church? For
fellowship? For edification? To serve? His message was,
"If you come for any other reason than the worship of
God, you are coming for the wrong reason."

I listened in rapt attention as he proceeded to recount
the Bible's descriptions of the worship that is taking
place around the throne of God — myriads of angels and
saints bowing in unending adoration, worshipping and
praising the Lord — crying out, "Holy, holy, holy, Lord
God almighty." He described the censers and incense
being offered with the prayers of the saints at the foot of
the Lord's golden altar.

It was all so glorious, and I know I was not alone in
feeling an acute longing and emptiness in my soul to
worship God in this way. This excellent sermon on the
heavenly worship described in Scripture was actually
counter-productive, since I (and I suspect many others
in that church) couldn't help but compare the scintillat-

ing splendor of the heavenly liturgy with the austere Presbyterian "service" we were attending.

Bob, Doug, and I discussed the sermon on the way home, and concluded sadly that we would have to wait for Heaven to truly worship God the way the blessed in heaven did. I remarked that it sure seemed that our Protestant worship services were not really worship at all, but only meetings where we could sing about the Lord, and hear preaching about the Lord. "I guess that's just the way it will have to be down here," I sighed.

The next week we shared with Doug how much John Michael Talbot's music had ministered to us. I said to him, half-jokingly, "You should be a monk, too! That's what you are." We laughed about it, the absurdity of the whole Catholic "monk" thing striking us all as very funny. I had no inkling that my offhand jest would penetrate his soul so deeply.

The next day he fixed me with a serious look and said, "You know, maybe that is what I am." He called the Roman Catholic Diocese of Oakland which referred him to the Anglican Church, since he was a Protestant. They told him that the Anglicans have orders of religious. Opening the telephone book, he picked out an Episcopal church. It seemed to be conservative, since it advertised their use of the *1928 Book of Common Prayer*. He called, and they invited him to attend a service to see if their spirituality was what he was seeking.

The next Sunday, my brother attended this Episcopal church, part of a small, conservative, "High-Church" Anglican diocese which had broken off from the liberal Episcopal Church in the late 1970's. He returned to our home that afternoon and recounted with astonished excitement that the pattern of heavenly worship that we had heard preached the previous week, he had just witnessed at the Anglican parish. It was the first church service in which he had experienced the worship of God through liturgy. Oh, I longed to go so badly! The more he explained it the hungrier I became for liturgical worship. I think my reaction surprised even Bob. I had not shared with him the details of my spiritual journey (much of which paralleled his own) so he hadn't realized the depth of my longing to know and to worship the living Christ.

A place to rest

John Michael Talbot's song, "The Lover and the Beloved," introduced me to St. John of the Cross, a 16th Century Spanish mystic who spoke of the "dark night of the soul." He showed me that the Cross is the consummation of the union of the Christ and his beloved the Church. While on the cross a soldier's lance pierced Jesus' side, which issued forth the blood and water that signified the Church. This fulfilled the work prefigured in Adam, who foreshadowed Christ (cf. Rom. 5:14) from whose side Eve was taken, born of the flesh and bone that the Lord drew from his wound (cf. Gen. 2:21-24).

After absorbing Doug's description of the Anglican Mass I knew I had to go and witness it for myself! Bob shared my desire to experience liturgical worship, so the following Sunday he and our children accompanied me to the Anglican service. The shock at what I saw was minimized by what my brother had previously told me of the meaning of the liturgy's outward forms such as the crucifix, incense, altar, candles, vestments, Mary, liturgical prayers, sanctuary lamp, and tabernacle, and even the bodily postures of kneeling and genuflecting. I was delighted and comforted and excited by what I found there.

Our initial visit to this church quickly led to our attendance on a regular basis. Several insights emerged in the first months of exposure to Catholic doctrine, filtered as it was through an Anglican lens. First, because of the incarnation, I realized that there is now humanity in the trinitarian Godhead. Second, I saw that in Communion, because of Christ's work on the cross and his Resurrection, his divine life deigns to indwell our humanity. That is what some theologians call the "holy exchange" of life. Christ is not only in us spiritually, but in Holy Communion he actually comes to us physically.

Our relationship with Christ is not just spiritual, but physical, too. The Incarnation of Christ crowned the union of the spiritual and the physical, found uniquely in human persons. Christ the God-man became the perfect example of the Father's delight in the human union of spirit and flesh. I now began to see that all of my Christian life I had been reinforcing a negative view of the physical aspect of man through my Calvinistic doctrine of the total depravity of man.

Another insight came when I recognized a flaw in the way Bob and I disciplined our children. It had always been difficult for me to teach them about the boundless love of God and at the same time, according to our Reformed theology, teach them that Christ died only for the elect and forgave only them. The rest of humanity, probably the vast majority, was "hated of God," as Calvin put it, and were damned to eternal separation from him. Since I had no way of knowing for sure if my children were numbered among the elect, how could I tell them truthfully that God was their Father and that he loved and had forgiven their sins? Correcting and training them through discipline was very awkward for me.

Nonetheless, we would go through our usual routine of telling God we loved him and asking him to forgive us, and then ask forgiveness of the one whom we had offended. Then I would tell them, "Since the Bible tells us that the rod of correction drives sin out of the heart, and because I love you, I must punish you." Sometimes the kids would ask me why I was punishing them if God had already forgiven them. I wanted to tell them, "Because you must pay for your sins; there is a just recompense to be paid, and the wrong must be righted. If you break the neighbor's window, you have to replace it. So, if you lie or disobey me, you must pay in order to right the account." But I couldn't really say all that because temporal payment for sins did not fit into our Calvinistic theology.

In my heart I knew I was being inconsistent, but I could never figure out how to avoid it, so I just put the subject aside until I could study the issue further. But it always bothered me. If God had forgiven us, why the need for the rod of correction? My common sense asked why mere words of repentance were not enough. Why did we need to suffer for our sins? The Reformed theology I had inherited told me I would never have to answer for my sins at the judgment seat of Christ, because God had already forgiven me for all my sins. But I could see throughout Scripture and in everyday life that there are always punishments meted out for sins that have been forgiven. Over time, the more I tried to make sense out of this inconsistency the more tormented I became.

My brother found in the company of these Anglo-Catholics a knowledge and appreciation of monasticism and a way to live out his call to a life of prayer. They were so helpful in counseling and directing him to pursue his desire to live a life of prayer, recognizing that this was a calling of God.

Happy at seeing my brother's peace, I began to read about monasticism, especially Thomas Merton's earlier works, such as his classic on the monastic life, *Seven Storey Mountain*. It was his autobiography, tracing his journey out of unbelief and into Christianity, his eventual entrance into the Catholic Church, and finally his retirement from the world when he became a Cistercian monk. It was one of the best books I had ever read. It introduced me to the reality that people did enter the Christian faith as Catholics, deliberately not choosing a Protestant denomination.

This was an eye-opener for me. I also learned that monks are not sickly failures who took refuge in the monastery because they could not make it in the "real world" and sought thereby to escape it. No, these men are very healthy, intelligent, even brilliant men who, to varying degrees, leave the world for the sake of the world, to deny themselves temporal goods for higher goods, and to give themselves, mind, soul, and body, to prayer and service for the salvation of souls.

Consecrated celibacy and monasticism is the living out of St. Paul's well-known exhortation to holiness: "I would like you to be free from concern. An unmarried man is concerned about the Lord's affairs — how he can please the Lord. But a married man is concerned about the affairs of this world — how he can please his wife — and his interests are divided. An unmarried woman or virgin is concerned about the Lord's affairs: Her aim is to be devoted to the Lord in both body and spirit. But a married woman is concerned about the affairs of this world — how she can please her husband. I am saying this for your own good, not to restrict you, but that you may live in a right way in undivided devotion to the Lord" (1 Cor. 7:30-35).

The monastic vocation to a life of consecrated virginity, obedience, and poverty is foreign to Evangelical piety. But the more I learned about Catholic asceticism the more I saw that it is the practical method of following our Lord's advice to the rich young man: "A man came up to Jesus and asked, 'Teacher, what good thing must I do to get eternal life?' . . . [Jesus responded] 'If you want to enter life, obey the commandments.' . . . 'All these I have kept,' the young man said. 'What do I still lack?' Jesus answered, 'If you want to be perfect, go, sell your possessions and give to the poor, and you will have treasure in heaven. Then come, follow me'" (Matt. 19:16-17, 20-21).

I cross the bridge

I began to sense that Anglicanism, although filled with beautiful liturgical traditions and "Catholic" doctrines, was not the destination of my pilgrimage. However close to Catholicism it came in outward form, it isn't actually Catholic. I knew that although the Anglican Church was a pleasant and instructive rest stop, it wasn't home.

Perhaps the most important factor in my journey toward Rome was my growing appreciation for liturgical worship— I was falling in love with it. The beauty and symbolism of the Anglican Eucharistic liturgy was everything I longed for in public worship.

My husband, Bob, had also come to realize the infinite value of the Mass as our Lord revealed Himself to him in the breaking of the Bread. Instead of the focus being just Christ-centered, it was now Trinitarian-centered: the soul's eyes beholding and worshipping the Father, through the Son, in the power of the Holy Spirit.

The Mass is a prayer to God the Father in the name of Christ our great High Priest who continually makes present his once-for-all sacrifice of Calvary to the Father (cf. Heb. 7:24-25, 9:24). At Mass, by a miracle of Christ's infinite grace, we are made present at the foot of the cross, so that we too may offer ourselves in union with him as a living sacrifice to our Heavenly Father. My reading of Catholic works on the Eucharist showed me a profound connection between the Old Testament Passover sacrifice (cf. Ex. 12:1-28) and the Mass.

The Passover sacrifice was not considered complete until the people had eaten the Passover lamb, whose blood, sprinkled on the doorposts and lintels of their homes, protected them from the Angel of Death. In the same way Jesus Christ our Lord, the true Lamb of God (cf. John 1:29, 36), invites us to partake of the sacrificial, eucharistic meal, his own Body and Blood. He promised this gift to his disciples (cf. John 6: 22-71), and he fulfilled his promise in the institution of the Eucharist at the Last Supper when he gave them his Body and Blood to eat and drink as the true Passover Lamb that would be sacrificed.

St. Paul explained the meaning of the Last Supper and the Real Presence of Jesus in the Eucharist: "The cup of blessing which we bless, is it not a participation in the blood of Christ? The bread which we break, is it not a participation in the body of Christ?" (1 Cor. 10: 16); "I received from the Lord what I handed on to you, namely, that the Lord Jesus on the night in which he was betrayed took bread, and after he had given thanks, broke it and said, 'This is my body, which is given for you. Do this in remembrance of me.' In the same way after the supper, he took the cup, saying, 'This cup is the new covenant in my blood. Do this, whenever you drink it, in remembrance of me.' Every time, then, you eat this bread and drink this cup, you proclaim the death of the Lord until he comes! This means that whoever eats the bread or drinks the cup of the Lord unworthily sins against the body and blood of the Lord. He who eats and drinks without recognizing the body eats and drinks a judgment on himself" (1 Cor. 11:23-29). As an Evangelical I had read these passages hundreds of times but they never made much of an impression on me. But now that I had been exposed to the theology of the Mass, the truth of the Catholic interpretation of these verses became immediately apparent to me.

I found that all early Church testimony is the same. The earliest Christians unanimously believed that the Eucharist truly is the Body and Blood of the Lord, and they believed that the Mass is a holy sacrificial meal through which they could partake of the Lord's Body and Blood.

The Real Presence of Christ Jesus in the Eucharistic sacrifice and meal is the center and focus of Christian life and worship, for daily we are given the awesome opportunity to offer ourselves and our intentions as a living sacrifice to the Father through Jesus the Son in union with him, dying with him, and receiving from his perfect sacrifice a meal by which we receive immortality and share in the very life of God. It is staggering, and the greatest privilege we can know on earth.

As I was busily studying Catholic teachings and checking them against Scripture to make sure they were "biblical," my brother, under the good counsel of the bishop of this new Anglo-Catholic diocese, spent a few months at a Roman Catholic Cistercian monastery in northern California. The bishop felt this would help him best discern whether or not monasticism was his true calling. It was an education for us too, as he would report back all he was learning.

One feeling that stands out in my mind was the sense of horror and betrayal I felt at having been deceived about the Catholic Church. For the most part the misinformation we had imbibed was unintentionally given us by sincere though ignorant Protestant preachers and writers. But I realized unhappily that some of these deceptions were knowingly perpetrated by "professional" anti-Catholic Protestants: most ex-Catholics, and some even ex-priests.

The shock of realizing that one's view of Church history is warped and based on wrong presuppositions is overwhelming. The average Protestant just assumes that the Church founded by Christ and the Apostles went astray and apostatized very early, and never really returned to doctrinal purity until the Reformation, almost 1500 years later. Many simply ignore or attempt to explain away the Lord's promises regarding the perpetuity and doctrinal integrity of his Church: "Thou art Peter, and upon this rock I will build my Church, and the gates of hell shall not prevail against it" (Matt. 16:18) and, "When he, the Spirit of truth is come, he will guide you into all truth" (John 16:23).

If my Protestant presuppositions were correct, the gates of hell *had* prevailed against the Church shortly after the apostolic era, and the Holy Spirit abandoned the Church. Either Christ let us down and deceived us by teaching us that there would be one Spirit, one faith, one baptism and one Church which would endure until the end of the world (cf. Matt. 28:20), or my anti-Catholic bias and interpretation of Scripture and Church history was unrealistic and unscriptural.

John Henry Newman, the famous Evangelical Protestant convert to Catholicism, once said, "Knowledge of Church history is the death of Protestantism." He was right. My study of the early Church showed clearly that it was Catholic in its beliefs and practices — in fact, it had begun calling itself "Catholic" at least as early as the end of the first century.

Ironically, while I was wrestling with Catholic doctrine I found the Catholic Church has always held and proclaimed (more clearly and vigorously than any Protestant denomination, I felt) key biblical doctrines such as the inspiration and inerrancy of Scripture, the atonement of Christ, salvation by grace alone, and the need to pursue holiness. I came to the conclusion that Catholics are real Christians; John Michael Talbot was not a fluke.

In the fall of 1991, my brother shared with us a cassette tape of Scott Hahn as he spoke of his conversion from being a Presbyterian minister to being a Catholic. Many of our theological and emotional struggles with Catholicism ceased as we learned that we were not alone. It was a great encouragement to hear the story of another Evangelical who had been staunchly anti-Catholic and who had experienced most of the difficulties with Catholicism that we were then dealing with. Another Reformed Evangelical had converted! This rousing conversion testimony gave us the emotional and biblical encouragement we needed to complete our journey to Rome. In particular, Hahn's explanation of the issue of justification and salvation (perhaps the single most difficult issue for me to deal with when it came to the Catholic Church) helped us see that the Catholic Church has always held to the biblical teaching in this area.

We realized that Martin Luther had deviated badly from historic Christian orthodoxy when he introduced his unbiblical theory of *sola fide* (justification by faith alone, apart from any works of obedience wrought by God's free gift of grace). It became clear that God's grace is infinitely more powerful than our sins. When we ask for his forgiveness and healing, he doesn't merely declare us righteous (as Luther thought), he makes us righteous. And by the grace of his Son Jesus Christ, we really become objectively beautiful and pleasing in his sight. As the Bible says, "For as the rain and the snow come down from heaven, and return not thither but water the earth, making it bring forth and sprout, giving seed to the sower and bread to the eater, so shall my word be that goes forth from my mouth; it shall not return to me empty, but it shall accomplish that which I purpose, and prosper in the thing for which I sent it " (Isaiah 55:10-11).

I came to see that through the Lord's free gift of grace Christians really become sons and daughters of God. This change is an intrinsic reality, not a mere extrinsic formality — the legal fiction Luther purported.

Bob and I continued attending the Anglican Church that fall, but at night, after the children were in bed, we burned the midnight oil, poring over Catholic books, magazine articles, and tapes. I began reading Fr. John Hardon's *The Catholic Catechism*, which I had checked out from the local library. The doctrines of the sovereignty of God, free will, grace, faith, Scripture and Tradition, the Church as a continuing incarnation of Christ's presence in the world, and Marian doctrines all fell into place one by one. Through the lucid writings of this holy Jesuit priest I became convinced that the doctrines of the Catholic Church were true. My soul was nourished and fortified by the Church's rich, mature, and time-tested system of faith and morals. It was like finding the pearl of great price.

I continued to grow in love for the Catholic Church as I witnessed the many examples of quiet, unrestrained charity that I saw in the lives of Catholics I encountered. I had never witnessed such a liberty of love in the Evangelical setting I knew, and wondered why this should be. Then one day in reading the Documents of Vatican II, I came upon a very important statement dealing with ecumenism, "'If we say that we have not sinned, we make him a liar, and his Word is not in us' (1 John 1:10). This holds good for sins against unity. Thus in humble prayer, we beg pardon of God and of our separated brethren, just as we forgive those who trespass against us." No wonder I had sensed from the first in my growing relationship with the Church a spirit of humility and charity toward separated brethren. Truly this was the fruit of repentance.

As Bob and I grew in love for the Church, I began to question why we as Anglo-Catholics were not part of the Catholic Church. As we questioned their "branch" and "via media" theories (the former being the Anglican concept that the "Catholic Church" is validly expressed in three branches, Roman Catholic, Anglican, and Orthodox; the second being that the Anglican Church was a viable "middle way" between Protestantism and the Catholic Church), we saw that though Anglicans were outwardly "Catholic," they were inwardly Protestant — they were living in a de facto state of "protest" against the Church of Rome by not submitting entirely to its doctrines and to its authority. The essential question was, "did Christ leave behind a fallible Church, capable of teaching error?" If so, we were left as orphans, insecure and fighting among ourselves without protection. But that option contradicts Jesus' express promise when he said, "I will not leave you orphans" (John 14:18). Increasingly, I wanted to be identified with "Holy Mother Church" as She is affectionately called by her children. I yearned to "go home" and claim the marvelous spiritual heritage and doctrinal certitude — the fullness of the Christian faith that had been mine all along.

After ten months in the Anglican Church, we as a family wanted to be identified with the Catholic Church. When we joined the Anglican Church, we thought we were joining the Catholic Church, or at least a living branch of it. But during the summer of 1991 we came to the sad realization that we were not yet in the Catholic Church. One statement in the excellent three-volume apologetics work, *Radio Replies* (Rockford: TAN, 1979), where the authors respond to a question on church unity, particularly struck me: "If you believe that the Church of England ought to be in communion with Rome, and is not, how can you justify yourselves in remaining where you ought not to be, in refusing to take that step personally which the corporate Anglican Church cannot and will not take?" After reading that, Bob and I never doubted the direction in which we had to go — into the Catholic Church.

We formally left the Anglican Church at the end of August and started preparations for our entry into the Catholic Church. We had worked out all the major Catholic dogmas, the Immaculate Conception of Mary being the last, but one of the most beautiful and spiritually edifying doctrines for the Christian. One night in September, I was brought to the realization of the role of Mary's intercession in our conversion, and what a prominent role it was. I was so grateful and humbled at the thought of God bringing us into his Church.

All along, I was very conscious that God had reduced me to being a little child, and I was being carried ever so tenderly into the arms of Mother Church. I started to praise God my Father for his tender and loving care for me over the past year, but I knew that this particular aspect of my care was not from God the Father. His job had been to reduce me to ashes in a loving, but firm way. God the Son, no, he was my Lord, my Master, my love, my Brother.

At first I concluded it could only be the work of the Holy Spirit. But that was not entirely right. His work was the light and fire of purification. No, the care I was given that brought me home to the Church after being open to the truth was the tender care of a mother who gently loves her child, covering and protecting it from all harm. Blessed Mother Mary! I very clearly sensed her strong maternal presence that night and her powerful intercessory work on my behalf, as well as that of the Son before the Father Himself.

The last week of October, 1991, my husband, Bob, our two older children, and I made our First Confession, and the entire family was conditionally baptized. And finally the next day, the Feast of All Saints at a Traditional Latin Mass, we were formally welcomed into the Catholic Church and received our First Holy Communion. There are no words to describe the joy and peace I felt having arrived at the end of my long and often painful journey home. After receiving the anointing of holy oil and receiving Holy Communion, no longer were we on the outside of the Church looking in, deprived of the life- and grace-giving power of the sacraments.

All my Christian life I had denied being the way God made me — a body (with sensory perception to approach God) as well as a soul (the mystical or spirit approach to God). The seven Sacraments are the outward visible signs of inward invisible imparting of grace to correspond with our physical body and spiritual soul. If we deny either aspect, physical or spiritual, we are unbalanced in our approach to Christ and his Church in this world. It appears that all Protestant misconceptions (communion of saints, the papacy, sacraments, the veneration of relics, images, liturgy, and the humanity of Christ) all revolve around Protestant refusal to acknowledge the external, physical expressions of the Christian religion.

We hosted a pot-luck dinner at our home afterward to celebrate. During the celebrations I quietly reflected on the workings of the Holy Spirit in my soul during the past year. He had worked in me in three ways for three ends. First, to pierce, purge, and humble me as at the start of my conversion. Second, to uplift, strengthen, and enable me to follow his leading. And third, to still my restless heart so I could hear him teach me the truth. The only response of gratitude I could make was to cry out to the Lord in the words of Psalm 131: "O Lord, my heart is not proud nor my eyes haughty, nor do I exercise myself in things too high for me. Rather, I have stilled and quieted my soul like a weaned child. Like a weaned child on its mother's lap, so is my soul within me." How I yearn to give back to God through his Church a tenth even of all he has given to me through the Church.

Most of our friends, the Fundamentalists, Evangelicals, and Reformed Protestants we knew and loved, were so shocked (and in many cases angered) by our conversion, they simply did not care to know why we chose the

Catholic Church. Their apathy sometimes made us feel lonely and frustrated. It hurt to realize that so few of our former friends were interested enough to ask us about the joys and pains of our search for the "fullness of the Christian faith." But since my conversion many Protestants have asked me "Why Catholicism?" I answer: "Because it is the truth — the fullness of the Christian faith; and because in it I can receive the sacraments, Christ's means of imparting grace through the ministry of his Church." I ask them, "How could you *not* be Catholic?"

When I selected Psalm 27:4 as my life's verse I didn't fully understand its meaning for my life. Now I do. "One thing have I asked of the Lord and this will I seek after: to dwell in the house of the Lord all the days of my life, to behold the beauty of the Lord and to pray in his Tabernacle." As a Catholic, I now dwell in the House of the Lord — his Church, his family. Each time I attend Mass, there in his house, "I behold his loveliness and pray in his tabernacle."

God's work of grace in bringing me and my family into the Catholic Church has been, in the words of author and fellow convert from Evangelical Protestantism Sheldon Vanauken, "a severe mercy." As a newly-adopted daughter of the Church, I give thanks to the Lord, for his mercy endures forever.

Oy!

Rick Conason

BEFORE YOU can understand why I became a Catholic you need to know something about the kind of Jewish family in which I was raised. And before you can understand the kind of Jewish family in which I was raised you need to know something about my grandparents, Emil and Cel.

They were both born to Jewish parents shortly after the turn of the century — Emil in Poland, Cel in America. She was the eldest daughter of the only Jewish family in Iowa (or so I was told). Emil's parents emigrated to the U.S. when he was about two years old, and they settled in Trenton, New Jersey. When Emil was twenty years old he made his way to New York City in search of the political and social stimulation to be had there.

New York in the Roaring Twenties was then, as it is now, a magnet for all stripes of liberalism, everything from avant-garde artists and poets, to left-wing intellectuals, political radicals, and atheists. Emil and Cel were quite at home in the political and social chaos that seethed around them. Both were close to notable figures of that era, such as Henry Miller (the author of such controversial works as *Tropic of Capricorn* and *Tropic of Cancer*), with whom they lived for some time. Emil joined the Communist Party, but left shortly thereafter, disillusioned because it had gotten too "Stalinist" for his taste. One by-product of his short-lived days as a Communist was the validation of his atheism. Emil always regarded himself as a Jew, but he did not believe in God. Cel, likewise, was strongly Jewish in a cultural sense, but she too was a devout atheist.

Around the time of his brief flirtation with Communism, Emil met Cel, who had been sent to New York by her parents to finish her schooling. They fell in love and were married shortly thereafter; he was twenty three, she was eighteen. They settled down to raise a family in one of Brooklyn's Jewish neighborhoods. Emil studied medicine and became a physician. Throughout his career he maintained his office in the heart of Greenwich Village which, even then, was the heart New York progressive liberalism. Cel, an accomplished artist, became a public school teacher.

My grandparents never lost their attachment to left-wing causes and politics. In fact, *the* defining characteristic of their social and political philosophy was liberalism (Look up the word "liberal" in the dictionary and you'll find Emil and Cel's picture). Their brothers and sisters, my great-uncles and aunts, also moved to New York for life, happiness, and the pursuit of liberalism. These great uncles and aunts included union organizers, Communists, and early supporters of Planned Parenthood. It was in this hot house of liberalism that my father was raised, inheriting the ideologies of his parents. He met my mom, they married, and began phase three of Conason Family Liberalism.

In the fullness of time I was born, and I grew up in Brooklyn. I attended the local public elementary school, took art classes at the Brooklyn Museum, and raised vegetables in a children's plot at the Brooklyn Botanic Garden. I ran with a boisterous group of neighborhood kids. Our free time was spent playing stickball and punchball, riding bikes, and roaming alleys like feral pack rats. My fondest childhood memories are of the many weekends spent with my family at Coney Island. (I can still regularly score over 300 at Skee-Ball, thank you very much.)

Our apartment was three floors above Emil and Cel's (of course I never called them Grandpa and Grandma, they were far too progressive for that sort of thing). It was here that I spent large amounts of time with them and the other relatives of their generation, becoming steeped in the liberal lore of my clan. I learned to have compassion for the worker, to be amused at the hypocrisy of religion, and to accept the political and social ideology espoused by my parents and relatives.

A typical family gathering at the Conason home: We children would run around the apartment playing while the adults gathered in the living room to talk. Well, "talk" is not really a forceful enough verb. They would argue for hours at the top of their lungs about politics, law, psychology, religion, art, etc. If it was controversial they would argue about it. Coming to a consensus was unimportant. The fun was in the arguing. One of my great aunts or uncles would often advance a position he or she did not agree with, simply to provoke an argument. There was, of course, one cardinal rule governing these proceedings: Since these contests were always and only between extreme left-wing views versus *radical* left-wing views, the only possible conclusions that could be drawn were liberal ones.

Religion had no place in our family life. We never prayed or read the Torah. We did not observe the Sabbath or any Jewish holy day except Passover, and this observance was as secularized as possible. A Conason Family Seder consisted of my great-uncle reciting in Hebrew the opening prayer over the wine. Then came the inevitable debates on politics, etc., while the traditional foods were eaten. Passover was a way for us to proclaim solidarity with our cultural roots — our Jewishness — but it was never regarded as a religious festival. We never attended Temple, and my only involvement with the religion of Judaism came when I attended Hebrew school.

My first year of Hebrew school was spent at a small, poor, Orthodox yeshiva. The next year I switched to a

large, affluent Reform yeshiva (Reform being the theologically liberal wing of Judaism), mainly because it had
a fully-equipped gym and swimming pool and, more
importantly, because all of my friends were teasing me
about going to the Orthodox Hebrew school. I vividly
remember the love and joy of the people at the Orthodox
yeshiva, as well as the fervor of their religious celebrations. I also recall my disgust at the watered-down Judaism of the Reform congregation as well as the hypocrisy
and coldness toward the faith I observed there. Compared to the vibrant piety of the Orthodox Judaism to
which I had been exposed, Reform Judaism seemed cynical and empty. In my third year of yeshiva I rebelled. My
parents wanted me to continue, but my religious upbringing was unimportant to them, so they didn't insist.
Sadly, I never finished Hebrew school, and I never made
my Bar-Mitzvah.

Emil died suddenly on April Fool's day, 1966. In July
of that year my family moved from Brooklyn to Great
Neck, an upper-middle class New York suburb. This
move, so soon after the loss of the man I never called
grandfather, was very difficult for me. I became a lonely,
confused teenager. My only friends were a couple of
other social losers like myself. The older I got the more
timid, insecure, gullible, and overweight I became. As
with many lonely and introverted youth, I took refuge in
books. I spent many an afternoon, not in the normal
rowdy pursuits of my junior high school peers, but in the
quiet of my bedroom, devouring books by the score.
Sure, I was a nerd, but at least I was a literate nerd.

During the late '60s era of pot-smoking, draft card-
burning, and psychedelic hippiedom, I went the way of
all teenage flesh: I rebelled against the morals and mores
of my parents' generation. And the really weird thing
about it all was that since my parents and their friends
were so left-wing the only direction toward which I
could rebel was *right*.

I became a conservative (Oh, how I loved throwing
that in my father's face when we argued). I sneered at

my family's quaint radicalism. I loathed their pro-social-ist leanings, and I aggravated them with my new-found enthusiasm for the Vietnam War. My rebellion knew no bounds. I openly supported Richard Nixon, joined Civil Air Patrol, and seriously investigated the prospects of attending the U. S. Air Force Academy. But this flirtation with the Right was short-lived.

My attitudes changed again during my junior year in high school. I began to exercise and lost weight, I made more friends, and even managed to find a girlfriend. The source of this metamorphosis was the discovery of the pleasures to be had in sex, drugs, and rock and roll. It didn't take much pressure for me to throw away my "I support Nixon" button, jettison my conservative views, and join my peers at the wallowing hole of drugs and immorality.

I didn't want my new friends to reject me — I wanted to fit in — so certain compromises had to be made. My "square" values had to be jettisoned. My opposition to recreational drug use had to go (this was easy once I discovered I liked drugs). Although I never went as far as my relatives, I embraced my heritage as a progressive, liberal New York Jew. One unforeseen side effect of this transformation was that I also developed a cynical and sardonic personality. Not surprisingly, this personality type is common in my family!

Other than what I learned at the yeshiva, my only contact with religion was when I ran across a Billy Gra-ham crusade now and then while watching television. Sometimes I'd wish that what he said about God were true, but I knew it was all fantasy. I had no time for Christ or his born-again followers and their "Jesus Loves You!" bumper stickers. The closest I came to faith was my support of Zionism. Although, oddly, I did not like many of the Jews I knew personally, I was convinced that the Jews were a special people — "The Chosen," as I was taught at the yeshiva — and that the State of Israel deserved special support.

By the end of high school, I wanted to get out of New York and see what might be out there lurking beyond the boundaries of the left-wing, atheistic Judaism that circumscribed my existence. I managed to get about as far away as possible from the concrete jungle by enrolling at Miami University in Oxford, Ohio, 40 miles from the nearest city. Miami University had 14,000 students and I knew only one other "New York Jew." The culture shock was hard to adjust to at first, but I stuck it out, and by my sophomore year I had grown to love it.

One new experience I had to deal with at Miami U was the campus contingent of "Jesus Freaks." Most of them belonged either to "Campus Crusade for Christ", or "Inter-Varsity Christian Fellowship." Although I had read about "Jesus Freaks," until I came to Ohio I had never met any. These clean-cut students would approach me and ask earnestly, "Have you accepted Jesus Christ as your personal Lord and Savior?" Given my citified Jewish background, I found them and their questions naive and ignorant, but also kind of cute (the way the Amish can be kind of cute, in their own way). Unlike many students who brushed them off with derision, I enjoyed talking to born-again Christians, mainly because I liked playing with their minds. I could refute their claims about Christ's divinity and messiahship (or so I thought), and my cynical nature loved to try to sow in their minds doubt about their Christian beliefs. Since I had been "wised-up" to religion by my parents and grandparents, I had a fun time wising-up these brainwashed followers of Jesus.

During my sophomore year I met Tom, a born-again Christian, who immediately struck me as a good and sincere person. He was a religion major, and that interested me. We argued about the existence of God, Jesus, and Christianity, and I played my usual mind games with him, but something unusual happened. Each time Tom and I debated religion I lost. He had convincing answers to atheistic arguments, and he raised points I could not seem to refute. Our discussions sometimes lasted for hours, and we met to talk several times each week. Gradually my attitude toward Christianity changed from cynical antagonism to curiosity. I became especially fascinated with the biblical prophesies regarding the apocalyptic Second Coming of Christ, popularized by Evangelical author Hal Lindsey in his best-seller, *The Late Great Planet Earth*. Tom was only too happy to give me such books to whet my appetite for learning about Christianity.

One evening Tom and I stayed up late in my dorm room discussing the Second Coming of Christ. I didn't believe in Jesus, but I was intrigued by the Christian claims regarding his return to earth that would be marked by the tremendous natural upheavals known as the Tribulation. After Tom left I went to bed but couldn't sleep. I kept thinking about our conversation and started to wonder. "What if there *is* a Messiah? And what if *Jesus* really is the Messiah. And what if he really *is* coming again soon to judge the world — me included. At that moment I heard a voice in my mind say clearly, "Zechariah 14."

"What?" I said to myself, startled. I knew Zechariah was a prophetic book from the Bible, but I had never read it.

"Zechariah 14," echoed again in my head.

"It's one in the morning. I'll read it tomorrow," I muttered to myself with exasperation and a little nervousness.

The voice was emphatic. "No. Now."

"Hah!" I thought to myself with relief. "I don't even own a Bible. I'll read it some other time." I turned over and tried to put the whole thing out of my mind and get some sleep. Then I remembered that Tom had accidentally left his Bible on my desk that evening (was it an accident?). Realizing I was not going to get any sleep anyway, I got up, took Tom's Bible into the bathroom (I didn't want my roommate to wake up and catch me reading the Bible), and started to look for Zechariah. I found it and thumbed to chapter 14. What I found leaped off the page:

"Behold, a day of the Lord is coming. . . . Then the Lord will go forth and fight against those nations . . . . On that day his feet shall stand on the Mount of Olives. . . . The Lord your God will come, and all the holy ones with him. On that day there shall be neither cold nor frost. . . . On that day living waters shall flow out from Jerusalem. . . . and the Lord will become king over all the earth; on that day the Lord will be one and his name one" (Zech. 14: 1-9).

I read the passage several times over and started to shake. It was a prophecy about the coming of Messiah. I tried to remain nonchalant as I shut the Bible and climbed back into bed. I said to the voice, "I don't know if you're real, and I don't know what just happened, but it's really blowing my mind. I can't deal with this now. Please let me go to sleep." Immediately I fell asleep.

Tired of running

Over the next several weeks, thinking about the Zechariah 14 incident didn't make me happy or peaceful — I was horrified! The last thing I was looking for was a relationship with God, and I had no desire to meet him. The prophesies in Revelation and the idea of Jesus were fascinating, of course, but I certainly had no intention of changing my life to meet his demands — I was having too much fun. I was depressed about the prospect of giving up my freedom if I became a Christian.

I did not go searching for Jesus, he came searching for me. And things began to happen quickly. He started to reveal himself in many little coincidental, yet unmistakable ways. I especially became aware of Jesus' presence all around me.

In conversations with Tom I tried my best to find the flaws in the claims of Jesus, but in vain. Although I didn't want to admit it to anyone, much less myself, in retrospect I see that I was becoming gradually aware that atheism was a sham; it's philosophical "proofs" against the existence of God were no match for the logic and clarity of Christianity. I saw too that Judaism had truly been fulfilled in Jesus the Messiah.

Due to my upbringing I was never able to be a religious Jew. Now I was becoming conscious of the fact that I had always felt a deep, unspoken longing for God and for his Torah, but these things had been denied me. As Tom showed me things in the Old and New Testaments I began to see that Jesus had not abolished Judaism; rather, he fulfilled it. And he offered me eternal life and happiness if I would accept him as my Lord and Savior. I knew I could no longer resist, nor did I want to anymore. I was tired of running from Jesus.

One brilliant spring day as I was returning to my dorm, I felt a gentle, yet irresistible urge to sit under a large, nearby shade tree. I looked up through the leaves at the clouds and blue sky and said, "I guess you're there after all." Then, simply and quietly I asked Jesus to come into my life as my personal Lord and Savior. The whole thing took less than two minutes, and when it was over I got up and went back to my room.

How mysterious are God's ways! I felt I had finally reached the end of my quest. I changed my major from pre-med to religion so I could learn more about my new faith. I told my friends and family about my conversion, and I tried to evangelize them. I went to Evangelical Bible studies and worship services. I called myself a Christian from that point on. But my heart did not change. My conversion was mainly intellectual. If I had known then the insults I would soon hurl at God, or foreseen the interior anguish I was going to undergo, I never would have dared respond to that call. Many "new Christians" backslide to some extent after their initial encounter with Christ, and I was no different. I started backsliding immediately.

That summer I went to Italy on a language study program, and I spent my free time like most of the other college kids kicking around Europe at the time: partying. When I returned to Ohio for my junior year, things got worse. I moved off campus into a "party house," I lost touch with Tom and the other Christians I knew, and I stopped going to Christian activities. I still called myself a Christian and believed in Christ; I just didn't live for Christ — I lived to satisfy my sensual appetites. I saw no reason why Christ should interfere with my fun. I saw nothing amiss with getting drunk or high and talking about Christ, or even "evangelizing" others while in such condition! In fact, I rather enjoyed doing so, and felt that being high gave me unique theological insights (much like Timothy Leary used to pretend about LSD).

When I graduated with a degree in religion I had no idea what to do with my life. I was drunk and high most of the time, and I couldn't think clearly enough to chart a course to anywhere except to the refrigerator for another beer. When my father suggested I apply to law school I jumped at the opportunity to delay for a few years having to decide what to do with myself. I was accepted into the law program at New York University School of Law.

Moving back to New York was weird. After four years of corn fields and pig farms, I had grown to like the quiet, rural atmosphere of Ohio. By contrast, the loud, frantic, dangerous chaos that is New York was hard to get used to again. I did my best to acclimate by diving headlong into the drug and music scene.

My relationship with Jesus grew more tenuous. I stopped talking about him or praying to him. I thought I was happy, but I was actually dying inside. Day by day I grew increasingly cynical, hostile, and belligerent. Other people could see what I could not. During my first year of law school, a fellow student told me that my classmates did not like being with me because of the anger and tension that was so visible in my life. Finally, toward the end of that year I was able to agree with her.

When I finally admitted to myself the depths of my unhappiness, I was given the grace to realize that the problem was the conflict between my belief in Christ and my sinful lifestyle. I knew I had to resolve this conflict or I would eventually die. The easiest thing to do, of course, was jettison my superstitious belief in God. But what if he really was real? In my magnanimity I decided to give God one more chance. I would put him to the test by going on a retreat to see if he would speak to me again. If God could not reveal himself to me on his own playing field, I would know he was false, and I could discard him. The only problem was, where to go on retreat? I did not know any Evangelicals I could call for a lead, but I did know a Catholic.

I mentioned my interest in making a retreat to Fr. Joseph Malagreca, a friend of mine and law school class-mate who was a priest from the Diocese of Brooklyn. We had gotten to know and like each other and met often at a local Greenwich Village espresso house to talk about religion. Although I had been calling myself Christian for four years, there were many basic Christian doctrines I had never accepted, such as the Trinity. Fr. Joe patiently and graciously listened to my babble, defended his be-liefs, and challenged me to consider the Catholic position on these issues.

When I asked him to recommend a good place for a retreat he steered me to "The People of Hope," a Catholic Charismatic covenant community in New Jersey. Al-though this group later became controversial, at that time it was a vibrant faith community under the leader-ship of Fr. James Ferry.

I wrote The People of Hope, and they agreed to accept me for a one week retreat in July at their young men's house located in a parish in a poor section of Newark. I knew nothing of Pentecostal Christianity, and my only experience with Charismatic gifts was witnessing one instance of tongues at a Campus Crusade for Christ meeting in college. Their response was so "Jesus-freaky" that I almost canceled.

It is impossible to describe the myriad, subtle ways Satan used to try to stop me from going on this retreat. Worldly cares and financial needs threatened my ability to take the time off. My current girlfriend informed me that we were through if I went. Opportunities to sample pleasures I had only dreamed of suddenly materialized. Shortly before the retreat, for example, I met a new friend who had access to drugs I had never tried before. One day, while he was visiting me, the phone rang. It was a young woman whom I had met socially six years before, but whom I had not talked to since. She asked to come over to my apartment. After she arrived, her less-than-chaste intentions were so obvious that my friend excused himself to "let nature take its course."

I never said "no" to these diversions and temptations, and I was fully willing to postpone my retreat if any need or pleasure conflicted with it. But mysteriously, without much will power on my part, on the appointed day I found myself at the front door of St. Antoninus Parish. Within ten minutes of my arrival, the entire group of young men (except me) were standing in the dining room with their hands in the air praising God in English and tongues. I wanted to get the heck out of there, but something made me stay to see what would happen next.

Although unbaptized, I participated in Mass and received communion. That night one of the priests took me aside and asked me to refrain from receiving Communion in the future. I reacted angrily. I used all of my new legal training to attack the priest and the Church. I "proved" beyond any reasonable doubt that the Church's practice regarding communion was wrong. Even worse, it was unfair because I wanted to receive and this stupid, legalistic regulation was hindering my search for God! The priest restrained his anger and remained patient with me, but didn't relent.

(I must take this opportunity to apologize to the priests in charge of the men's house for my behavior that week. I was obnoxious. All of the cynicism and hostility pent up inside me for those many years started to come out. But I also experienced intermittent periods of happiness and fellowship with the other retreatants. Above all, I was jealous of the peace and joy I saw in their lives. I wanted that peace and joy terribly, but I could not bring

myself to accept their faith, unless it were actually true
— happiness alone wasn't enough.)

In a rage I went into the chapel where I threw myself
on the ground before the altar and in tears poured out to
God my frustration and anger and misery. After awhile
I opened my Bible to Matthew 12 and read, "You brood
of vipers! how can you speak good, when you are so
evil?" I was stunned. I realized that I was wrong and that
I had to apologize to the priest. I also realized that God
was angry with me.

Many other things both good and bad happened that
week and, by the end of it, I was an emotional wreck. I
knew I was not ready to return home so I approached
one of the fathers and he kindly arranged for me to spend
an extra week at People of Hope's main retreat house
located on beautiful grounds at St. Elizabeth Ann Seton
College in Convent Station, New Jersey. When I got
there, God wasted no time. Again and again he revealed
himself in powerful and unexpected ways.

The first significant event was the gift of another
Bible reading, Micah 7:9, "I will bear the indignation of
the Lord because I have sinned against him until he
pleads my cause and executes judgment for me." This
finally forced me to admit to myself the true nature of
my life during the prior four years. It had been one of
sin, blasphemy, and yes, evil. It also made me starkly
aware that my eternal salvation was in serious jeopardy
unless I sincerely repented of my sins. The problem was
that I needed to repent, but I couldn't. I just was not sorry
for having done all those things. They were so much fun
and I did not want to stop doing them. I wanted to have
God and my fun too.

For several nights I fell asleep crying from frustration
because I could not feel remorse over my actions. Finally,
one night, I became aware of the merest hint of remorse
in my soul, and I offered it to God for what it was worth.
It must have been enough.

The next day during Mass I felt a gentle urge to get
on my knees and pray. I remained kneeling and crying

quietly for the remainder of the Mass. When Mass ended, several people asked me if I was feeling okay. All I could say was "Do you know what it is like to be told by God that you have offended him, and then be told that you are forgiven?" I will never fully understand how I knew this, but I knew that Micah 7:9 was now behind me. I felt that God and I could start over. My spiritual aridity was gone, and once again I became aware of his presence.

One evening I took a walk. When I glanced at my watch and saw that the doors of the building would soon be locked for the evening I hurried to get back. Suddenly, I heard the Lord's voice speaking to me. He said very clearly and firmly, "Down." The next moment I was flat on my back. Despite the power I was experiencing I was acutely aware that I had a choice. I could say "yes," or I could get up and leave. I chose to stay.

The voice spoke to me again: "Relax and let me heal you." I worried for a moment about the doors that were going to be locked soon, but the voice repeated, "Relax and let me heal you." "Yes," I said and lost consciousness. I awoke a few minutes later and got back to the building just as Sister was locking the door. She opened the door, looked at me and said, "Rick, what happened to you?"

"What do you mean?" I replied.

"You look different," she said.

I stared. "What do you mean?"

"You don't look worried anymore."

And I wasn't.

For the remainder of the week, God continued to pour his blessings on me and he began to prepare me to return to the outside world where dangers, old habits, and temptations were waiting for me. I knew I would have to face them, and I was somewhat scared to, but by the end of the second week I knew it was time.

I returned home on Sunday morning. The first thing I did was "cleanse" my apartment. I ripped apart, smashed with a hammer, and threw out every item I could find related to my former lifestyle of sex and drug debauchery. By the grace of our Lord, I never returned to the worst of those sins, although I have had plenty of other sins to deal with in my life, and these sins did leave vestiges against which I still have to struggle.

I began to pray and read Scripture at home. I steadfastly avoided the temptation to get back together again with the girlfriend I had broken up with, and I let certain other morally dangerous friendships lapse. Most importantly, I realized the need to get into a Christian community for support, and I started looking for one. The only community I knew of was The People of Hope, so I made the long trip to Newark each week to attend their weekly prayer meeting while I looked for fellowship closer to home.

I was extremely grateful to the People of Hope for showing me that God existed and that he was present in the Catholic Church. I still felt, however, that Catholicism was merely one of many ways to God, and possibly not the best way. After all, Roman Catholicism had all those odd practices and beliefs I just couldn't accept. And though I accorded the Catholic Church a sort of primary place in my search, I didn't limit my search to it. I looked at Evangelical and Pentecostal Protestantism in its many varieties (and I got into the habit of devotedly watching several well-known T.V. evangelists, in particular, I'm sorry to say, Jimmy Swaggart).

My search took me through several church communities. None seemed to be the right one. No matter how good the singing or preaching, or how warm the fellowship, in the depths of my spirit I felt that something was missing in the Protestant churches. Although the people were extremely loving and spiritual, it was only at Catholic gatherings that I had a sense of completeness. So I started to lean towards the Catholic Church. If you had asked me why, my answer would have been "I'm trying to follow where the Holy Spirit is leading me." Only in retrospect can I see the doctrinal factors that were so crucial to my journey of faith.

By far, the most important of these factors was the Catholic doctrine of apostolic succession. I came to see that the unbroken apostolic authority in the Church was the sure sign of God's guidance. Its *lack* would mean that Jesus had left his people shepherdless, but I knew he didn't work that way. Given the powerful guidance I had received from God, I could not accept the notion that he didn't or wouldn't provide the same sort of direct guidance for his Church.

I was also compelled by the holiness I found in the lives of the Catholic saints I read about. Many Protestants I knew or had read about were good devout Christians, but their spirituality and heroic virtues simply couldn't compare with the likes of Francis of Assisi, Teresa of Avila, or Augustine. And although the Catholic saints were very different from each other in temperament, learning, and spirituality, they had one thing in common. All were utterly convinced that the Catholic Church was the only true Church. I reasoned that if these great Christian men and women believed this, it very likely was true.

Understanding the nature of Christ's Church was also a crucial point for me. Protestantism regards the Church as an amorphous, invisible, "mysterious" collection of believers. Catholicism, on the other hand, teaches that Christ's Church is indeed mysterious — since it is the mystical Body of Christ (cf. Rom. 12:3-8; 1 Cor. 12:12-26) — but it is also visible and recognizeable, like the city on the hill about which Jesus spoke (Matt. 5:14). Given my experiences with God, I could no more accept the idea of a strictly invisible Church than I could the idea of the Church surviving without the guidance of the magisterium through apostolic succession.

There were still many Catholic practices and doctrines that I didn't feel I could understand or accept. So I continued to study Catholic teaching, and one by one my objections fell by the way. In addition to my growing spiritual conviction, I gained the intellectual certitude that the Catholic Church was true.

Above all, I prayed. Ironically, when I prayed for guidance about making a formal entry into the Church by accepting baptism, I felt the Lord was telling me, "Not now. You're not ready just yet." I was peaceful about this, although I wasn't sure what I needed to do to be "ready" to become Catholic. I believed the doctrines, and I wanted to be a Catholic and to receive the sacraments, but I felt held back by something. I felt I had some unfinished business to take care of first.

I felt a deep desire and need to enter into a sort of Lenten vigil of penance for my sins. I sensed that before I could enter the Church I had to stand outside the gates for awhile in a state of prayerful and penitential preparation for my union with Jesus and his Church. I reminded myself wryly that this was only fair. After all, I had kept God waiting for all those years, and now it was only just that he make me wait a bit, too.

In the Fall of 1979, I was praying in front of the Blessed Sacrament at Our Lady of Guadalupe church in Manhattan, where I had been getting to know the pastor. I was angry with a family member for something he had done which was not really his fault, but for which I blamed him. As I prayed, I made a conscious decision to forgive him. At that moment something in me was changed — no, *healed.*

I felt a sense of peace. Not only had I forgiven my relative, I experienced a strong conviction that the Lord had forgiven me of all my sins. The line from the Our Father wafted through my mind: "Forgive us our trespasses as we forgive those who trespass against us." I felt free, liberated! And I knew that it was time for me to formally enter the Catholic Church.

After a brief period of preparation, I became a Catholic at the 1980 Easter Vigil Mass at Our Lady of Guadalupe Church. I was baptized, confirmed, and I received my First Holy Communion. My joy at finally coming home was not diminished in the least by the fact that most of the Mass was celebrated in Spanish (which I do not understand!).

Much has happened since that glorious Easter eve. I graduated in 1980 from law school, passed the bar, and began my practice as an attorney at law. Most important was the day I married Edwina, a beautiful Episcopalian woman (she also converted to the Catholic Church 8 years after our marriage). In 1987 our son James arrived. He is a terrific little boy, the apple of our eye (usually).

Cel passed away in 1990 after a long illness. Although I have no evidence of this, God assured my spirit that she and Jesus worked things out before her death, and this has been a great comfort to me. My relations with the rest of my family have remained cordial, but slightly strained. Everything is fine as long as we don't discuss religion or politics — a near-impossible feat for our clan.

Perhaps the hardest lesson I've had to learn in my years as a Catholic is that although the Lord gives us innumerable helps to avoid falling into sin, he doesn't take away our sinful nature (what theologians call concupiscence). Like everyone, I still have to struggle against temptations to sin, as well as struggle to ward off the effects of my earlier life of sin, but as a Catholic I now have access to the sacraments — the mightiest arsenal of weapons against sin available to mankind.

As a Catholic I know I have Jesus *in* me as I go forth each day to fight the daily battle against my selfishness and human weaknesses. This, I believe is the essence of the beauty and power of the Catholic Church, and why it has attracted, and will always attract, people to it. In it alone can men and women find the sacramental gifts that Jesus wants to give us for the perfection of our lives and for the salvation of our souls. It is here that I can truly live out the family covenant of grace that the Lord God promised to my Father Abraham. It is through the grace of Christ, found in its fullness in the Catholic Church, that my Judaism is fulfilled and perfected.

Jesus constantly challenges me, indeed all of us, to move forward. The "Miracle of Convent Station" was only a beginning. God changed my life, but he did not change the kind of person I am. Each period of growth follows my familiar pattern: apathy, resentment about having to change, procrastination, grudgingly accepting the change, backsliding, and repenting.

There's a verse that describes me perfectly: "I can will what is right, but I cannot do it. For I do not do the good I want, but the evil I do not want is what I do. So I find it to be a law that when I want to do right, evil lies close at hand. For I delight in the law of God, in my inmost self, but I see in my members another law at war with the law of my mind and making me captive to the law of sin which dwells in my members" (Rom. 7: 18-19, 21-23). I've reflected often on this passage and about how appropriately it sums up my life. Even today, I sometimes find myself resisting God's nudges to grow in virtue and holiness, even though I know that growth will be good for me and that I will be happier for it.

The great mystery is why Jesus puts up with me. The answer can only be love — an infinite love that is totally undeserved by me. When I wasn't looking for him, and even when I was *fleeing* from him, the Lord showed himself to me. When I tried to ignore him, he clobbered me with his grace. When I procrastinated, he gave me a gentle but firm shove in the right direction. When I turned away from him in rebellion, he respected my free will and let me go; but when I hit bottom, he was there waiting with mercy and forgiveness, ready to bring me back home again.

Faced with God's infinite mercy and patience with my sinfulness and obstinacy, I can only respond with the words of another Jew, St. Paul: "Wretched man that I am! Who will deliver me from this body of death? Thanks be to God through Jesus Christ our Lord!" (Romans 7: 24-25).

Into the Crimson Light

T.L. Frazier

THE EASTER Vigil Mass on Holy Saturday is quite an impressive event, especially for the non-Catholic. For the nervous catechumen awaiting full communion into the Catholic Church, as I was that evening, it is absolutely overwhelming. Whiffs of incense filled my nostrils and diffused the light which flickered from the many candles around the sanctuary. The effect was transporting.

My attention was drawn to the side of the pulpit where there was a particular candle which seemed larger than life. On it were affixed two Greek letters, *Alpha* and *Omega*, the first and last letters of the Greek alphabet. The candle was obviously intended to represent Christ who is described in the New Testament as the *Alpha* and *Omega*, the beginning and the end, as well as the light of the world. But I also saw in those two Greek letters another appropriate meaning; for while I was that evening beginning a new life as a Catholic, I was also ending an old one as a "born again" Fundamentalist. I reflected on my past and the circumstances that had brought me to that Easter Vigil.

I was truly a child of the times. Like many other post baby-boomer children born in the Age of Aquarius, my parents divorced and I had been bounced between my mother's and my father's home. I had a brother four years my junior who mostly stayed with our mother. Perhaps it was because the divorce occurred as I was entering adolescence that I felt the absence of my father much more keenly than did my brother.

Being this human pin-ball obviously had an influence on my psychological make up. I changed schools frequently and the concept of normal, long term relationships became something of an abstract ideal to me. On the other hand, I became rather proficient at introducing myself.

Amidst all the chaos, craziness and occasional violence in the home, I had one odd refuge I would turn to: the public library. Like most small children, my mother would read to me and I used to so enjoy this I would often beg her not to stop. Wearied and exasperated at my persistence, she'd tell me that one day I would go to school, learn to read, and then I could read books perpetually if I were so inclined. And so I did.

Books are marvelous things. In a book one can journey to distant lands and different epochs. One can ride the battlefields of Persepolis, explore the cold reaches of space or the innermost recesses of the human psyche. All are equally accessible. What one need not deal with in a book is the present, the here and now immanence of one's own life. As I entered adolescence, I found this to be the most appealing quality of books.

Like most teenagers, what I seemed to want most was escape from coarse reality. My peers chose alcohol, marijuana and cocaine. In junior high school, I too tried some of these avenues of escape, attending school on several occasions intoxicated or high. Early on, however, I decided I didn't possess the temperament for substance abuse and I turned instead toward literature as an alternative form of escapism. The book became my Mephistopheles, an intimate to whom I'd sold my soul in order to possess a literary "reality" as illusory as Faustus' Helena. Yet this Mephistopheles too in the end delivered nothing more permanent or substantial than Hell. So instead of LSD, the drug of choice at the time, I sold my soul to the Musae.

The moral upbringing I had received was quite con-voluted, being chiefly constituted of the contradictory clichés of the liberal ethos prevalent during the '60s and '70s. Two such paradoxical gems are, "All values are relative, there are no absolutes;" ergo, "It is absolutely wrong to impose values on others." Needless to say, there was a profound spiritual vacuum within me due to these irrational moral beliefs I'd inherited. I began searching during my teenage years for a definitive measure of good and evil. I was searching for a standard which was absolute and immutable where all around me seemed contingent and variable, something transcend-ing myself and the secular society around me and thereby allowing me to place it in an overall perspective. In short, though I wasn't aware of it at the time, I was searching for a god.

In my senior year of high school I was living with my father, who in many ways had become a stranger to me when he remarried and had started another family. Still, by and large, things had been going well that year. I was working in a hospital and had there met a girlfriend who was in college, which was nice as I had a reasonable determination to pursue college myself.

Yet felicity would not endure for long. Over the Christmas season my father and I had a brawl over some trivial issue which sent him searching for a physician to attend to his bloody nose and sent myself in search of a new home. Violence was no stranger to our family. My father was shocked that I would return his blows, though, for he had never struck his own father. Yet even my earliest recollections were that my father had used violence against our family, and there was nothing in my malformed conscience to prevent me from turning it back on him once I reached six feet, 170 pounds. I felt little remorse. After all, hadn't I learned this method of conflict resolution from him?

This is not to imply I wasn't devastated by this clash with my father. I was forced to abandon my job, school, companions, and girlfriend as I moved to my mother's home in another city. My hurt, though, was mostly self-centered. I went to my upstairs bedroom in my mom's house and, protesting the general Christmas cheer, threw a one-man pity party in my own honor lasting several days. I did what was natural for me in such circumstances: I reached for a book. And which one chanced to be at hand? None other than the Book of books itself, the Holy Bible.

The Bible wasn't entirely unknown to me. When I was thirteen I had once tried to read the Gospel of Matthew, but got bogged down in the Sermon on the Mount. Jesus' moralizing seemed unprogressive and unrealistic to me. I was the product of a secular culture and the much vaunted sexual revolution, so my perception of the world clashed markedly with the world-view I found in the Gospel. I had been taught that "virtue" was safe-sex and my concept of "nobility" could be exemplified as assisting a maid-in-distress to procure an abortion.

The humanism and moral naturalism I had imbibed at the hands of my parents and teachers led me to prefer the pagan wisdom of Homer, Ovid, and Virgil to Christian truth, as exemplified by Jesus' Sermon on the Mount. Paganism emphasized the natural over the supernatural. The gods were made in man's image and likeness, not vice versa. Christianity, by emphasizing the supernatural and asserting that man is created in God's image and likeness, appeared to have it all backwards.

But this particular Advent, after being thrown out of my father's home, I was in such an agitated state of mind that I put aside my pagan outlook and was willing to approach the Bible with an open mind. Disillusioned with all I had been taught by family and secular society, I was looking for answers and was willing to radically alter whatever I had previously held true if the Bible could provide those answers. With this attitude I picked up the book and commenced reading (for reasons I can't now recall), not the Gospel of Matthew, but the Gospel of Luke which shows a slightly different side of Jesus' personality.

I was immediately absorbed by the story of Christ. I was struck by how Jesus was constantly misunderstood, even by those nearest to him. I was amazed at how people were always attempting to exploit Jesus to their own ends and by how Jesus extended love and acceptance to everyone, though he himself was often met with rejection and even hatred. He came to his own but his own received him not. What teenager could not identify with this, with feeling misunderstood, exploited, rejected and unloved? I noted how Jesus especially loved the outcast of the world, the dregs of society, those who had made a failure of their lives. The thought crossed my mind that perhaps Jesus could love even me.

The turning point for me occurred when Jesus was heading toward Jerusalem to meet what he knew to be certain death. Expressing love even for his own murderers, as he approached the city he cried out, "Oh Jerusalem, Jerusalem, you who kill the prophets and stone those sent to you, how often have I longed to gather your children together as a hen gathers her chicks under her wings, but you were not willing. Behold, your house is left to you desolate. I tell you, you will not see me again until you say, '*Blessed is he who comes in the name of the Lord.*'"

I could feel Jesus' hurt and anger at this final rejection which would lead to the cross. I wept with him. At that moment I made a solemn covenant to forever be his friend and follower. I accepted his claims upon me and looked to him alone for my salvation. I had found a friend from whom I could not be separated.

I carried a Gideon's New Testament wherever I went and my nose was in it constantly. In only six months I read the entire Bible through from cover to cover except for the Psalms. The Bible had become my sacrament. Through it Christ was made present to me and I was able to fellowship with him. It was a communion of a non-eucharistic sort yet in many ways no less intense.

As what meager religious instruction I had previously received in my nominally Christian family was from liberal Presbyterian churches (of which I have generally fond memories of youth groups and other social activities), I found a local Presbyterian church in the neighborhood with the intention of learning more about Jesus, the Bible and the religious conversion I had experienced. In return, I wanted to throw into the church all my new-found zeal and energy. I soon discovered, though, that I was moving at a much more fervent pace than the rest of the congregation and I quickly lost interest.

While I tried to keep an open mind to what everyone had to say on the religious issues I was endeavoring to resolve, I became more and more inclined toward Fundamentalism. I had concluded that liberal Protestantism was less driven by a thirst for objective truth than by subjective emotional compulsions. It was a pick-and-choose, smorgasbord Christianity where whatever happened to be unpalatable to twentieth century Western tastes could be rationalized away with a little theological hocus-pocus. In a sense, the Liberal in his endeavors to avoid orthodoxy came to be associated in my mind with the child who hides his food under the place mat in an attempt to fool his parents into believing he really cleaned the whole plate. As I was perfectly willing to eat whatever my Father set before me, I found myself rejecting liberal Protestantism and moving towards Evangelical para-church organizations like Young Life, Campus Crusade for Christ and the Navigator Bible Study groups.

After high school I decided to join the Air Force and this afforded me the opportunity to travel around the country and meet different types of Christians. Fundamentalism was virtually omnipresent in the military in the early 1980's and this ultimately confirmed me in the direction I was already heading. It was also while in the Air Force that I formed my first impressions of Catholicism.

I didn't question that the Catholic Church as a historical institution had its origins in Jerusalem on the day of

Pentecost, as recorded in the second chapter of the Acts of the Apostles. Yet most of the Catholics I had known seemed more like unregenerate heathen than those original Christians who turned the world upside down for Jesus. It seemed to me that somewhere along the historical road the Christian Church had strayed from the straight and narrow path into paganism and the end result was Catholicism, a mongrelized form of Christianity. I knew that Christ promised not even the gates of hell would prevail against his Church (Matt. 16:18), that he would remain with the Church to the end of time (Matt. 28:20), and that the Holy Spirit would lead it into all truth (Jn. 16:13), nevertheless, this didn't disturb my conviction that the Holy Spirit had somehow been overcome by paganism and that Fundamentalists had somehow emerged from this divine debacle as the "faithful remnant."

I was certainly anti-Catholic, but I wasn't the sort of nefarious knave usually associated with the term. I wasn't anti-Catholic in the sense that I went out of my way to bait Catholics or attack Catholicism. I was more passively anti-Catholic in that I was deeply concerned about the salvation of my Catholic friends. If I hated anything, I hated what I perceived to be the errors of Catholicism which I felt in many instances, as for example the Marian doctrines, amounted to outright blasphemy.

I remember visiting my first Catholic church while being stationed at Lowery Air Force base in Denver, Colorado. One afternoon a girlfriend and I were walking in downtown Denver when I noticed across the street a beautiful Catholic church which reminded me of the Anglican cathedrals I'd seen while in England. Later that afternoon we came across that church again on our way back to the base and I decided to enter it to see what it was like inside. Going through the large doors was like parachuting into an alien world. There were strange Catholic paraphernalia everywhere: boxes for offerings, candles, fonts of water, and things for purposes I could only wonder at. Ahead were doors which I presumed led into the sanctuary. I cautiously approached and opened one of these doors.

We were met with pitch blackness. My girlfriend and I, though apprehensive, resolved to proceed inside anyway. Thus, with one hand clutching hers and my other feeling along the wall, I entered this seeming Temple of Doom. After my eyes adjusted to the darkness, I perceived what looked like pagan idols staring down on us menacingly from niches in the walls overhead. Looking toward the front of the church, my attention was drawn to an eerie blood-red flame which, for some reason, reminded me of the day of Pentecost when the Holy Spirit descended on the Church in tongues of fire. I decided we should try to make for that flame. We felt our way further along the wall and I saw that bathed in this red light was a raised altar upon which, I had no doubt, primitive sacrifices were performed.

We approached the altar and began circling it. I remember my heart was gripped by not a little fear and I asked myself, "What sort of obscene rites could possibly be performed here?" Then suddenly from behind us this voice cut through the darkness, "Get the @#$&*! away from the @#$&*! altar!" For a brief moment I thought we might have encountered the demonic. I believe we were as startled by the foul language as the discovery that we weren't alone. Never had I heard such language used in any church before! We turned and were confronted by some man who had emerged from the dark, perhaps a janitor, and then we were rather unceremoniously bounced out. From this little field trip into a Catholic church I obviously went away with some skewed notions about Catholicism.

I eventually settled into becoming a Baptist. Life was Sunday school at 10:00 a.m., worship service at 11:00 a.m., and various Bible studies through the week. On Wednesday evenings we would have a revival at 7:00 p.m. which was of recommended attendance, and on Saturdays we went door to door spreading the Good

News of Protestant Fundamentalism. All those truly saved wouldn't dream of missing Saturday evangelization, or "witnessing" as we called it, lest the impression be given that one were back-sliding into apostasy. This may indicate one had never really been a Christian to begin with, despite all assurances given to the contrary at the altar-call that one was indeed forever saved. This is the idea that a Christian is "once-saved-always-saved," that one is eternally secure because one has received Christ by faith in an act of the will through sincerely praying a "sinner's prayer." According to this Fundamentalist dogma, no sin committed after getting "saved," no matter how heinous, will deny one access to heaven at death. Indeed, if one were truly saved, one would never commit such acts. A Christian might back-slide into sin, but he will ultimately repent. If he doesn't, he was never a Christian to begin with—even if he had been one's pastor or spiritual mentor all one's life.

Yet many "born-again" Fundamentalists, people who have sincerely believed they were forever saved and had received solemn assurances to this effect from their pastor, have later been declared by the same pastor never to have been saved to begin with! I myself was once told this on live talk radio by a Baptist pastor after I became Catholic. If I had ever *really* been saved, he said, I would never have become a Catholic. From the pastor's perspective, how did he know I wasn't simply backslidden? He didn't. Really there is no way to distinguish between a "backslidden" Christian and an absolute non-Christian in this sort of reasoning, even after the straying member returns to the fold. In fact, the highly personal and subjective nature of this concept of salvation leads most thoughtful Fundamentalists to decline passing judgment on whether the person sitting next to them in the pew, though perhaps an old friend, is really a "Christian" or not. One never knows, that person may someday become a Catholic!

Nor is it even possible for one to be certain that he himself is actually saved. Not only is self-deception always possible, but people also change over the course of their lives and what a person may honestly and even fervently believe at one point may be doubted later on. A friend of mine who had been active in witnessing and daily Bible reading developed some personal problems in his life and gave up these practices. Lacking faith at that moment, he questioned whether he had really had genuine faith when he accepted Christ, and so was unable to decide whether he was backslidden or had ever been saved at all.

How ironic that a doctrine designed to give one eternal assurance can, during a difficult period of life when one especially needs his Christian Faith, leave one doubting whether he was ever a Christian to begin with! It's an "assurance" which assures the believer that the elect will assuredly go to heaven, but can't assure him that his "born again" experience was authentic and thus that he's assuredly among the saved. This and the fact that scores of biblical passages deny this notion[1] (saying that only by enduring to the end will we be saved[2]) have likely helped foster the general perception of Fundamentalism as a religion for those a touch less than quick-witted.

As a Fundamentalist, I was ever being exhorted by my pastor to check everything from doctrine to mere personal preference against Holy Writ. And as a bookworm I found this a quite congenial task. Like the Bereans evangelized by St. Paul, I searched the Scriptures daily. I believe it was ultimately this practice which undermined my faith in the "born again" religion.

Having visited a wide variety of Protestant churches and trying to understand the differences which divided the assorted Protestant bodies, I came to realize that

---

[1] Cf. Rom. 11:22; 1 Cor. 11:32; 15:2; Col. 1:21-23; 1 Tim. 4:16; 2 Tim. 2:11-13; Heb. 3:12-14; 6:4-6; Jas. 1:12.
[2] Cf. Matt. 10:22; Jn. 15:6; Rev. 2:10-11, 26.

honest and sincere people could legitimately interpret the Bible in many different ways. True, not all the diverse doctrines claiming scriptural warrant could survive close scrutiny, but neither was it right to say that what constituted "biblical Christianity" was self-evident. For example, the Presbyterian Church baptizes infants, whereas Baptists feel the practice is sheer foolishness. Any literate person, I and my Fundamentalist peers would argue, can see the New Testament knows nothing of infant baptism. Yet was it true, I wondered, that Presbyterians and all other Protestant denominations who practice infant baptism were really such mental midgets as to be unable to perceive this upon a fair reading of the Bible? I doubted it. And upon pursuing the scriptural reasons for the practice of infant baptism, I found they were quite good ones and I eventually changed my position on the issue. Still, the resolution of the question wasn't self-evident from the Bible. This, I came to realize, was because the Bible isn't a comprehensive textbook of systematic theology with a section entitled "Baptism."

Fundamentalists feel baptism shouldn't be administered to anyone below the age of reason. This idea is largely derived from the Fundamentalist understanding of both salvation and baptism rather than any biblical text which explicitly states, "Thou shalt baptize only adults," though the vehemence with which we insisted on "believer's baptism" would lead one to think we'd discovered at least that much. But if baptism is the means of entering into the New Covenant, as circumcision was for entering the Old Covenant (Col. 2:11-12), and if one keeps in mind that under the Old Covenant a male child was to be circumcised while an infant (Gen. 17:12-14), then the issue of infant baptism takes on a whole different complexion.

The baptismal covenant which was offered to the people of Israel and to their children (Acts 2:38-39) was to be no less inclusive than the Old Covenant they had known all their lives, including even infants (cf. Luke 18:15-17). If the Church changed the Old Covenant practice and began to exclude children below some theoretical "age of reason," it would have created a controversy as large as that of circumcising Gentiles converts. And yet the New Testament gives no hint the subject was ever even brought up, much less debated.

In pagan society, the religion of the head of the house was normally adopted as the religion of the entire household, including the children. The Church never challenged this and baptized infants heedless of any unscriptural rule about an "age of reason." When the Gospel was first preached to the Gentiles, we see entire households baptized, which would include all the babies and, if there were servants, the servants' babies as well (Acts 16:15, 31-34; 1 Cor. 1:16).

Thus there was never any controversy in the early Church over the practice until the third century when the Council of Carthage (A.D. 252) condemned the novel proposition that baptism ought to be postponed until the eighth day after birth. St. Cyprian of Carthage and his colleagues at this council wrote in a letter to Fidius: "As to what pertains to the case of infants: you said that they ought not to be baptized within the second or third day after their birth, . . . In our council it seemed to us far otherwise. No one agreed to the course which you thought should be taken. Rather, we all judged that the mercy and grace of God ought to be denied to no man born." So the council retained the ancient practice, essentially reaffirming what Origen (A.D. 185-253) had said, that "The Church received from the Apostles the tradition of giving baptism even to infants."[3]

I was beginning to have difficulties with many Baptist dogmas. I concluded that there was no evidence in the New Testament for the Baptist notion of altar calls and praying a "sinner's prayer" which saves one forever

[3] *Commentaries on Romans* 5:9.

from perdition. No such prayer is recorded in the Bible as being a normative part of Church life. But I did see that the first Christians "devoted themselves to the teaching of the Apostles and to the communal life, to the breaking of the bread and to the prayers" (Acts 2:42). Obviously, "the breaking of the bread and to the prayers" (Greek: *tai klasei tou artou kai tais proseuchais*) was something other than the traditional Baptist after-church potluck hosted by the Ladies Auxiliary. This verse, along with Acts 20:7, says that the Lord's Supper, or *Eucharist* in Greek (literally "to give thanks," as in John 6:23), was a central part of Christian Sunday worship described in the New Testament. "Why wasn't it a part of ours?" I wondered. This thought really plagued me.

One afternoon I was reading the Gospel of John when something Jesus said caught my attention for the first time. It contained graphic eucharistic language: "I am the bread of life. Your ancestors ate manna in the desert, but they died; this is the bread that comes down from heaven so that one may eat it and not die. I am the living bread that came down from heaven; whoever eats this bread will live forever; and the bread that I will give is my flesh for the life of the world. . . . Amen, amen, I say to you, unless you eat the flesh of the Son of Man and drink his blood, you do not have life within you. Whoever eats [Greek: *trogon*] my flesh and drinks my blood has eternal life, and I will raise him up at the last day. For my flesh is true food, and my blood is true drink. Whoever eats [*trogon*] my flesh and drinks my blood remains in me and I in him. Just as the living Father sent me and I have life because of the Father, so also the one who feeds [*trogon*] on me will have life because of me. This is the bread that came down from heaven. Unlike your ancestors who ate and still died, whoever eats [*trogon*] this bread will live forever" (Jn. 6:48-58). The normal Greek verb meaning "to eat" used throughout this passage, *phagon*, is suddenly replaced by *trogon*, meaning literally to crunch or gnaw. The real, corporal function of eating is obviously being stressed. Also, the tense of the verb *trogon* implies a continuous consumption of the body and blood of Christ.

So as death was introduced by eating the forbidden fruit, now life is restored by eating the "bread of life," that is, Christ's flesh. I knew the Catholic Church taught that the bread and the wine used in celebrating the Last Supper became the real body and blood of Christ. Professional anti-Catholic Jack Chick had disclosed as much to me in his comic books in which he lampoons the Eucharist as the "Cookie Christ." While it's easy to ridicule the Eucharist, I saw that this passage in John was best understood in light of the ancient Catholic belief.

1 Corinthians 5:7-8 came to mind where Paul says, "For indeed Christ our Passover was sacrificed for us. Therefore let us keep the feast." As the Lord's Supper is the only "feast" Christians celebrated, this implied a regular celebration of the Eucharist as the New Testament Passover, the Passover being a ceremonial meal the Israelites had to eat in order to be saved from "the destroyer" which killed the first-born among the Egyptians (Ex. 12:1-42). Recalling that in Acts 2:42; 20:7 and 1 Corinthians 11:20-21, the Christians used to celebrate the "breaking of the bread and the prayers" whenever they met, I became even more uneasy. Could Catholics possibly be right? Could the Eucharist be the normative Christian worship where, as Jesus said, "whoever eats my flesh and drinks my blood has eternal life", saving us from the "destroyer"?

I found the import of 1 Corinthians 11:27-32, that those who fail to discern "the body and blood of the Lord" in the Eucharist would eat and drink condemnation upon themselves, refuted the Baptist dogma that the actual body and blood of the Lord were not to be discerned in the Eucharist. In fact, if the Eucharist were merely a "symbol" lacking efficacy, Paul's stern warning to the Corinthians concerning its improper observance seemed incomprehensible: "That is why many among you are ill and infirm, and a considerable number are dying." What other Christian "symbol" ever carried the death sentence for its ill treatment?

Moreover, 1 Corinthians 10:16-17 says that our communion, or fellowship (Greek: *koinonia*), in the body and blood of Christ in the Eucharist is the basis for the Church's own *koinonia*—each member of the Body of Christ being at one with each other (cf. Rom. 12:4-5 and 1 Cor. 12:12-26). Certainly our fellowship with the body and blood of Christ in the Eucharist couldn't be less real than our fellowship with one another, especially, as St. Paul says in this passage, if the Eucharist is the very basis for the Church's fellowship.

If the Church as the Body of Christ isn't merely a symbolic *koinonia*, then the Eucharist as the Body of Christ couldn't be merely a symbolic *koinonia* either. To uphold the Fundamentalist position, one must maintain that the Church itself is only symbolic like the Eucharist. But could a merely symbolic Church be the salt of the earth and the light of the world (Matt. 5:13-16)? The thought was absurd.

The Fathers know best

As time went on, I slowly began to lose faith in the Fundamentalist religious system to interpret Scripture in an objective manner. I commenced looking for an alternative interpretive authority to the Fundamentalist pastors I had so trusted. I needed to start thinking independently. It seemed that I needed to interpret the Bible not as a twentieth century American but as a first century Easterner in Galatia or Syrian Antioch would. I remember wishing I possessed a commentary from the ancient Church so I could get a clue as to how they understood the Bible. But it was only a passing whimsical thought.

In the library one day I ran across a book of ancient Christian literature. I was ecstatic. I had been wanting to see early Christian writings to help me gain the ancient Christian perspective from which to study the Word of God. I began studying the epistles of St. Ignatius, a convert of the Apostle John and second bishop of Antioch. In the year A.D. 110, Roman soldiers were leading Ignatius to Rome where the lions awaited him. Along the way, he wrote several letters to churches along his route, encouraging them in the faith. These letters were regarded so highly by the early Christian community for their witness to the apostolic Faith that they were even held by many to be part of the New Testament, frequently being bound with the apostolic writings.

Writing to the church at Smyrna, a major Christian center in Asia Minor, Ignatius condemned heretics who denied that Christ had an actual physical body, likely referring to Docetism. (This was a form of the Gnostic heresy. The Apostle John may have had these same people in mind when he penned 1 John 1:1-4.) To refute them, Ignatius wrote, "They [the heretics] even absent themselves from the Eucharist and the public prayers [cf. Acts 2:42], because they will not admit that the Eucharist is the flesh of our Savior Jesus Christ which suffered for our sins and which the Father in his goodness afterwards raised up again" (7:1).

I believe I nearly suffered cardiac arrest. This was the bishop of Antioch, the city where Jesus' followers were first called Christians (Acts 11:26) and a major center of Christianity. This was a man who had heard the Good News from the lips of the Apostle John himself, the very Apostle who had written that graphic Eucharistic passage in his Gospel (Jn. 6:48-58). Writing merely ten or fifteen years after the death of St. John, Ignatius refers to the "real presence" of Christ in the Eucharist as though it were common knowledge throughout the Church! Indeed, if Christ weren't really present in the Eucharist, Ignatius' whole apologetic argument would have come to naught. To the church at Ephesus, Ignatius wrote that they were "to obey [the] bishop and clergy with undivided minds and to share in the one common breaking of the bread—the medicine of immortality and the sovereign remedy by which we escape death and live in Jesus Christ for evermore" (20:3). I had been taught that salvation was centered on praying a "sinner's prayer," yet the early Christians were teaching we "live in Jesus Christ for evermore" in the Eucharist, which is called the "medicine of immortality." This was patently intolerable to my Fundamentalist temperament.

But then, to heap insult on injury, Ignatius explained, "The sole Eucharist you should consider valid is one that is celebrated by the bishop himself or by some person authorized by him. Where the bishop is to be seen, there let all his people be, just as wherever Jesus Christ is present, there is the Catholic Church."[4] That Ignatius called the Church "Catholic" had a profound psychological effect on an anti-Catholic like myself.

I suspected some diabolical mischief was afoot to subvert the true Evangelical Faith, and so I decided to make a thorough study of all the early Christian literature I could find. Much to my shock, not one Christian writing in the early Church viewed the Lord's Supper as a mere symbol that failed to do what it symbolized. Indeed, the early Christians had a very "Catholic" sacramental theology.

I read the *Didache*, an early Syrian Christian church manual (A.D. 60-140), an allegory called *The Shepherd*, written by a Roman Christian named Hermas (A.D. 148), Pope Clement's epistle to the church at Corinth commanding them to reinstate some presbyters they had thrown out (A.D. 96, probably while the Apostle John was nearby at Ephesus), as well as Justin Martyr's two apologetic works and his *Dialogue with Trypho* (A.D. 155). Finally, there were the twin treasures *Against Heresies* and *Proof of the Apostolic Preaching* by Irenaeus, the bishop of Lyons and the celebrated student of Polycarp (the bishop of Smyrna who, according to Irenaeus, had "known [the apostle] John and others who had seen the Lord").

---

4 *Epistle to the Smyrnaeans* 8:1-2.

After reading everything I could lay hands on coming from the ancient church, concentrating especially on the second century, I started developing a theology more closely resembling traditional Catholicism or Eastern Orthodoxy. Reading a book of Church history, I remember being impressed by the authoritative role Pope Victor I (A.D. 189-198) played in the second century during the Quartodeciman controversy over the date on which Easter was to be celebrated.

I was also impressed by the fact that during the early trinitarian and christological controversies, after the patriarchs of Alexandria, Jerusalem, Antioch, and Constantinople had succumbed to one heresy or another, only the papacy remained constant in witnessing to the orthodox Faith. This and the obviously prominent role in the New Testament of St. Peter, to whom the pope claims to be the successor, inclined me toward Catholicism.

Soon after I had become a Baptist, my pastor preached a sermon on Matthew 16:13-19. Here Jesus made Simon Peter the rock on which he would build his Church: "When Jesus came into the coasts of Caesarea Philippi, he asked his disciples, saying, 'Whom do men say that I the Son of Man am?' . . . And Simon Peter answered and said, 'Thou art the Christ, the Son of the living God.' And Jesus answered and said unto him, 'Blessed art thou, Simon Bar-Jona: for flesh and blood hath not revealed it unto thee, but my Father which is in heaven. And I also say unto thee [singular], that thou art Peter [Greek: *petros*], and upon this rock [Greek: *petra*] I will build my church; and the gates of hell shall not prevail against it. And I will give unto thee the keys of the kingdom of heaven; and whatsoever thou shalt bind on earth shall be bound in heaven; and whatsoever thou shalt loose on earth shall be loosed in heaven.'" This, my pastor informed me, was the key passage on which Catholics base the papacy: Peter was made the earthly pastor of the universal Church and the popes, Peter's successors, continue this ministry.

According to my pastor, who was attempting to debunk the Catholic position, "this rock" (*petra*) refers not to Peter, who is called *petros*, but to Christ himself (cf. Rom. 9:33; 1 Cor. 10:4; 1 Pet. 2:8). Thus, according to him, there is a contrasting of the word *petros*, a stone or detached rock in Greek, with *petra*, meaning a boulder or a mass of rock upon which large fortresses were built.

At Caesarea Philippi there was such a *petra*, a looming wall of rock 200 feet high and 500 feet wide with, instead of Christ's Church, a marble temple dedicated to Caesar on the top and sanctuaries for Pan near the bottom.[5] The point was also made in the sermon that only God was called "rock" in the Old Testament. My pastor wisely rejected the interpretation that "this rock" refers to Peter's confession of faith which occurs two verses earlier. Grammatically, "this rock" must refer back to the nearest noun, which would be Peter and not his confession of faith.

The first problem I noted was that it isn't entirely true that "only God was called 'rock' in the Old Testament." Picking up a simple concordance revealed that Abraham is called the rock from which the Old Covenant people of God were hewn in Isaiah 51:1-2. I found the comparison between Abraham, the rock whose name was also changed by God (Gen. 17:5), and Simon Peter, the rock on which the new, spiritual Israel is to be built, to be intriguing. It suggested that Jesus might be deliberately echoing this idea from Isaiah and making Peter the new Patriarch of the New Covenant people of God. My pastor's explanation of Matthew 16:18 had far more glaring flaws, however.

---

[5] An excellent biblical and archeological analysis of the connection between this rock cliff at Caesarea Philippi and Christ's words to Peter in Matthew 16:18-19 is found in Stanly Jaki, *And On This Rock* (Manassas: Trinity Communications, 1987).

The main problem was John 1:42: "Then [Andrew] brought [Simon Peter] to Jesus. Jesus looked at him and said, 'You are Simon the son of Jona; you will be called *Kephas*' (which is translated Peter [*petros*])." Simon Bar-Jona wasn't renamed *petros* at all, but *Kephas* (sometimes rendered as *Kepha* [cf. 1 Cor. 1:12; 3:22; 9:5; 15:5; Gal. 2:9]). Aramaic was the common language of Palestine at the time and *Kepha* is the Aramaic word for "rock," meaning both an ordinary rock and an exceptionally large one. Thus Jesus, who almost certainly spoke to the twelve in Aramaic and not in Greek, would have said to Simon Peter in Matthew 16:18, 9, "Thou art *Kepha* and on this *Kepha* I will build my church." The proper translation of *Kepha* into Greek would ordinarily be *petra*; however *petra* is a feminine noun and can't be used to refer to a man. Hence the masculine ending "*os*" would need to be substituted when referring to Simon Peter, giving us *Petros*.[6] In this case the distinction between *petra* and *petros* in the Greek is merely a question of gender, not of meaning.

Actually, if the Evangelist had intended to contrast Peter the "stone" with Jesus the "Rock," the obvious word to use for Simon Peter would have been *lithos*, the more common Greek word for stone or small rock. This would also have eliminated any possible confusion between Peter and Jesus. On the other hand, the deliberate use of *petros* and *petra* points to an attempt to translate an Aramaic pun into Greek, which of course is precisely what Catholics contend. Interestingly, Jesus himself is called *lithos* (e.g., Matt. 21:42, 44) four times more often than he's called *petra* (12 times to 3, a fact which doesn't

---

6 As John makes clear in John 1:42, the Greek text of which reads: "*Su ei Simon ho huios Ioannou, su klethese Kephas (ho hermeneuetai Petros)*"—"Thou art Simon the son of John, thou shalt be called *Kephas* (which is translated Peter)".

dissuade Peter from characterizing all believers as "stones" [*lithoi*] in 1 Peter 2:5).

At that time, though, I was naturally inclined to believe my pastor and so I began doing research into Matthew 16:18 assuming I would eventually arrive at the same conclusions he had. What I found, though, hardly assuaged my difficulties.

A Baptist proves that Peter was the first pope

Nearly every major Protestant commentary on Matthew written within the last half-century concurs that Simon Peter is the rock upon which Christ promised he would build his Church in Matthew 16:18.[7] What I found especially enlightening were the comments of Baptist Scripture Scholar D.A. Carson, who contributed the commentary on Matthew in the theologically conservative *Expositor's Bible Commentary*.[8] Carson lists five reasons why the exposition of Matthew 16:18 given by my pastor couldn't be correct, stating that "If it were not for Protestant reactions against extremes of Roman Catholic interpretation, it is doubtful whether many would have taken 'rock' to be anything or anyone other than Peter."[9]

Carson adds a brief paragraph about the "extremes" in the Catholic understanding of Peter's role in the New Testament, such as infallibility. Unfortunately, he fails to consider Luke 22:32 where Christ said that he had prayed especially for Peter and that, after Peter's own conversion, Peter is commissioned to strengthen his

---

7   E.g., Craig L. Blomberg, *New American Commentary*; R.T. France, *Tyndale New Testament Commentaries*; W.F. Albright and C.S. Mann, *The Anchor Bible*; David Hill, *The New Century Bible Commentary;* Howard Clark Kee, *Interpreter's One Volume Commentary on the Bible*; and H.N. Ridderbos, *Bible Students' Commentary.*

8   Grand Rapids: Zondervan, 1984, Frank E. Gaebelein, ed., vol. 8.

9   Ibid., 368.

brethren in their faith. Given the fact that Peter is given "the keys of the kingdom of heaven" in Matthew 16:19, as well as the rabbinical function of binding and loosing, the *halakah* (rabbinical pronouncements, including exorcism, legislation, discipline, and excommunication) of the community, it seemed inconsistent for him to deny that Peter had a special teaching office as a sort of chief rabbi. Peter received from Christ this binding and loosing authority separately from and before the other disciples (cf. Matt. 16:18 with Matt. 18:18). Alone among the disciples, he is given the keys of the kingdom, keys commonly signifying in the ancient world absolute power over a home, city or kingdom. In pagan mythology, keys were given to Pluto, Persephone, Eache, Anubis, and Hecate to control admittance into the Netherworld.

The prophet Isaiah used the metaphor of keys in reference to the authority of the powerful office in ancient Israel, the master of the palace (Hebrew: *asher al habbayith*), the highest post in the land: "The key of the house of David I will lay on his shoulder; so he shall open, and no one shall shut; and he shall shut, and no one shall open" (Isa. 22:22). This verse is echoed in Matthew 16:19.

I came to understand papal infallibility by recognizing that Jesus had promised to send the Holy Spirit to lead us "into all truth" (Jn. 16:13), which, if this promise means anything at all, is a promise of infallibility in matters of spiritual truth. The successor of St. Peter, as the "chief rabbi" holding the keys of the universal Church against which hell can't prevail, possesses this particular charism of the Spirit in its entirety, so that the Church can be assured that what is being taught in matters of faith and morals is true. This is not to say that the Pope can "invent" doctrine out of thin air, which had been my impression, but that under certain determined circumstances the Holy Spirit guides (not "inspires") the Pope in defining "the faith that was once for all entrusted to the saints" (Jude 3). This is what happened at Caesarea

Philippi when no one could agree on Jesus' identity and Peter received, "not from flesh and blood," but from the Father the definitive christological confession. It made sense to me that our Lord didn't leave his flock vulnerable to every wolf coming along with a heresy on his lips and a Bible verse to sweeten its taste. This is why Jesus made Peter the pastor of his sheep (Jn. 21:15-17).

Careful not to go too far toward the Catholic position, Carson added that "The text [Matt. 16:18] says nothing about Peter's successors."[10] But I knew the other passages which do indicate a succession of the Petrine office. It has long been recognized, as alluded to above, that Matthew 16:18-19 is modeled on Isaiah 22:20-25 where Eliakim is given the "key of the house of David" to be prime minister over Israel, "a father to those who live in Jerusalem and to the house of Judah." This office, which some have compared to the office of vizier held by Joseph in Egypt (Gen. 41:40; cf. 2 Kgs. 15:5; 18:18; 1 Kgs. 18:3), was second in prerogatives and authority only to the monarch himself and was hereditary (i.e., there were successors). If Peter's apostolic office was the fulfillment of this Old Testament type, I thought, then there could be little question that Peter's office also had successors.

It was one of the Church's earliest Popes, St. Clement, writing to the church at Corinth around A.D. 96, who left little question in my mind that the ancient Church regarded the succession of bishops from the Apostles as highly important. Clement appeals to the memory of the two martyrs, Peter and Paul,[11] and explicitly states that the Apostles appointed bishops and made provisions for their succession, adding that "our sin is not small if we eject from the episcopate those who have blamelessly and holily offered its sacrifices [i.e., the Eucharist]" (44:4). He then exhorts the Corinthians to reinstate the

---

10   Ibid., 368.
11   *Epistle to the Corinthians* 5:3-7.

204 / Surprised by Truth

clergy they had ejected from their ministry on the basis that the priesthood, like the Gospel itself, is something established by Christ and handed down from the Apostles.

In the same epistle, Clement exercises the Petrine authority to bring order back to the Corinthian church: "But if some be disobedient to the words which *have been spoken by him* [Christ] *through us,* let them know that they will entangle themselves in transgression and no little danger . . . So you will afford us great joy and happiness if you are obedient to what *we have written through the Holy Spirit*" (59:1; 63:2). Clement appears to claim a sort of divine authority, and yet, in spite of the somewhat imperious tone and the claim to divine authority, the Corinthians welcomed this "papal intervention." Indeed, not only was it welcomed, the great Church historian and bishop of Caesarea, Eusebius (A.D. 260-339), writes, "I have evidence that in many churches this epistle was read aloud to the assembled worshippers in early days, as it is in our own."[12]

The unique status of the church at Rome was unmistakable in the second century church. In his letter to that church, Ignatius of Antioch (d. 110) lauds it as "worthy of honor, worthy of blessing, worthy of praise, worthy of success, worthy in its holiness, and presiding in love, named after Christ, named after the Father, . . . those who are united in flesh and spirit in every one of his commandments, filled with the grace of God without wavering, and filtered clear from every foreign stain." And that's just part of the greeting! Though Ignatius never hesitated to exercise his pastoral influence in other churches he wrote to, he declines in this instance, saying simply, "I am not commanding you as did Peter and Paul."[13] Rather, he says, "You have never envied any-

---

[12] *Ecclesiastical History,* book 3, 16.
[13] *Epistle to the Romans* 4:3.

one; you taught others. But I desire that those things may stand fast which you enjoin in your instructions."[14] So, at the very dawn of the second century, the church at Rome is "presiding in love" over the Church.

Around A.D. 182-188, Irenaeus of Lyons wrote a classic work entitled *Against Heresies.* In a passage which has been much debated by scholars, he maintains that the church at Rome is the best standard of orthodoxy: "Since, however, it would be very tedious, in a volume such as this, to reckon up the successions of all the churches, we do put to confusion all those who, in whatever manner, . . . assemble in unauthorized meetings; [we do this, I say,] by indicating that tradition derived from the apostles, of the very great, the very ancient, and universally known church founded and organized at Rome by the two most glorious apostles, Peter and Paul; as also [by pointing out] the faith preached to men, which comes down to our time by means of the succession of bishops. For *it is a matter of necessity that every church should agree with this church,* on account of its preeminent authority, that is, the faithful everywhere, inasmuch as the apostolic tradition has been preserved continuously by those [faithful men] who exist everywhere."[15] Irenaeus then proceeds to list the succession of the bishops of Rome to his own day, adding, "In this order, and by this succession, the ecclesiastical tradition from the apostles, and the preaching of truth have come down to us. This is a most complete proof of the unity and identity of the life-giving faith, which has been preserved in the Church from the apostles until now and handed down in truth."[16] One can hardly miss the significance here attached to the succession of the popes.

[14] Ibid. 3:1.
[15] Ibid. 3:3:2.
[16] Ibid. 3:3:3.

I started visiting Catholic parishes in order to talk to priests. The Catholic chaplain at the Air Force base I was then stationed at in New Mexico seemed more interested in helping me work through my questions than the civilian priests in town who, instead of discipling me, simply wanted to dump me into a program called RCIA (Rite of Christian Initiation of Adults). The chaplain was a brave soul, daily enduring my sincere yet pointed questions. ("If Mary was 'ever-virgin,' what of the brothers and sisters of the Lord mentioned in Mark 6:3? What about indulgences? What about . . . ?") He eventually invited me to participate in a weekday Mass in his small chapel. Never having seen a Mass before, I accepted the offer.

There were no more than half a dozen people at Mass that morning and there was an atmosphere of intimacy that was slightly intimidating to an outsider, though to be sure, everyone tried to make me feel welcome. I again saw the blood-red light above the altar and was told it meant that the Eucharist, Christ's sacramental presence, was being reserved behind the altar in a box called the tabernacle. The light was blood-red to signify Christ's redemptive sacrifice through which we have been delivered from darkness into the peace of his Kingdom "by the blood of his cross" (Col. 1:13, 20).

The chaplain then entered and the liturgy commenced. Somehow it all had a certain familiarity to it, almost as though I had heard it all before. I was pleased that Catholics actually sang the Psalms (as the ancient Jews intended them to be) and not merely discoursed upon them as in Baptist services. Then came the celebration of the Eucharist. I knew from my study of the New Testament and from the second century Church Fathers that the Eucharist was truly the Body, Blood, Soul, and Divinity of Christ. Consequently I felt considerable anticipation when this truth would no longer be something read about in a book, but would be realized only a few feet in front of me.

We chanted the *Sanctus*: "Holy, holy, holy Lord, God of power and might, heaven and earth are full of your glory. Hosanna in the highest. Blessed is he who comes in the name of the Lord. Hosanna in the highest", and then we all fell down on our knees. Again, that ring of familiarity. Where had I heard this before? It then dawned on me: this was the heavenly liturgy as revealed in Isaiah 6 and Revelation 4. I had never before been in a church that had taken Scripture so seriously as to structure its worship on the heavenly liturgy revealed in the Word of God.

But that was not all. The *Sanctus* reminded me of that day long ago when I first read the words, "I tell you, you will not see me again until you say, *'Blessed is he who comes in the name of the Lord.'*" Jesus was coming to me again as he had that day when St. Luke first introduced him to me in the Word. Only this time he was coming in the Sacrament. Jesus was now personally inviting me to the wedding feast of the Lamb (Rev. 19:9).

After Mass, I remember feeling as though I had worshipped God for the first time. One part of me wanted to beat down the doors to get into the Catholic Church. Instead I wound up in a two-year RCIA course which was intended to give me a deeper understanding of the Catholic Faith. It failed miserably in this admirable aim. The text used was the highly defective *Christ Among Us*, and I concluded that the acronym RCIA must really mean "Roman Catholic Ignorance Amok." Disappointed, I eventually dropped out of RCIA to learn Catholicism on my own. I read Catholic books on Church history, liturgics, patristics, Sacred Scripture, spirituality, and theology. A very helpful book was Dr. Ludwig Ott's *Fundamentals of Catholic Dogma*.[17]

The liturgy and the presence of Christ in the Eucharist were realities I couldn't shake from my mind. In truth, I was a Catholic the moment I left that first Mass.

---

[17] Rockford, IL: TAN, 1974.

After a few more years of study, I decided that I was truly prepared to make a commitment to the Catholic Church. It wasn't easy giving up some of my Fundamentalist beliefs. *Sola Scriptura*, the dogma that Scripture *alone* is authoritative, over against the Catholic belief in the authority of Scripture and Tradition,[18] was a doctrine I gave up only with fear and trembling; yet, by abandoning this unscriptural invention, I regained two thousand years of authentic Christian teaching. Not a bad exchange when one thinks about it.

After leaving the Air Force, I moved to California and started college. I found the local Catholic church and wound up yet again in RCIA, which I decided to endure this time as a penance for my past misdeeds. The RCIA director mercifully allowed me to enter the Church that Easter, which was only a few months away.

Recalling my promise to follow Christ wherever he would lead me, I found he had led me to the Catholic Church. On the Easter Vigil that Holy Saturday I would be conditionally baptized (Jn. 3:5; Acts 22:16), confirmed (Acts 8:14-17; 19:1-6; Heb. 6:2) and, what I had been longing for, receiving my first Communion (cf. Jn. 6:22-61; 1 Cor. 11:23-29). I had been baptized already as a Baptist, but I frankly felt uncomfortable entering eternity with a baptism administered by someone who called the Bride of Christ the "Whore of Babylon" and the Vicar of Christ the beast whose number is 666. I thought I'd cover my bases, and ask to be baptized conditionally.

The Easter Vigil which saw me meditating on that giant candle was indeed the consummation of a long journey. That evening I found myself loving the light shining from that Easter candle. Thinking back to the time I approached with such trepidation the blood-red light in that darkened church in Denver, I thought how

---

[18] Cf. 2 Thess. 2:15 and 1 Cor. 11:2.

ironic it was that what frightened me so much was in reality the sign of Christ's real presence in his Church. Trying so desperately to escape the darkness which surrounded me in my youth, the Father had led me by his Word to the light which shines forever above his altar in the Catholic Church.

Protestants often ask me why I became a Catholic. I reply that Scripture states the Church is the mystical Body of Christ and Christ is its head (Eph. 1:22-23; Col. 1:18). One can't have a personal relationship with the Head as Lord and Savior in its fullness if one doesn't embrace the Body as well. One can't decapitate Jesus from the Body and expect to have a "personal" relationship with just the severed head. That isn't what Jesus intended for us (cf. Jn. 17:20-23). In the Acts of the Apostles we read about an organized Christian community lead by the Holy Spirit, a visible Church which St. Paul could call "the pillar and foundation of truth" (1 Tim. 3:15), not merely a bunch of individualists running around with Gideon Bibles and "Just Me and Jesus" attitudes. As a Fundamentalist I couldn't claim to belong to a visible Church which is "the pillar and foundation of truth." As a Catholic I now can.

My message to my Fundamentalist friends is this: The Catholic Church is the Bride of Christ, joined to our Lord as one in the bond of the Holy Spirit. Listen: "The Spirit and the bride say, 'Come!' And let him who hears say, 'Come!' And let him who thirsts come. And whoever desires, let him take of the water of life freely" (Rev. 22:17). Here you will find the Faith once and for all delivered unto the saints. Here you will find one Lord, one Faith, one baptism, one God and Father of all—one holy, catholic, and apostolic Church.

The Bible Made Me Do It

Tim Staples

FROM THE time I was ten years old, I wanted to be a preacher like Billy Graham and my Baptist pastor. I dreamed of preaching in the pulpit on Sunday morning and leading people to Jesus Christ. Other kids wanted to be firemen and policemen, I wanted to be a preacher.

Though in my early teenage years I drifted away from my faith with the advent of parties and girls, as is the case with so many young people, I came back to Christ through the Assemblies of God when I was eighteen and rediscovered my boyhood desire to be a preacher.

After leaving high school, shortly after giving my life back to Christ, I decided to enter the Marine Corps, in order to save money for college and gain some much needed discipline. This decision proved to be a blessing. Being stationed in different parts of the United States allowed me to become involved, in my off-duty hours, with many different Protestant churches and ministries. I was involved with street evangelization and leading Bible studies. I led young Christian singles groups and a detention center outreach.

Then my dream came true. Just after I left the Marine Corps, I was asked to serve as a part-time interim youth pastor at the Assemblies of God church where I worshipped. After about six months of this work, the elders of the congregation offered to make the job a permanent full-time position. They also offered to pay my way through Bible college while I was in the ministry. I was elated!

There was one problem. During my last year in the Marines I met Matt Dula, a Catholic who really knew his faith. I didn't know a whole lot about Catholics, but I did know two things: Their beliefs were not biblical, and they were not Christians. Anti-Catholicism is a staple in the diet of many Assemblies of God churches, and growing up I gorged myself on the many horror stories I heard about the errors of "Romanism."

When I first met Matt and we started talking about religion, I assumed he would be another poor Catholic that I could help get "saved the Bible way." I was in for quite a surprise. I started an argument that lasted my entire final year in the Marine Corps. In spite of the jousting, we became good friends. But when it came to religion, Christian charity would often go out the window.

I thank God that Matt had enough knowledge of and love for his faith, to give me intelligent answers about Catholicism. If it were not for him, I would not be Catholic today. I pray that my testimony will encourage Catholics to defend the Faith when challenged by non-Catholics. I thank God for letting me encounter a Catholic who was willing and able to contend for the Faith (Jude 13).

Unfortunately, before meeting Matt, I had encountered many Catholics who were ignorant of their beliefs and often indifferent toward their Church. Their apathy was just another sign to me that the Catholic Church was not the true Church of Jesus Christ.

I was never shy about my faith in Jesus Christ. When I met Matt I immediately asked him if he was a Christian. He said he was Catholic. "Ha!" I scoffed to myself. "I'll set *him* straight." And the argument commenced. Matt didn't match me verse for verse (Fundamentalists are encouraged to memorize as much Scripture as they can), but for a Catholic he did a pretty good job! Every time I raised an objection against Catholicism his answers were always reasonable and often downright compelling. What startled me was that his explanations were invariably grounded in Scripture.

I always took the offensive, attacking Catholic teachings, and poor Matt could hardly get a word in at all. I'd lob one scriptural grenade after another until he'd be exasperated by the sheer number of my objections. (Many Protestants are skilled at delivering scriptural one-liners which seem to disprove a given Catholic belief. Unfortunately, these succinct arguments often require a lengthy response. It's important for Catholics to learn how to give short, biblical responses to Fundamentalist objections. This will get their attention.)

I must have seemed like a stubborn mule, but I didn't try consciously to be obstinate. I simply *knew* I was right and he was wrong. I had no respect for Catholics because of their lack of scriptural knowledge and because they held to doctrines I had been taught were unbiblical.

The concept that the Catholic Church might be right about anything was just not a possibility, as far as I was concerned. Nope. Fundamentalist Protestantism was the truth, and I knew it. I had everything planned out: When I left the Marine Corps I was going to enter the ministry. I didn't want anything to spoil the plan I was sure the Lord had given me. But the Lord had other plans for me.

When I attacked Catholic formula prayers as violating the Lord's condemnation against "vain repetitions" (Matthew 6:7), he asked if I thought a wife would object to her husband repeating the words, "I love you." "Would that be vain repetition?" he asked. "In the same way, we Catholics tell God we love him over and over again in our prayers." This gave me pause. I had to admit to myself that hymns we sang at our worship services often were just repetitions of the words "praise God," or some other prayerful phrase. Why were these repetitions somehow allowable for the Assemblies of God? I asked. But Catholics were *not* allowed to do the same?

Matt reminded me that even the angels described in Revelation 4:8 are eternally in the presence of God, repeating the prayer "holy, holy, holy, Lord." I was forced to admit that this repetition is not only not "vain repetition," it is biblical repetition.

When I objected to the Catholic belief in the perpetual virginity of Mary, Matt had a response that was devastating to my argument. I asked how he explained the fact that Matthew 13:55 lists the "brothers" of Jesus as James, Joses, Simon, and Judas (this verse was one of my favorites for making a Catholic squirm). He pointed out that Luke 6:15-16 reveals that James and Joses, though elsewhere called "brothers" of Jesus, are here shown to be the sons of Alphaeus (cf. Matt. 10:3, 27:56) whose wife Mary was actually the blessed Virgin Mary's sister, or perhaps her cousin (cf. John 19:25). These "brothers" were actually Jesus' cousins. The term "brother" is often used to mean "cousin" or some other type of kin in Scripture. How embarrassing to be shown up by a Bible-quoting Catholic!

But even if those men were Jesus' cousins, I thought, Scripture says that Jesus was Mary's "firstborn," implying she had other children afterwards (Matt.1:25). Matt reminded me that the text did not say they had marital relations — that was simply my interpretation. And "firstborn" is a ceremonial title given to the firstborn male child who inherited a unique birthright from his father (cf. Gen. 25:33). An only child could have this title just as validly as the firstborn of many brothers.

I was also bothered by the word "until" in Matthew 1:25 until Matt pointed out that the word "until" (Greek: *heos*) does not imply anything about what came after the incident being described. He cited 1 Corinthians 15:25 which says that Christ "must reign, *until* he has put all enemies under his feet." Obviously, this does not mean Jesus ceases to reign after all his enemies have been put under his feet (cf. Luke 1:33).

What's your authority?

I objected to many Catholic doctrines during our discussions, but one afternoon Matt turned the tables and challenged me to defend *my* ecclesiology. "If everyone in the Church has the same authority, as you claim" he asked, "who has the final authority to settle disagreements over the correct interpretation of Scripture? Isn't that the role of the Church?"

I answered by defending *sola scriptura*, the Protestant doctrine that Scripture alone is God's infallible binding revelation for his Church. "*Scripture* is our teacher!" I chided Matt, "not any pope or council." I quoted 1 John 2:26-27: "These things have I written unto you concerning them that seduce you. But the anointing which ye have received of him abideth in you, and ye need not that any man teach you: but as the same anointing teacheth you of all things, and is truth, and is no lie, and even as it hath taught you , ye shall abide in him"; and Matthew 18:19-20, "If two of you shall agree on earth as touching any thing that they shall ask, it shall be done for them of my Father which is in heaven. For where two or three are gathered together in my name, there am I in the midst of them." Based on these and similar verses I believed that all Christians have the same authority given by Christ through the Holy Spirit, and the true Church is where any two or more of these Christians gather together.

Matt grinned. He had been waiting for me to say that. In response he simply read aloud the entire passage of Matthew 18 (rather than just the two verses I wanted to emphasize [19 & 20]). In this text, Jesus explains how to deal with a Christian who falls into sin or error. If he will not listen to an individual's admonishment, two or more witnesses should confront him, "so that in the mouth of two or three witnesses every word may be established." If he refuses to listen to them, they are to refer the issue to the Church. And "If he refuses to listen even to the Church, treat him as you would a Gentile or a tax collector" (Matt. 18:16-17). In other words, the Church has the final say. In fact, it has the authority, given it by Christ, to excommunicate someone for sin or heresy.

Immediately after this teaching on the final authority of the Church to settle such issues Jesus delivers another promise regarding the Church's authority: "Amen, I say to you, whatever you bind on earth shall be bound in heaven, and whatever you loose on earth shall be loosed in heaven" (v. 18). Matt asked me to explain how the Church could fulfill the Lord's command to decide issues authoritatively if the Church is not infallible.

"Furthermore," he pressed, seeing that I was on the ropes here, "given all the conflicting opinions among Protestants on essential doctrinal issues, how can you possibly say that the Bible is the supreme authority when the Bible cannot interpret itself? Whose interpretation are we to go by?" Matt pressed further by quoting Hebrews 13:7: The faithful must "obey them that have the rule over [them], and submit; for they watch for [their] souls."

This Scriptural definition of an authoritative Church hierarchy really shook me! For the first time, I didn't have a ready retort. I was speechless, stumped by the logic of his question.

Matt suggested I look at Acts 15 and 16 which describes a doctrinal and pastoral controversy that threatened to tear the early Church apart. Questions about the Mosaic Law and about admitting Gentiles into the Church proved so vexing that the Apostles and elders of the Church called a council to consider these questions. "And certain men which came down from Judea taught the brethren, and said, Except ye be circumcised after the manner of Moses, ye cannot be saved. When therefore Paul and Barnabas had no small dissension and disputation with them, they determined that Paul and Barnabas, and certain other of them should go up to Jerusalem unto the apostles and elders about this question" (Acts 15:1-2).

Matt pointed out that the council did not appeal to Scripture alone to settle the difficulty (this would have been difficult with only the Old Testament to refer to, since none of the New Testament had been written yet). "Isn't it true that the Church decided the matter, as the Lord commanded in Matthew 18? And doesn't this magisterial authority also fulfill what Jesus promised his disciples, and by extension the Church, "He who listens to you listens to me, and he who rejects you rejects me?" (cf. Luke 10:16; cf. Matt. 10:40).

He also pointed out Jude's warning to the Church (Jude 11) where Jude condemns those intruders who are following after the "rebellion of Korah" (Jude 3-11). What was this rebellion? I looked at Numbers 16, the passage to which Jude is refering, and found that Korah and his followers were condemned and punished by God for their rebellion against the priests who had been appointed to preside over the People of Israel. Matt asked me how I explained the fact that Jude was warning the Church against those who rejected the authority of the New Testament Church's hierarchy if the New Testament Church had no authoritative hierarchy.

I was stumped.

He was right, of course. I couldn't think of a single argument that would get around the biblical evidence that the New Testament Church hierarchy had the authority to speak for Christ on doctrinal and pastoral issues. What's more, Jude's warning coincided with Jesus' warning to the churches of Asia Minor who rejected the decisions of the Council of Jerusalem(cf. Acts 15): "Repent; or else I will come unto thee quickly, and will fight against thee with the sword of my mouth" (Rev. 2:16; cf. Acts 16:1-8).

A few days later I tried to use 1 John 2:27, which says that we need not have any man teach us, but the Holy Spirit will teach us. "Doesn't this verse imply that we don't need a Church to tell us what to believe and how to act?" I asked, knowing all the while what a weak argument this was. Matt explained that the Holy Spirit speaks preeminently through the Church, so that when the Church teaches officially, it is not mere human teaching but the Holy Spirit guiding the Church.

Then he reminded me of Acts 15:28, "It is the decision of the Holy Spirit and of us not to place on you any burden beyond these necessities." The apostles then sent Paul and Silas, "who handed on to the people for observance the decisions reached by the apostles and presbyters in Jerusalem" (16:4). He pointed out that these Church decrees were "necessary things" that were binding on the consciences of all Christians. They were not free to reject what the Church taught without, in the same act, rejecting Christ himself (cf. Luke 10:16). Matt also quoted Paul's statement, "Although we were able to impose our weight as apostles of Christ . . . we were gentle among you" (1 Thess. 2:7).

I was chagrined that a Catholic was able to use the very passages I quoted to prove *his* case. I was being biblically outmaneuvered by a Roman Catholic! Since Matt knew of my plans to be a Protestant minister, he asked me whether I believed my interpretations of Scripture would be infallible. "Of course not." I responded. "I'm a fallible, sinful human being. The only infallible authority we have is the Bible."

"If that's so," he countered, "how can your interpretations of Scripture be binding on the consciences of the members of your congregation? If you have no guarantee that your interpretations are correct, why should they trust you? And if your interpretations are purely human in nature and origin, aren't they then merely traditions of men? Jesus condemned tradtions of men which nullify the Word of God. If it's possible, as you admit, that your interpretations may be wrong — you have no infallible way of knowing for sure — then it's possible that they are nullifying the Word of God."

"Wait a minute!" I said to myself. "Attacking 'traditions of men' is supposed to be my line. It's my job to expose the Catholic Church's unbiblical traditions." The problem was, I had no way to argue around the Catholic position. The more Matt and I talked, the more I saw that the Catholic Church didn't pull its beliefs out of thin air — it had a biblical basis for them. I might not agree with the Catholic model of authority but I couldn't argue with the fact that it had very strong Scriptural support.

The most frustrating thing about our discussions was that Matt never appealed to any Church tradition or any papal teaching; he stuck strictly to Scripture. He didn't have to rely solely on the Bible, he could have brought forward a mountain of evidence for Catholicism from Church history, but he was willing to meet me at my level and use Scripture alone.

This exchange compelled me to study Protestant scholars on the issue of the role of the Church. William Barclay's commentary on Matthew 18:15-18 gave me an example of the confusion and lack of consensus I found. This is one of the most difficult passages for Protestants to harmonize with *sola scriptura*. Jesus' conferral of special authority on the hierarchy of the Church fit the Catholic model perfectly, not the Protestant one.

I was dismayed at Barclay's attempt to avoid the force of this passage: "It is not possible that Jesus said this in its present form. Jesus could not have told his disciples to take things to the Church, for it did not exist; and the passage implies a fully developed and organized Church with a system of ecclesiastical discipline. . . . And the last verse actually seems to give the Church the power to retain and to forgive sins. Although this passage is certainly not a correct report of what Jesus said, it is equally certain that it goes back to something he did say. Can we press behind it and come to the actual commandment of Jesus?" (*Daily Study Bible, Matthew*, vol. 2, 186-187).

Barclay's argument was indicative of the gyrations many Evangelical scholars go through to integrate those troublesome "Church authority" texts with the Protestant doctrine of *sola scriptura*. They ranged from absurdly implausible interpretations to the more candid yet thoroughly heretical "solutions" (like Barclay's) which denied that Jesus and the apostles actually said the things attributed to them in the text. The more I studied this issue the more unsettled I became. I began to question whether my denomination, the Assemblies of God, could lay claim to being the authoritative Church described in the New Testament.

One day Matt asked, "Tim, why do you believe in the inspiration of Scripture?" My response was, "Because the Bible says it's inspired. 2 Timothy 3:16 says, 'All Scripture is given by inspiration of God.'" Then Matt showed me the fallacy of circular reasoning that flawed my response. I was right, of course; Scripture is inspired, but I hadn't proved it by citing 2 Timothy 3:16. The mere fact that the Bible claims to be inspired doesn't prove that it is. Plenty of other "holy books" claim to be inspired: the Qur'an, the Book of Mormon, the Hindu Vedas, just to name three.

Matt explained that Catholics and Protestants alike have received the testimony of the Church that Scripture is inspired. The Church did not make the books of the Bible inspired, of course, but it is the trustworthy witness God uses to attest to Scripture's authenticity and inspiration.

As a Pentecostal, I did not like the Calvinistic view that Scripture "confirms itself" as inspired in the hearts of those who read it with a sincere heart. That was too subjective to be an accurate test, and reminded me of Mormonism's "burning in the bosom" method of proving the Book of Mormon's divine origin.

The only other argument I could think of was to show that the Old Testament prophecies had been fulfilled in Jesus Christ. Didn't that historical and prophetic reliability prove the inspiration of Scripture? No it didn't. To believe that one would still have to trust the New Testament in what it told us about Jesus.

In less than a year, I had gone from utter confidence that I would convert another misguided Catholic to Christ, to wanting to get out of the Marines and away from him so I could salvage my dreams of being an Assembly of God pastor! I was beginning to get nervous.

One by one, what used to be my best arguments to "disprove" Catholic beliefs, were being defused.

Call no man 'father'

I had always thought that by calling their priests "father," Catholics violate the Lord's command: "Call no man your father upon the earth: for one is your Father, which is in heaven" (Matt. 23:9). Matt pointed out that in context Jesus is saying we must not give honor to men that belongs to God alone, and must not regard any human as taking the place of our Father in heaven. He showed how my Protestant aversion to the Catholic custom of calling priests "father" was biblically untenable by pointing out that Jesus calls Abraham "father Abraham" in Luke 16:24, as Paul does repeatedly in Romans 4.

In fact, Paul made the startling statement that, "Even if you should have countless guides to Christ, yet you do not have many fathers, for *I became your father in Christ through the gospel*' (1 Cor. 4:14-15). Matt explained that this passage sums up the theological reason why Catholics call priests 'Father.' Also, the deacon Stephen, under the inspiration of the Holy Spirit, addressed the Jewish priests and scribes as "my fathers" (Acts 6: 12-15, 7:1-2). And the other New Testament writers addressed men as "father" (cf. Rom. 4:17-18; 1 Thess. 2:11; 1 John 2:13-14). I found myself acknowledging that this Catholic practice in no way conflicted with the Bible, but my crass literalism did.

No one can forgive sins but God alone!

The Catholic belief in the sacrament of confession and their practice of confessing sins to a priest had always grated on me. I challenged them by saying "Only God can forgive sins. No one has to go to a mere sinful man to be forgiven. We go directly to God!" Matt quoted Jesus' words, "Peace be with you. As my Father has sent me, so I send you. And when he had said this, he breathed on them, and said, 'Receive the Holy Spirit.' Whose sins you forgive are forgiven them, and whose sins you retain are retained'" (John 20:21-23). Jesus gave this authority to forgive sins to men acting in his name. In legal terms we would say he gave them power of attorney.

In 2 Corinthians 2:10 Paul said (as the King James properly translates the text), "[I]f I forgave anything, to whom I forgave it, for your sakes forgave it I in the person of Christ." Paul also said, "And all this is from God, who has reconciled us to himself through Christ and given us the ministry of reconciliation, ... So we are ambassadors for Christ, as if God were appealing through us" (2 Cor. 5:18-20). I saw that I had no biblical basis for rejecting the Catholic doctrine of confession to a priest.

My objection was based on what I perceived as the absurdity of the Catholic proposition, rather than on any scriptural grounds. "How could Jesus be saying that a mere man can forgive sins? This is ludicrous, only God can forgive sins!" Matt said he believed it because the Bible said it. "What was so difficult about that?" he needled me with mock solemnity. (It wasn't pleasant to have a Catholic steal my lines like that.)

Be fruitful and multiply

The one issue that Matt and I could agree on was abortion, so we could always retreat to this common ground when things got too heated. From abortion the topic slipped over one day to contraception, which I had always assumed was a non- issue. My church had classes on which types of birth control to use, and I didn't think twice about it.

Matt quoted Genesis 38:6-10: "And Judah took a wife for Er his firstborn, whose name was Tamar. And Er, Judah's firstborn, was wicked in the sight of the Lord; and the Lord slew him. And Judah said unto Onan, Go in unto thy brother's wife, and marry her, and raise up seed to thy brother. And Onan knew that the seed should not be his; and it came to pass, when he went in unto his brother's wife, that he spilled it on the ground, lest that he should give seed to his brother. And the thing which he did displeased the Lord: wherefore he slew him also."

The question I asked was why was Onan killed by God. At first, I posited the possibility he may have been killed for disobedience to the law stating he must "raise up seed" for his brother, but Matt effectively demolished that possibility when he pointed out that in verse 26, Judah was guilty of not being willing to "raise up seed" for another, but he was not killed. Onan's sin must have been in "the spilling of the seed."

Matt quoted Romans 1:26 giving his reasons why contraception, like homosexuality is sinful. These actions change, "The natural use into that which is against nature." It was already obvious to me that the purpose and nature of conjugal love is both unitive and procreative.

It was also obvious that homosexuality eliminates the procreative aspect of the conjugal act (although sodomy cannot be properly called a "conjugal act"). But now I also saw how this principle also applies to contraception. Contraceptive conjugal union is sinful precisely because, by not being open to the possibility of new life, it distorts and misuses the Lord's gift of conjugal love, rendering it sterile and incapable of fulfilling its total purpose.

After a lot of Scripture study and reading other Catholic works on this subject I was sold on the Catholic position. We had found another issue we could agree on. Ephesians 5:32 teaches that marital love is a living symbol of the loving, spousal relationship between Jesus and the Church — a loving relationship that is ever-creating and ever unifying. I recalled the constant reminder in the Old Testament that children are precious blessings from the Lord (Psalms 127:3-5), and that it is God who opens the womb (Gen 30:22).

So often, when it comes to the vagaries of moral theology and its practical everyday outworkings in the lives of Christian men and women, Protestant pastors are forced to say that the Bible is silent on the issue so "every man must do what is right in his own eyes." Christ did not intend such lack of doctrinal certitude for his flock.

This lack of clear and authoritative teaching ability among Protestant pastors and theologians presented itself to me as yet another example of how the principle of *sola scriptura* fails as a sure guide to truth. The Protestant denominations began to resemble less and less the authoritative teaching Church described in Acts 15.

Traditions of God vs. traditions of men

Matt often told me how much authentic Christian truth I was missing out on because I denied the Church's tradition which could so enrich Scripture for me. He said my views would remain incomplete without this gift of God. As a Fundamentalist, tradition had always carried a negative connotation for me. I connected "tradition" with Jesus' stern condemnation of "traditions of men" which nullify the Word of God (Matt. 15:9).

Until Matt and I began to hammer away at *sola scriptura* I hadn't noticed the Bible's positive discussion of traditions. For example, Paul commanded the first Christians to "stand firm and hold fast to the traditions that you were taught, either by an oral statement or by a letter of ours" (2 Thess. 2:15). Here Paul says that divine Revelation comes to us in both written and oral form, and both are equally binding. I noticed too that this text says that the written Word is a subset of the overarching category of Tradition.

Other passages dealing with tradition helped me gain an appreciation of the biblical role of divine revelation preserved in the Church's oral Tradition. For example, Paul said, "I praise you because you remember me in everything and hold fast to the traditions just as I handed them on to you" (1 Cor. 11:2; see also Luke 10:16; 1 Thess. 2:13; 2 Tim. 2:1-2).

This is a hard saying! Who can listen to it?

The Catholic doctrine of the Eucharist was particularly bothersome to me. In the past my argument was mainly an assault against the absurdity of the Eucharist just as my objection to confession had been. But in the past, it had worked! "You Catholics think you are going to eat God? Don't you realize how ludicrous that is?" Luke-warm or ignorant Catholics would back down from my challenges against the Eucharist, in some cases because they really did not believe it. But Matt did believe this and was prepared to use the Bible to show why.

My objection pivoted on a single passage (it was actually the only one on which I could my base my objection): "It is the spirit that gives life, while the flesh is of no avail. The words I have spoken to you are spirit and life" (John 6:63). I argued from this that the Lord was speaking metaphorically not literally when he said things like "this is my body" and "unless you eat my flesh and drink my blood you have no life in you." How could Jesus possibly have meant that we should actually eat his literal flesh and blood? Matt challenged me to show him a single example in Scripture where "spiri-tual" means metaphorical or symbolic. I couldn't. "The fact that Jesus said his words in John 6 are 'spirit and life' does not mean that he was speaking symbolically," Matt explained. In response to the Jews' grumbling about his talk of "eating his flesh and drinking his blood," Jesus said, "I solemnly assure you . . . my flesh is *real* food, and my blood is *real* drink" (v. 53, 55).

The text says that his teaching was so difficult for some that many of them "returned to their former way of life and no longer accompanied him" (v.66). When this occurred Jesus didn't say, "Wait, folks! You misunder-stood. I just meant you have to come to me and believe in me as your personal Lord and Savior. You don't think I really meant you have to *eat* my flesh and drink my blood, do you?" No. Jesus let them leave and then turned to his disciples and said, "Do you also want to leave?" (v. 67). Peter answers for all who believe the Lord's

Eucharistic teaching, even though we don't fully comprehend it or aren't totally comfortable with it: "Master, to whom shall we go? You have the words of eternal life. We have come to believe and are convinced that you are the holy one of God" (v. 68-69).

To understand why Catholics see John 6 as literal, not figurative, one must consider its context. Earlier in the chapter Jesus says, "No man can come unto me, except it were given unto him of my Father" (v. 65). You can only see this truth if it has been supernaturally revealed to you because "the natural man receiveth not the things of the Spirit of God: for they are foolishness to him: neither can he know them, because they are spiritually discerned" (I Cor. 2:14). Words of spirit and life can only be understood in the spirit.

And what about the apostles? If Jesus had been speaking figuratively here, Paul is certainly no help in clarifying the matter when he says such things as: "I speak as to sensible men; judge for yourselves what I say. The cup of blessing which we bless, *is it not a participation in the blood of Christ?* The bread which we break, *is it not a participation in the body of Christ?* ...Whoever eats the bread or drinks the cup of the Lord unworthily shall be guilty of the body and blood of the Lord.... For anyone who eats and drinks without recognizing the body, eats and drinks damnation on himself" (1 Cor. 10:15-16, 11:27, 29). Paul surely seemed to take Jesus' words literally! I saw for the first time that the Catholic Church had a strong — a very strong — biblical basis for its teachings on the Eucharist. What would later convince me of the truth of the Catholic claims was the fact that the early Church Fathers unanimously taught the literal Real Presence of Christ in the Eucharistic elements. Their testimony cinched it for me.

As I worked through these and other issues I began to get nervous. With each discovery that the Catholic Church had compelling biblical reasons for its teachings I became more alarmed. Things were going too fast. I was actually beginning to consider the possibility that the

Catholic Church might be right. With a shudder I told myself to slow down and find some answers from some Evangelicals who could show me the errors in Catholic thinking that I had somehow missed.

At the very least, I reassured myself, whenever I'd get those troublesome "Catholic" thoughts, the Romanists were dead wrong about their Marian doctrines. That subject alone would make it impossible for me to ever become Catholic. Somehow, though, no matter how sternly I told myself this, I couldn't seem to shake the growing fear that I was going to discover the Catholic Church was right on everything.

I desperately did not want that to be true, but I couldn't figure out how to avoid the compelling biblical and logical arguments in favor of the Catholic Church. I felt like I was in that proverbial canoe without a paddle to help me push against the current. Worst of all, as I felt myself borne along faster and faster toward some unknown destination, I could hear the rumble of a huge waterfall somewhere in the distance. And the rumble was growing louder. "Please God," I prayed, "Show me the truth, but don't let the truth be Catholic!"

Searching for a tunnel at the end of the light

To my delight and relief, just when I thought I would go crazy with all these "what if" thoughts about the Catholic Church, I heard that Dr. Walter Martin, one of my favorite Evangelical apologists, was going to debate a Jesuit priest on "The John Ankerberg Show" (a Fundamentalist TV apologetics program).

"Hooray!" I exulted. Walter Martin was an excellent debater and a vigorous defender of classical Protestantism. I had (and still do have) a strong admiration for his ability to twist his opponents like pretzels with his knowledge of Scripture and his forceful, aggressive personality. I had never heard of Mitchell Pacwa before, but I was confident that Dr. Martin would destroy him, and in the process lead me back to my senses. I eagerly awaited the evening of the debate.

I sat in front of the TV, Bible in one hand, notepad in the other. The exchanges were lively and sometimes humorous, Martin was at his usual aggressive best, but I quickly saw that it would not be the rout I had expected. They went head to head on a number of controverted issues: justification; the sacraments; Marian doctrines; papal infallibility; calling priests "father"; and *sola scriptura*. By the end of the debate I was stunned. Not only had Pacwa refuted all of Martin's arguments, he had pinned Martin to the wall on a number of issues, and it was obvious that Martin had no way of responding.

The unthinkable had happened. The best spokesman for Evangelical "biblical" Christianity had gone up against an average Jesuit priest and lost. Worse yet, Pacwa's biblical and historical arguments reinforced everything Matt had told me. Instead of liberating me from the lure of Catholicism, this debate merely confirmed all of my fears that Protestantism might be wrong and Catholicism might be right. I was terrified at the implications that presented themselves to my mind.

Not long after the Martin/Pacwa debate my tour in the Marine Corps ended. I was finally free from daily contact with Matt and all of his Catholic arguments that were haunting me. It's so ironic that when I first met Matt I couldn't wait to argue religion with him, I was so confident that I was right and he was wrong. By the time we parted ways, I dreaded getting into such discussions with him. But I still had to deal with Fr. Pacwa's arguments.

In an effort to clear my head, I threw myself into ministry work at my home Church. It was at this time that I was asked to be interim youth pastor, and outwardly things were going great. This was the fulfillment of a childhood dream. But I couldn't enjoy it. The Catholic Church was wrecking everything!

Slowly, almost imperceptibly, the Catholic faith was becoming the most important thing to me. But as I came to realize this, my unease increased. The battle that raged in my soul was lonely and painful. With whom could I share these doubts and suspicions? No one in my congregation or circle of friends would have understood or accepted my quandary. I was torn between a deep love for the people and piety of the Assemblies of God and a growing sense of conviction that the Catholic Church was the fullness of the truth. I was faced with a decision that I couldn't put off indefinitely: How could I be a leader in my church, if I didn't know what I believed anymore?

I watched the Martin/Pacwa debate tapes repeatedly, studying each side's arguments carefully, searching for a chink somewhere in the Catholic armor. I wanted badly to agree with Dr. Martin, but the more I watched, the more I had to agree with the Catholic positions. Father Pacwa convinced me of the biblical basis for the Catholic positions on the communion of saints and justification. And one by one, as Martin raised them, Pacwa put to rest many of the myths and misconceptions I had always believed about Catholic Marian doctrines.

He explained the doctrine of the communion of saints using 1 Corinthians 12 where Paul described the Church as the body of Christ. He made the statement that as Christians we are more united to each other through Christ than a finger is united with a hand. Christ himself makes us one body. I had always known this to be true, but Father opened up an entire new understanding of this for me. He did this in several steps.

First, he showed me in the Bible how Christians are commanded to help one another and love one another as members of a family, and to see their interdependence as members of a single body. Paul said, "As a body is one though it has many parts, and all the parts of the body, though many, are one body, so also Christ. For in one spirit we were all baptized into one body . . . If one part suffers, all the parts suffer with it; if one part is honored, all the parts share its joy. Now you are Christ's body, and individually parts of it" (1 Cor. 12:12-13, 26-27).

Second, Christians do not cease being members of Christ's body at death. I was taught as a Protestant that there is some sort of separation between Christians that occurs at death. "We cannot pray to them or for them because they are with Jesus," I was assured. Why does "being with Jesus" mean they are separated from us? There is no Scripture verse that says this.

A Christian is even more radically joined to God, and therefore more radically joined to the other members of the body of Christ, when he goes home to heaven. He is freed from the constraints of sin; his faith has given way to perfect knowledge, and he is perfectly enabled to love and pray for the other members of the Body of Christ.

Most importantly, since in heaven he has been perfected in righteousness by the blood of Christ, his prayers are very powerful, much more so than they ever could have been while he was here on earth. When this fact is seen in light of James 5:16 — "The prayer of a righteous man has great power in its effects" — the Catholic doctrine of asking the saints for their intercession is undeniably the biblical teaching.

2 Maccabees shows that long before Christ the Jews prayed for the deceased and knew that those who died in a state of friendship with the Lord could pray for them (cf. 2 Macc. 12:42-46, 15:12-15). Even though I did not then accept the canonicity of 1 and 2 Maccabees, I had to acknowledge its historicity. Orthodox Jews still pray for the repose of the souls of their dead friends and relatives. Father opened my eyes to see the souls in heaven are not dead; they are alive (cf. Luke 10:38) and they are intimately concerned with our spiritual welfare (Heb. 12:1). Scripture confirms this again and again. On the mount of transfiguration in Luke 9:30-31, Moses and Elijah appear with Christ, and involved with our salvation. Revelation 5:8 shows saints in heaven interceding with God for us and God responding to their prayers. Revelation 8:5 depicts the angels doing the same. Hebrews 12:22-24 tells us that when we "come unto Mount Sion" in prayer, we do not just come to God, but also to "the spirits of just men made perfect." These are all members of our "family in heaven" (Eph. 3:15).

Blessed art thou among women

The single most difficult Catholic doctrine for me to accept was Mary's role in the Church. I had been taught to believed that Catholics worship Mary and the saints. In the debate Father Pacwa had to refute this claim over and over again with Dr. Martin. He explained that Catholics don't worship anyone but God, but they do honor and revere their elder brothers and sisters who have served Christ and are now with him in heaven. The Church encourages the practice of asking Mary and the saints to pray for us, just as we would ask fellow Christians on the earth to pray for us.

I had always believed that asking Mary to intercede for us conflicted with the Bible's teaching that Christ is the "one mediator between God and man" (cf. I Tim. 2:5). When Martin made this objection Father responded that the opposite is true. It does not take anything away from Christ's authority and glory when Christians preach the gospel to those who had never heard the good news. "How shall they hear without a preacher?" (Romans 10:14). This is acting as a mediator. Or what about when we pray for one another to effect change that would not occur unless we prayed? The Bible is clear that God grants gifts, "through the prayers of many" (2 Cor. 1:11). In fact, the Bible is clear that when Christians offer "supplications, prayers, petitions, and thanksgivings . . . for everyone," these things "are good and pleasing to God our savior" (1 Tim. 2:1,3). I came to see that Mary's role as a heavenly "prayer warrior" is completely biblical. [1]

When I began to see the Church as a body — as St. Paul repeatedly describes it — it was as though scales fell from my eyes. I no longer had a problem with hon-

---

[1] A thorough explanation of the biblical reasons for praying to Mary and the saints is found in Patrick Madrid's article, "Any Friend of God's Is a Friend of Mine," *This Rock* magazine, September 1992, 7-13.

oring my brothers and sisters in Christ. In fact, when I honor them I am honoring Christ and the marvelous beauty he has wrought in them! I saw that in honoring God's work of grace and beauty in Mary Catholics are fulfilling the biblical prophecy she uttered: "All generations shall call me blessed. The Mighty One has done great things for me!" (Luke 1:48-49). The greatest honor God ever paid to a human being he paid to Mary when he invited her to become the mother of Jesus, the Second Person of the Blessed Trinity. No Catholic could possibly heap more honor and exaltation on Mary than the Lord had already done.

I also labored under the misconception that by their Immaculate Conception doctrine, Catholics denied that Mary needed a savior. Father Pacwa set Walter Martin and me straight when he quoted Mary's own words in Luke 1:47: "I rejoice in God my savior!" Mary *indeed* needed Christ as her savior. From the moment of her conception the Lord saved her by the grace of Christ's death on the cross, shielding her from the ravages of sin. That he would do this for her was only fitting, in light of her mission to be the mother of Jesus, the Ark of the New Covenant who had been chosen to carry the Word of God in flesh in her womb.

If the Old Testament ark had to be pure, how much more the New Testament Ark (cf. Luke 1:43, 2 Samuel 6:9). If John the Baptist was "filled with the Holy Ghost, even from his mother's womb" (Luke 1:15) to prepare him to prepare the way of the Lord, how much more would Mary need grace to prepare her body and soul for the august task of carrying God himself within her! Not only does the reference to her being the ark of God imply her sinlessness, but the angel Gabriel names her "one who has been perfected in grace" (Luke 1:28).

I also objected to the title "Mother of God," arguing that since Mary only gave Jesus his humanity; she was only his mother "after the flesh." But Elizabeth addressed her as the "mother of my *Lord*," not "the mother of my Lord's body." It is true that Mary gave Jesus only his human nature, but this is true of any human mother or father — they only give us our bodies — God is the creator of the soul. Furthermore, a mother gives birth to a person, not a nature. Mary gave birth to a divine Person, not a human nature.

For by grace you have been saved through faith . . . it is not of works

Many Protestants accuse the Catholic Church of teaching a system of salvation based on human works independent of God's grace. This is not true.

The Church does teach the necessity of works, but so does Scripture. The Church condemns the notion that salvation can be achieved through "works alone." Nothing, whether faith or works, apart from the grace of God, can save us. It is works of grace that we do as a result of the grace of God moving us to act and helping us to bring the meritorious acts to their completion.

Father Pacwa summed it up nicely when he explained that we are saved by grace through faith which works by love (cf. Gal. 5:6). But we must choose to allow God's grace to work through us. He does not force us to "continue in grace" (cf. Acts 13:43). This made sense to me, but I was still confused by Paul's emphasis on salvation being a past-tense event: "For by grace you *have been* saved" (Eph. 2:8). And then there was 1 John 5:13: "These things have I written unto you that believe on the name of the Son of God; that ye may know that you *have* eternal life."

Father cleared up both of these problems. He agreed that salvation is in a sense a completed action in the life of all who have been baptized (Matt 16:16, Rom. 6:3, Gal. 3:27). But salvation is also spoken about in the present tense, for example, Paul says, "The message of the cross is foolishness to those who are perishing, but to us *who are being saved* it is the power of God" (1 Cor 1:18). Salvation is also described as a future event: "He who endures to the end *will be saved*" (Matt. 10:22).

I did an exhaustive word study on the Greek terms related to the English word "justification," and I found that not only is it inextricably linked to the issue of sanctification (the two concepts are actually one and the same thing) the Bible also speaks of justification in the past, present, and future tenses, implying that it is an ongoing process of sanctification in the life of each believer: "Therefore, since *we have been justified* by faith, we have peace with God through our Lord Jesus Christ" (Rom. 5:1); [we are] "being justified freely by his grace through the redemption that is in Christ" (Rom. 3:24); and, "But if, in *seeking to be justified* in Christ, we ourselves are found to be sinners, is Christ then a minister of sin? Of course not!" (Gal. 2:17).

What can separate us from the love of Christ?

Fundamentalists claim to have an absolute certainty of their salvation. But in the debate Father Pacwa demonstrated that, while Christians have a moral assurance of salvation — meaning that God will always remain faithful to his promise of eternal life for those who love and obey him (cf. 2:11-13) — the Bible explicitly says that Christians do not have an *absolute* assurance of salvation.

Paul said "It does not concern me in the least that I be judged by you or any human tribunal; I do not even pass judgment on myself; I am not conscious of anything against me, *but I do not thereby stand acquitted*; the one who judges me is the Lord. Therefore do not make any judgment before the appointed time, until the Lord comes, for he will bring to light what is hidden in darkness and will manifest the motives of our hearts, and then everyone will receive praise from God" (1 Cor. 4:4-5). Other verses which show this are Romans 11:22; Hebrews 10:26-29; and 2 Peter 2:20-21.

In Matthew 5:19-30, Jesus first tells us that there are "least commandments" that a person can break and still go to heaven, though he will be "least in the kingdom of heaven." And then he tells us of sins that leave a man "in danger of hell fire." St. Paul gives us a number of lists of deadly sins about which he says, "They which do such things shall not inherit the kingdom of God" (Galatians 5:21, see also Eph. 5:5-7 and 1 Cor. 6:9-10).

Into the lions' den

By this point in my study I had seen the handwriting on the wall. I knew I had to decline the offer of taking the full-time position of youth pastor at my Assemblies of God Church. I still was officially a Protestant but I was growing more and more convinced that the Catholic Church was right.

In what some might see as a dangerous act of "tempting the Lord," I decided to put the Catholic Church to one last test at a place where I knew the toughest questions would come. I enrolled for studies at Jimmy Swaggart Bible College (JSBC) in the fall of 1987. I had not given up completely my dream of being a minister; there was still a faint glimmer of hope that I could be shown the error of Catholicism. I figured that if Jimmy Swaggart's people couldn't do the job of demolishing the claims of Rome, no one could.

With all of the studying I had done previously, I became known for my knowledge of apologetics. On my own I was studying the early Church councils that defined orthodox Christology and Trinitarian doctrines, so when a Sabellian "Jesus only" movement arose on campus, a number of my classmates came to me for help. I found that I could refute these anti-trinitarian arguments largely because I had been studying how the early Catholic apologists did so in the first five centuries of the Church. There was no need for me to "reinvent the wheel"; I simply gave them a dose of good old Catholic theology — and they loved it!

I was amazed to find myself in two classes back to back that taught entirely different positions on the Trinity. The first taught orthodox trinitarian theology. The second taught that God the Father has a body and God the Holy Spirit has a body. The first class taught that

Jesus was the eternal Son of the Father. The second taught that he was the eternal Word who became the "Son" only at the incarnation. I remember going to lunch with a young lady one day and she was very distraught. She said to me in despair, "I thought I knew what I believed about God, but now I'm not sure what I believe."

The confusion I discovered at JSBC, contrasted with the Catholic doctrine I had been studying, made Rome look that much more attractive. I intensified my study of the early Church Fathers. If the Catholic Church *was*, in fact, the fourth-century syncretistic invention of emperor Constantine, as Jimmy Swaggart taught and as I had always believed, perhaps writings of the earliest Christian theologians and apologists would clear up my Catholic delusions. This was my last hope.

I took Jimmy Swaggart's challenge: "We would like to challenge the Catholic church to demonstrate that the saints and martyrs of the first three hundred years accepted the beliefs and practices of the Catholic church as it exists today . . . All of the Early Church fathers were evangelical and Pentecostal and had no association with what is now recognized as the Roman Catholic church."

I acquired a copy of J.B. Lightfoot's *The Apostolic Fathers* and devoured it. I went to the library on campus and began to study the lives and works of other Fathers of the Church, examining their writings and checking their theological arguments against what the Greek text of Scripture said. I researched all of the early councils of the Church. To my dismay, all I found was Catholic truth. I could not believe Brother Jimmy could have read what I read and issued his "challenge."

The writings of the Church Fathers clearly show that the early Church was Catholic long before the time of the Emperor Constantine. St. Ignatius, bishop of Antioch who knew St. John and who wrote in A.D. 110, speaks of the Church of Rome having primacy. He said the Roman Church has "the presidency of love." A shiver went up my spine when I read these words from Ignatius: "Let no man do aught of things pertaining to the Church apart from the bishop. Let that be held a valid Eucharist which is under the bishop or one to whom he shall have committed it. Wheresoever the bishop shall appear, there let the people be; even as where Jesus may be, there is the Catholic Church."

Reading William Eerdman's *Handbook to the History of Christianity*, which I purchased from Swaggart's bookstore, I hoped to find a more accurate (or a more Protestant) version of this history, but even he acknowledges Irenaeus's giving primacy to Rome. He does not agree with Irenaeus, but he does give us the historical fact. He also tells of Victor I, who was a very powerful second-century pope. He does not explicitly say Victor exercised pastoral authority over the whole Church as bishop of Rome, but this conclusion is implicit in his statement that Victor "threatened to excommunicate the Asian Churches over the Quartodeciman dispute."

He relates that Stephen, bishop of Rome in the 250s, claimed his authority derived from Jesus' promise to Peter in Matthew 16:18. Around the year A.D. 250 Cyprian, bishop of Carthage, wrote, "And again [Jesus] says to [Peter] after his resurrection, 'Feed my sheep.'

"On *him* he builds the Church, and to him he gives the command to feed the sheep; and although he assigns a like power to all the Apostles, yet he founded a single chair, and he established by his own authority a source . . . for that unity. . . . If someone does not hold fast to this unity of Peter, can he imagine that he still holds the faith? If he desert the chair of Peter upon whom the Church was built, can he still be confident that he is in the Church?"

Under the weight of so much Scripture and now the Church Fathers, I could no longer argue against the authority of the Catholic Church. I realized that I had to become a Catholic. The only questions that remained were "when?" and "how?"

Imagine what it would be like to go public with the plan to become Catholic at Jimmy Swaggart Bible College. My friends could see the direction in which I was headed, and they were concerned for me. I was "worked on" by them at every meal. I was grilled by professors. In fact, I nearly got called in to see Jimmy Swaggart himself. Instead, I had a confrontation with the faculty "expert" on Roman Catholicism: Andrew Caradagas, a former Catholic priest who was teaching Church History at JSBC.

Our discussion was quite an adventure. He had no idea I had done the kind of study I had. He attempted to persuade me of the error of Catholicism by telling me there were no popes until the fifth century. His face turned colors when I began to rattle off quotes from the Fathers long before the fifth century speaking of the authority of the bishop of Rome. He claimed the Eucharist was a medieval invention. I quoted the 1st- and 2nd-century writings of Fathers such as Ignatius, Justin, and Irenaeus on the subject of the Real Presence of Christ in the Eucharist. The sad part is, I knew he knew better than to say those things.

As we moved from doctrine to doctrine it became evident that he had not left the Church for doctrinal reasons. He admitted that he had some "bad experiences" in the Church that had led him to leave.

Our conversation ended on a sharp note as he snapped that the Catholic Church I was reading about "existed only on paper." He warned me that I would be very disappointed in the "real Catholic Church." As we parted he peered at me and muttered, "You're not going to *become* Catholic; you *are* Catholic!" I left his office with mixed feelings of sadness and relief. There was nothing I could do for him, and there was certainly nothing he could do for me.

There was no one at JSBC who could answer my objections and I think it was then that it really fully dawned on me that I must become a Catholic. I have never felt so alone in my life. I knew I would have to break up with my staunchly Protestant girlfriend; I'd be estranged from my Protestant family, most of whom I had "led to Christ." I would be at odds with all of my friends at school and at home. But most painful was the realization that by becoming a Catholic I would forever forfeit my life-long dream of being a pastor.

I was extremely depressed, and I remember coming back to my dorm room one night, exhausted from an all-day argument about Catholicism with my friends. I collapsed on my bed, slid down to my knees and looked up to the ceiling with tears filling my eyes. "Lord! Help me!" I cried out in anguish.

After a few moments I felt the strong urge to ask Mary to pray for me. "I don't know if I am doing this right, Mary. I don't know what's going to happen, but please help me! Please pray for me!" At that moment, the peace and joy of Christ flooded my heart. I almost *felt* the prayers ascending to God from Mary, my newly-found mother. It was as though Jesus had given his own mother to me just as he had done for John at the foot of the Cross. I have never doubted the Catholic Faith since that day. The pilgrimage did not become easier, but I knew that I was not alone anymore. The Lord and his Mother were helping me all along.

When I left school and went home, I told my family and the members of my church that I was converting to the Catholic Church. On the first night I was home, I talked to my mother and my brother from about 10:00 until 8:00 the next morning. At first my decision was very difficult for them to accept, but we continued to discuss my reasons for becoming Catholic.

By God's grace, these discussions with my staunchly-Protestant family members has borne much good fruit. I am forever grateful that God enabled me to help my mother, my father, and my two brothers (one of whom is now studying for the priesthood at St. Charles Borromeo Seminary, Philadelphia) join the ranks of the Catholic faithful.

The Lord asked me to give up everything and follow him, no questions asked. But he also has been true to his promise to repay a "hundredfold" those who give up everything for him. The joy and peace that I now experience, the doctrinal certitude that I now possess, and the tremendous graces that are mine in the sacraments, especially in the Holy Eucharist, are riches far beyond anything I expected.

As I look back on my journey to the Catholic Church, sometimes I still cannot believe it all really happened. The pilgrimage was difficult and painful. And I marvel at God's tenacity and patience in leading me to the Catholic Church — I fought against it every step of the way. I had despised for so long the Catholic belief in Mary's intercession. But when I finally gave in to her loving call, bidding me follow Christ her son wherever he might lead me, I knew she was saying to me, "Do whatever he tells you" (John 2:5).

Once home in the Church I felt the sweet consolation of the truth those Christians in Antioch must have felt when the apostles read the decrees of the first Church council. "They rejoiced for the consolation" (Acts 15:31) of knowing the Church had spoken; the dispute was ended.

And I can say that the former priest at Jimmy Swaggart Bible College was wrong. I love the real Catholic Church with all my heart and soul and strength.

Confessions of a 1980s' Jesus Freak

Dave Armstrong

I WAS RECEIVED into the Catholic Church in February 1991 by Fr. John Hardon, an act which, as recently as a year earlier, would have seemed to me absolutely inconceivable. Not much in my background would have indicated this surprising turn of events, but such is the way of God's inscrutable mercy and providence.

My initial exposure to Christianity came from the United Methodist Church, the denomination in which I was raised. The church we attended, in a working-class neighborhood of Detroit, appeared to me, even as a child in the early 1960s, to be in a steady decline. The most striking evidence of this was the fact that there were few children and teenagers in that congregation; the average age was about fifty. (Later, in my studies as an Evangelical, I learned that shrinking and aging congregations were one of the marks of the deterioration of modern mainline Protestant denominations.) As it turned out, our church folded in 1968. Rather than seek out a new congregation in which to fellowship, I slid quietly into apathy and for the next nine years rarely attended church.

My early religious upbringing was not totally without benefit, though. My parents imparted to me a respect for God which I never relinquished, a comprehension of his love for me, and an appreciation for the sense of the sacred and for basic moral precepts.

At any rate, for whatever reason, I didn't sustain an interest in Christianity at this time. In 1969, at the age of eleven, I first came in contact with the quintessential altar call of Fundamentalist Christianity at a Baptist Church which we visited two or three times. I went up front to get "saved," perfectly sincere, but without the knowledge or force of will required (at least not by the typical Evangelical standard) to carry out this temporary resolve to follow Jesus Christ.

During this period, I became fascinated with the supernatural, but unfortunately, it got channeled into a vague, catch-all occultism. I dabbled, with great seriousness, in ESP, telepathy, the Ouija Board, astral projection, even voodoo (with a vicious gym teacher in mind!). I read about Houdini and Uri Geller, among others.

Meanwhile, my brother Gerry, who is ten years older than I am, converted, in 1971, to "Jesus Freak" Evangelicalism, a trend which was at its peak at that time. He underwent quite a remarkable transformation out of a drug-filled rock band culture and personal struggles, and started preaching zealously to our family. This was a novel spectacle for me to observe. I had already been influenced by the hippie counterculture, and had always been a bit of a nonconformist, so the "Jesus Movement" held a strange fascination for me, although I had no intention of joining it.

I prided myself on my "moderation" with regard to religious matters. Like most nominal Christians and outright unbelievers, I reacted to any display of earnest and devout Christianity with a mixture of fear, amusement, and condescension, thinking that such behavior was "improper," fanatical, and outside of mainstream American culture.

During the early 1970s I occasionally visited Messiah Lutheran Church in Detroit where my brother attended, along with his "Jesus Freak," long-haired friends, and would squirm in my seat under the conviction of the powerful sermons of Pastor Dick Bieber, the likes of which I had never heard. I remember thinking that what he was preaching was undeniably true, and that if I were to "get saved," there would be no room for middle ground or fence-sitting. Therefore, I was reluctant, to say the least, because I thought it would be the end of fun and fitting in with my friends. Because of my rebelliousness and pride, God had to use more drastic methods to wake me up.

In 1977 I experienced a severe depression for six months, which was totally uncharacteristic of my temperament before or since. The immediate causes were the pressures of late adolescence, but in retrospect it is clear that God was bringing home to me the ultimate meaninglessness of my life — a vacuous and futile individualistic quest for happiness without purpose or relationship with God. I was brought, staggering, to the end of myself. It was a frightening existential crisis in which I had no choice but to cry out to God. He was quick to respond.

It so happened that at Easter 1977 the superb Franco Zeffirelli film "Jesus of Nazareth" (still my favorite Christian movie) was on television. I had always enjoyed Bible movies, such as "The Ten Commandments." They brought the biblical personalities to life, and the element of drama (as an art form) communicated the vitality of Christianity in a unique and effective way. Jesus, as portrayed in this movie, made an extraordinary impression on me, and the timing couldn't have been better. He seemed like the ultimate nonconformist, which greatly appealed to me. I marveled at the way He dealt with people, and got the feeling that you could never expect what He would say or do — always something with unparalleled insight or impact.

I began to comprehend, with the help of my brother, the heart of the gospel for the first time: what the Cross and the Passion meant, and some of the basic points of theology and soteriology (the theology of salvation) that I had never thought about before. I also learned that

Jesus was not only the Son of God, but God the Son, the Second Person of the Trinity, which, incredibly, I had either not heard previously, or simply didn't comprehend if I had heard it. I started to read the Bible seriously for the first time in my life (the Living Bible translation, which is the most informal paraphrase).

It was the combination of my depression and new-found knowledge of Christianity that caused me to decide to follow Jesus as my Lord and Savior in a much more serious fashion, in July 1977 — what I would still regard as a conversion to Christ, and what Evangelicals view as the "born-again" experience or getting "saved." I continue to look at this as a valid and indispensable spiritual step, even though, as a Catholic, I would, of course, interpret it somewhat differently from the way I did formerly. Despite my initial burst of zeal, I again settled into lukewarmness for three years until August 1980, when I finally yielded my whole being to God, and experienced a profound renewal in my spiritual life.

Throughout the 1980s I attended Lutheran, Assembly of God, and non-denominational churches with strong connections to the "Jesus Movement," characterized by youth, spontaneity of worship, contemporary music, and warm fellowship. Many of my friends were former Catholics. I knew little of Catholicism until the early 1980s. I regarded it as an exotic, stern, and unnecessarily ritualistic "denomination," which held little appeal for me.

I wasn't by nature attracted to liturgy, and didn't believe in sacraments at all, although I always had great reverence for the "Lord's Supper" and believed something real was imparted in it.

On the other hand, I was never overtly anti-Catholic. Having been active in apologetics and counter-cult work (specializing in Jehovah's Witnesses), I quickly realized that Catholicism was entirely different from the cults, in that it had correct "central doctrines," such as the Trinity and the bodily Resurrection of Christ, as well as an admirable historical legitimacy: fully Christian, albeit vastly inferior to Evangelicalism.

I was, you might say, a typical Evangelical of the sort who had an above-average amateur theological interest. I became familiar with the works of many of the "big names": C.S. Lewis, Francis Schaeffer, Josh McDowell, A.W. Tozer, Billy Graham, Hal Lindsey, John Stott, Chuck Colson, *Christianity Today* magazine, Keith Green and Last Days Ministries, the Jesus People in Chicago, *Cornerstone* magazine, InterVarsity Christian Fellowship (a campus organization), as well as the Christian music scene. All in all, they were quite beneficial influences and not to be regretted at all.

My strong interest in evangelism and apologetics led me to become, with my church's permission, a missionary on college campuses for four years. I also got involved in the Pro-Life movement, and eventually Operation Rescue. It quickly became apparent to me that the Catholic rescuers were just as committed to Christ and godliness as Evangelicals. In retrospect, there is no substitute for the extended close observation of devout Catholics. I had met countless Evangelicals who exhibited what I thought to be a serious walk with Christ, but rarely ever Catholics of like intensity. I began to fellowship with my Catholic brethren at Rescues, and sometimes in jail, including priests and nuns. Although still unconvinced theologically, my personal admiration for orthodox Catholics skyrocketed.

In January 1990 I launched an ecumenical discussion group which I moderated. Three knowledgeable Catholic friends from the Rescue movement, John McAlpine, Leno Poli, and Don McSween, started attending. Their claims for the Church, particularly papal and conciliar infallibility, challenged me to plunge into a massive research project on that subject. I believed I had found many errors and contradictions throughout history. Later I realized, though, that my many "examples" didn't even fall into the category of infallible pronouncements, as defined by the Vatican Council of 1870. I was also a bit dishonest because I would knowingly overlook strong historical facts which confirmed the Catholic position, such as the widespread early acceptance of the Real Presence, the authority of the bishop, and the communion of the saints.

In the meantime, I embarked on an extensive reading program of Catholic apologetics books, as well as the many tracts and booklets produced by Catholic Answers. I kept an open mind and a teachable heart as I studied Scripture along side these Catholic works, occasionaly checking Evangelical commentaries and apologetics works to see what their rebuttals to the Catholic claims might be. I was amazed at how compelling the biblical and historical case for Catholicism was — how unanswerable its claims were — and as my understanding of Catholicism grew, my respect for it grew also. Providentially, my study began with *The Spirit of Catholicism* by Karl Adam, a book too extraordinary to summarize adequately here. It is, I believe, a nearly perfect book about Catholicism as a worldview and a way of life, especially for a person acquainted with basic Catholic theology. I read books by Christopher Dawson, the great cultural historian, Joan Andrews, a heroine of the Rescue Movement, and Thomas Merton, the famous Trappist monk. Each impressed me deeply.

My three friends at our group discussion continued to calmly offer replies to nearly all of my hundreds of questions. I was amazed. The Catholic Church seemed to have everything so well thought out — it was a marvelously complex and consistent belief system unparalleled by anything I had ever encountered in Evangelicalism. But mere complexity was not what drew me Romeward. In fact, many Evangelicals (myself included, at that point) take pride in the fact that their gospel is so simple. But the more I studied the theological details of the Christian faith, as expressed, for example, by the early Church Fathers of the first five centuries, the more it became clear that the Gospel is both complex and simple.

The principles of the Gospel — such as the Trinity, the divinity of Christ, salvation by grace alone, and baptismal regeneration — can be articulated in very simple terms, but explaining and exploring them is anything but simple. (Prove this to yourself by pulling down from the shelf the writings of theologians such as Athanasius, Augustine, and Thomas Aquinas, and see the tremendous detail they go into as they labor to explain the doctrine of the Trinity: One God in Three Persons. They wrote *volumes* explaining the meaning of that deceptively simple, five-word formula — the most central doctrine of the Catholic faith.

The more I studied Catholic teachings in the light of Scripture, the more troubled I became. I was bothered by the universal Protestant acceptance of contraception after I recognized how utterly anti-biblical this practice is. I came to believe, in agreement with the Church, that once one regards sexual pleasure as an end in itself, then the so-called "right" to abortion is logically not far away. My Evangelical pro-life friends might easily draw the line, but the less spiritually-minded have not in fact done so, as has been borne out by the sexual revolution in full force since the widespread use of the Pill began around 1960.

Once a couple thinks that they can thwart even God's will in the matter of a possible conception, then the notion of terminating a pregnancy follows by a certain diabolical logic devoid of the spiritual guidance of the Church. In this, as in other areas such as divorce, the Church is ineffably wise and truly progressive.

I was shocked to learn that no Protestant denomination had permitted contraception until 1930, when at its Lambeth Conference the Anglican Communion announced it no longer viewed it as sinful. Since then, every single Protestant denomination has followed suit. What ensued was the inevitable progression from allowing contraception to allowing abortion. My growing awareness that artificial contraception was wrong solidified into outright certainty when I read *The Teaching of*

Humanae Vitae, by John Ford and Germain Grisez. It convinced me of the moral distinction between contraception and Natural Family Planning, and in so doing pushed me over the edge into accepting the Catholic position on sexual issues.

By rejecting birth control I had adopted a very "un-Protestant" position, but I was still far from becoming Catholic. Despite the many other obstacles that remained, I was falling prey to Chesterton's principle of conversion: that one cannot examine Catholicism and not develop an admiration for it — an admiration that almost invariably leads to becoming convinced of its truth.

Meanwhile, my wife Judy, who was raised Catholic and became a Protestant before we dated, had also been convinced of the wrongness of contraception, independently of my studies. By July 1990, then, I believed Catholicism had the best moral theology of any Christian body, and greatly respected its sense of community, devotion, and contemplation.

The walls came tumbling down

My attraction to the beauty of the Church's moral and mystical theology facilitated my conversion process. The more I read about the Church's teachings the more I admired them; they rang true deep within my soul, beyond, but not opposed to, the rational calculations of my mind — what Cardinal John Henry Newman termed the "Illative Sense."

My Catholic friend, John, tiring of my constant rhetoric about Catholic errors and unscriptural additions through the centuries, suggested that I read John Henry Newman's *Essay on the Development of Christian Doctrine.* This book demolished the whole schema of Church history which I had constructed. Up to that point I assumed (without any evidence to support the notion) that early Christianity was "Protestant" and that Catholicism was a later corruption. I thought the corruption reached its zenith in the late Middle Ages rather than the time of

Constantine in the fourth century, which is the more common view of Evangelicals.

Martin Luther, so I reckoned, had discovered in *"sola scriptura"* the means to scrape the accumulated Catholic barnacles off of the original lean and clean Christian "ship." Newman, in contrast, exploded the notion of a barnacle-free ship. Ships always got barnacles. The real question was whether the ship would arrive at its destination. Tradition, for Newman, was like a rudder and steering wheel, and was absolutely necessary for guidance and direction. Newman brilliantly demonstrated the characteristics of true developments, as opposed to corruptions, within the visible and historically continuous Church instituted by Christ. I found myself unable and unwilling to refute his reasoning, and a crucial piece of the puzzle had been put into place — Tradition was now plausible and self-evident to me.

Thus began what some call a "paradigm shift." While reading the *Essay* I experienced a peculiar, intense, and inexpressibly mystical feeling of reverence for the idea of a Church "one, holy, catholic and apostolic." Catholicism was now thinkable and I was suddenly cast into an intense crisis. I now believed in the visible Church and suspected that it was infallible as well. Once I accepted Catholic ecclesiology, the theology followed as a matter of course, and I accepted it without difficulty (even the Marian doctrines).

My Catholic friends had been tilling the rocky soils of my stubborn mind and will for almost a year, planting "Catholic seeds," which now rapidly took root and sprouted, to their great surprise. I had fought the hardest just prior to reading Newman, in a desperate attempt to salvage my Protestantism, much like a drowning man just before he succumbs!

I continued reading, now actively trying to persuade myself fully of Catholicism, going through Newman's autobiography, Tom Howard's *Evangelical Is Not Enough*, which helped me appreciate the genius of liturgy for the first time, and two books by Chesterton on Catholicism.

At about this time I had a conversation with an old friend, Al Kresta, who had also been my pastor for a few years, and whose theological opinions I held in very high regard. I admitted to him that I was seriously troubled by certain elements of Protestantism, and might, perhaps (but it was a far-fetched notion) think of becoming a Catholic. To my amazement, he told me that he, too, was heading in the same general direction, citing, in particular, the problem that the formulation and pronouncement of the canon of Scripture poses for Protestants and their "Bible-only" premise. These types of unusual "confirming" events helped to create a strong sense that something strange was going on during the bewildering period just preceding my actual conversion. Al was in such a theological crisis (as was I), that he resigned his pastorate within two months of our conversation.

Also at this time I had the great privilege of meeting Fr. John Hardon, the eminent Jesuit catechist, and attending his informal class on spirituality. This gave me the opportunity to learn personally from an authoritative Catholic priest, who is a delightful and humble man as well.

After seven tense weeks of alternately questioning my sanity and arriving at immensely exciting new plateaus of discovery, the final death blow came in just the fashion I had suspected. I knew that if I was to reject Protestantism, then I had to examine its historical roots: the so-called Protestant Reformation. I had read about Martin Luther, and considered him one of my biggest heroes. I accepted the standard Protestant textbook myth of Martin Luther as the bold, righteous rebel who stood against the darkness of "Romanist tyranny, superstitious ritualism, and unbiblical traditions of men" that had been added on to the original, "pure" Christianity described in the book of Acts.

But when I studied a large portion of the six-volume biography of Luther, by the German Jesuit Hartmann

Grisar, my opinion of Luther was turned upside down. Grisar convinced me that the foundational tenets of the Protestant Revolution were altogether tenuous. I had always rejected Luther's notions of absolute predestination and the total depravity of mankind. Now I realized that if man had a free will, he did not have to be merely declared righteous in a judicial, abstract sense, but could actively participate in his redemption and actually be made righteous by God. This, in a nutshell, is the classic debate over justification.

I learned many highly disturbing facts about Luther; for example, his radically subjective existential methodology, his disdain for reason and historical precedent, and his dictatorial intolerance of opposing viewpoints, including those of his fellow Protestants. These and other discoveries were stunning, and convinced me beyond doubt that he was not really a "reformer" of the "pure," pre-Nicene Church, but rather, a revolutionary who created a novel theology in many, though not all, respects. The myth was annihilated. I was *un*convinced of the standard Protestant concept of the invisible, "rediscovered" church. In the end, my innate love of history played a crucial part in my forsaking Protestantism, which tends to give very little attention to history, as indeed is necessary in order to retain any degree of plausibility over against Catholicism.

At this point, it became, in my opinion, an intellectual and moral duty to abandon Protestantism in its Evangelical guise. It was still not easy. Old habits and perceptions die hard, but I refused to let mere feelings and biases interfere with the wondrous process of illumination which overpowered me by God's grace. I waited expectantly for just one last impetus to fully surrender myself. The unpredictable course of conversion came to an end on December 6, 1990, while I was reading Cardinal Newman's meditation on "Hope in God the Creator" and in a moment decisively realized that I had already ceased to offer any resistance to the Catholic Church. At the end, in most converts' experience, an icy fear sets in, similar to the cold feet of pre-marriage jitters. In an instant, this final obstacle vanished, and a tangible "emotional and theological peace" prevailed.

In the three years since I converted, some astonishing things have occurred among our circle of friends. I claim no credit for these happenings, other than maybe a tiny influence, but rather, marvel at the ways in which God moves people's hearts. Four people have returned to the Church of their childhood and three, like myself, have converted from lifelong Protestantism. These include my former pastor, Al and his wife, Sally, one of my best friends and frequent evangelistic partner, Dan Grajek and his wife Lori, Dan's longtime friend Joe Polgar, who had lapsed into virtual paganism for years, another friend Terri Navarra, and Jennifer, the daughter of a friend, Tom McGlynn. Additionally, another couple we know converted to Eastern Orthodoxy, a second is seriously thinking about the same, and a third couple may convert to Catholicism.

Many of our mutual Protestant friends view these occurrences with dumbfounded trepidation. One of my former pastors, in the most heated encounter since my conversion, called me a "blasphemer" because I believed there was more to Christian Tradition than simply that which is contained in the Bible! Another good friend, a Baptist minister, said that although I had made a terrible mistake, I was still saved because of his belief in eternal security! All in all, it has, thankfully, been fairly smooth sailing among our Evangelical Protestant friends. Many ignore our Catholicism altogether.

I believe that all Catholics can share in such experiences as I've been describing, in the sense that each new discovery of some Catholic truth is similarly exhilarating. As we all grow in our faith, let us rejoice in the abundant well-springs of delight, as well as instructive times of suffering which God provides for us in his Body, fully manifested in the Catholic Church. I feel very much at home in it, as much as could be expected this side of heaven.

All Detours to Rome

Al Kresta

THEY SAY all roads lead to Rome. I must have trav-
eled every one of them before I got there. The Lord
allowed me to wander through nominal Catholicism,
adolescent hedonism, psychedelic mysticism, occultic
rigorism, evangelical Protestantism, and finally, into the
gracious fullness of Catholic truth. There were many
detours along the way, but I'm home now.

I rejected Evangelical Protestantism for biblical and
historical reasons and embraced the Catholic Church,
but I owe Evangelicalism a great deal. Its inventiveness,
vibrancy, and forceful presentation of Christianity is in
many respects unmatched by the Catholic Church in
America. We Catholics have a lot to learn from our
Evangelical friends. But we need to pray hard for them
too.

Tragically, Evangelicalism is a reform movement that
forgot the Catholic Church it was seeking to reform. It
produces some great wine but spills it for want of wine-
skins. It generates fire but gets burned because it can't
settle on a fireplace. It manages to convert many goats to
sheep but leaves them wandering without the shepherds
Jesus has appointed for them.

I was born into a Catholic family in 1951 in New
Haven, Connecticut, the oldest of five children. I don't
remember my parents ever discussing things sacred.
They had plenty to say, often with the business end of a
sturdy paddle, about generic morality, embodied in the

Golden Rule and the Ten Commandments, but they didn't talk to us about sacred things.

That's not to say my young life was bereft of the transcendent. After my first confession I was so overwhelmed by the love and forgiveness of God, a sense of purity of heart and giddy delight, that as I walked down the church driveway I imagined I might be lifted from the earth and caught up to heaven. A friend suggested that I was probably just glad it was over. Nah. When does performing a duty raise one to rapture?

Adolescent doubt — the "common doom," as Melville called it — hit me hard, and I turned to the pleasures of wine, women, and song (known to my generation as "drugs, sex, and rock & roll"). My teenage years began with my classmates electing me class president and "most likely to succeed." They ended with the courts imposing a two-year suspended sentence for heroin possession and my high school pushing me out the door with a 1.8 grade point average.

By the time I had graduated from high school my hedonism and intellectual laziness had exacted a fearful toll on my Christianity: I had no religion, no interest in God, and I regarded the Catholic faith I had inherited from my parents to be totally irrelevant.

This moral and spiritual drifting went on for a year or so, but in a quirk of grace, my sense of the sacred was reawakened during three LSD experiences in 1969. I became conscious of God again, and that made me nervous. I felt him calling me. So I quit drugs cold-turkey and became a metaphysical vagabond, a theological homeless person with the tin cup of my mind stretched out in supplication, in hopes that someone would drop some truth in there.

I hitchiked around the country, flopping at the feet of any guru or charlatan who would offer me answers to life's big questions. In Miami I met Swihart, an "alien from Venus" who ran a science fiction bookstore and taught classes on past life regression. In a small Michigan town I sat at the feet of Beulah, a 300 pound grandmother of a multitude who, when in her trances, dictated cosmic revelations that always began with the reminder, "I am the Queen of Life." In Kalamazoo, Michigan, a saffron-clad flock of Hare Krishnas, reeking of patchouly oil and incense, danced after me, forcing a copy of the *Bhagavad Gita* into my hands. In Memphis, the cultic group Children of God prophesied that the Comet Kohoutek would strike the earth in 1974, wiping out much of humanity (I was interested in this group briefly, but when 1974 came and went with nary a cosmic collision, I pushed on). In the Catskill Mountains, I was intrigued by a tattered copy of the Jehovah's Witnesses' *Watchtower* magazine that warned me to prepare for Armageddon in 1975. By January 1, 1976 my mild interest in that group had evaporated.

Limited space cuts short my meanderings through the bizarre spiritual menagerie of those years: pennies falling from heaven at Woodstock, Scientology peddled aggressively on the streets of New York, Edgar Cayce's dreams and predictions, astral projection, seeing angels on blank TV screens, dream analysis courses, and assorted vegetarian diets.

In 1971 I moved to Michigan to live with a community that went by the rather infelicitous moniker,the I AM Religious Activity (IARA). We were strict vegetarians, celibate, abstaining from alcohol, drugs, vaccinations, onions, and garlic (Don't ask me to explain the last two items; it had to do with attracting "discarnate entities").

By practicing rigorous occultic discipline we hoped to purify our bodies and ascend from the earth like Jesus. We were taught that Jesus was but one of hundreds of fully purified "ascended masters" who, from the vantage point of their higher planes of consciousness, directed the spiritual evolution of the human race. They dictated instructions for us disciples through their "Accredited Messengers" in Chicago, that is, the higher ups in the IARA.

Before long I hit a few obstacles. First was my inability to live according to the group's rigorous laws. We were expecting to maintain perfect harmony in our feelings, thinking that doing so would charge the life energy flowing through us with positive qualities and thus, hasten the purification of our bodies and souls.

But anger, lust, and discouragement regularly alternated with more mellow emotions, and some days I found myself frustrated and feeling doomed to failure in my bid to become an ascended master.

One day I dropped by the Kalamazoo Public Library, bent on finding some spiritual book that could help me. I spotted Thomas á Kempis's *Imitation of Christ* "Of course!" I thought. "For 2,000 years, the Christian Church has been trying to produce people like the Ascended Master Jesus. Surely, they must have a few tips that can help me." I sat down in my carrel to read and meditate.

Within a few minutes a disheveled, fiftyish man wandered over. He circled my carel once, twice, three times (perhaps he thought it was the wall of Jericho). Finally, he intoned, "You'll never do it."

"Never do *what*?" I asked, taken aback.

"You'll never be like Jesus. "

I started to argue with him, annoyed by his arrogance, but I quickly realized he wasn't being arrogant. In spite of his dowdy appearance, he was rather graceful and humble as he explained that men cannot achieve peace with God by their own efforts. I needed to become like a child, he said. I had to call upon Jesus, and he would save me. Though there was no denying the extraordinary timing of his intervention, his assertion didn't faze me right away.

The second snag I hit on my way to godhood was seeing the sheer profusion of ascended master sightings. Oddball groups claiming to have been started by this or that master were everywhere. They all taught a broadly similar worldview (all is one, all is god, you are god, and you'll realize it in the new age that is dawning *if* you purchase this cassette tape course for only $499) but they abounded in contradictions. None agreed on when and where the masters were appearing, or to whom they had given authority, or which master was legitimate and which was merely an impostor. Also, the messages varied greatly. Most were insipid, sentimental, convoluted, or simply downright stupid. These exalted beings may have been able to raise their bodies from the earth and into the astral plane, but few could have gotten higher than a D in Logic 101 and freshman English Comp.

The third problem was that I had begun to fear I might be on the wrong side of things. In 1973, shortly after I enrolled at Michigan State University, I started reading the Bible. I was bothered by all the warnings about false gods, false prophets, false teachers, false dreamers, angels who had left their first estate and had become demons, false visions, false apostles, Satan appearing as an angel of light, false interpretations of Scripture, and, most unsettling of all, false christs. As fogged as my brain was with what's now known as "New Age" philosophy, I saw that it's impossible to believe that all religions are compatible with each other and, at the same time, call some religionists "false prophets." Yet the Bible, one of the most ancient and revered religious scriptures, claimed that some religions *were* false.

One evening I took my supper in the MSU student union, where a financially distressed, vegetarian student could get a bowl of broccoli for 35¢, a dinner roll for a nickel, and as much free pickle relish as he could eat ("Relish rolls" were a staple in my diet in those days). Depressed over my inability to sort out these issues, I sat down at a table in a far corner, wanting to be left alone; but I wasn't for long.

Halfway through my meager meal, I noticed three hippie-type young people come sauntering into the cafeteria. A dreadful feeling foretold an imminent encounter with them; I dropped my eyes to my broccoli, trying to be inconspicuous. No luck. A few moments later, three pairs of scuffed and dirty earth shoes appeared in front of my table. I looked up, my eyes traveling over patched jeans, tie-dye tee-shirts, "Jesus loves you!" buttons, and long, unkempt hair. "Have you met Jesus?", the one on the right asked me.

"Oh yes," I managed in a falsely calm voice that concealed the pounding of my heart. "He's my master, and he guides me through the I AM presence,"

Silence for a moment. They obviously had no idea what the I AM presence was. Another chimed in, "But has he washed you in his blood? Is he your Lord?"

The "Jesus Freaks" evangelized me, telling me that I didn't know the real Jesus, that I was a sinner, and that I needed Jesus if I wanted to be truly happy and avoid the "Lake of Fire" reserved for the devils and those who don't accept Jesus. My response was to pretend that we really believed the same thing, if viewed from the vantage point of the ascended masters. When I returned to my apartment, hoping I might find some divine "message" that would calm my aggravation about the encounter, I opened the Bible and decided I'd glean some message from wherever the page happened to fall open.

Bad move. I flipped open to Isaiah 47:8-10: "Now then listen, you wanton creature, lounging in your security and saying to yourself, ' I AM,' and 'there is none besides me.' Disaster will come upon you in full measure in spite of your many sorceries and all your potent spells. . . . Your wisdom and knowledge mislead you when you say to yourself, 'I AM, and there is none besides me.'"

I felt cold for a minute and started to tremble. This passage was describing me — no, it was *addressing* me! I knew this was no coincidence. The Jesus Freaks had been right.

On Saturday, March 9, 1974, I began a trip to the Mayflower Bookshop, East Lansing's occult bookstore. I tried to shake off the feeling of guilt I had been feeling since I chanced upon Isaiah 47, but with little success. So I was on my way to pick up some New Age books, hoping they might reconcile the Christianity of the Bible and my personal philosophy.

I was anxious and tense as I walked down Grand River Avenue toward the center of town. Ironically, even though I was running from Jesus, I was also praying to him. "Jesus, Jesus, Jesus," I said, "What does the Bible mean? Show me which books to get so I can understand it better. Help me do the right thing."

This gorgeous spring day had lured thousands of students out from their dorm rooms, and the streets were jammed with them. Just ahead of me I spotted a young man who stood near a storefront handing out what I assumed were Christian tracts. I continued my agitated praying and stepped to the curb to avoid him. Over the years I had learned to avoid zealous, usually pugnacious, Christians who handed out tracts in public places.

I reached the corner and waited for the light to turn green. When it did I breathed a sigh of relief. Confrontation with another simplistic, tiresome, Christian who had no idea how to help me enter more deeply into a study of the Bible, had been averted — or so I thought. As I brushed past him I felt a tapping on my shoulder. I turned with a grimace, and there he was: grinning widely, hand extended toward me, clutching a tract. "Hey, man, you need this," he said, as he pressed the slip of paper into my hand.

I didn't miss a step. I stuffed the tract in my pocket and hurried on, leaving him behind in a knot of pedestrians. A few moments later curiosity set in. I pulled the tract out and read the title: "Do you want to know why some people can't seem to understand the Bible?" That opening line from the Pacific Garden Mission's tract was like a mallet blow on my forehead. I felt like I had been suckerpunched. Some people glory in such divine intervention, I wanted to throw up.

I sat down on a bus bench and read the tract, knowing, somehow, that I was crossing some kind of important hurdle. By the time I finished, I knew what I had to do. When I got home I tossed out all my occult literature and paraphernalia. Evangelicals might say I had had a "born-again" experience; Catholics might say I had appropriated the implicit faith of my childhood. All I know is that at that moment, on that bus bench, I rejected the

New Age Movement and all its empty philosophy and became a follower of the Jesus Christ of the Bible.

I'm sometimes asked why I didn't return to the Catholic Church at that time. I bore no hostility, and don't wish to be harsh now, but the Bible became my authority and in the Catholic Church I didn't hear what I thought of as "biblical" preaching. Catholics I met seemed tentative and timid about their faith. The Bible spoke of Christians who were willing to risk martyrdom for their belief in Christ. The Catholics I met didn't even seem willing to risk embarassment for their beliefs. Another thing that disturbed me was that so many were spiritual crybabies, always grousing about the Church's teachings on artificial contraception, divorce and remarriage, and abortion. Other Catholics I met would stress how much their Church was changing, as though they were ashamed of their past. I wanted something doctrinally solid and permanent, and as far as I could see, the Catholic Church, in those years just after Vatican II, didn't appear to fit the bill.

I became a Christian again, and as is the case with many new, exuberant converts, I immediately became active in"ministry." Within a few months a group of friends and I started an independent fellowship called Church of the Word. The Bible, expounded in the original languages, was our only authority. We didn't have membership, our doctrine was minimal, a variant (or so we thought) of C.S. Lewis's "Mere Christianity." We viewed the Church as a voluntary association of spiritually like-minded Christians. The person and work of Christ, his divinity, the Atonement, Resurrection, Ascension, the Holy Spirit, and our need as sinners to personally appropriate by faith Christ's work on the Cross, composed the core of our "creed" — everything else was secondary. This doctrinal minimalism made evangelism easy. The less you believed, the less you had to explain and defend.

I became deeply attracted to Sally Morris, one of my converts, and we later got married. A few years before my re-commitment to Christ, one of Sally's cousins had joined The Way, International, whose founder had authored *Jesus Christ is Not God*. About two years after our 1977 wedding, Sally's family asked me to write up a critique of the group. During this research I first seriously questioned "Bible-only" Christianity.

In reviewing the beliefs of the primitive Church, I noticed that the Church Fathers didn't hesitate to invoke biblical authority, but they never tried to prove their case by the Bible alone. They also appealed to an authoritative Church tradition handed down through a succession of bishops that could be traced all the way back to the apostles themselves. I decided to check some Evangelical commentaries on the writings of the early Church Fathers. One, written by Protestant theologian Louis Berkhof, said, "It is frequently remarked that in passing from the study of the New Testament to that of the Apostolic Fathers one is conscious of a tremendous change. There is not the same freshness and originality, depth, and clearness"[1] In Berkhof's opinion, the Fathers were not innovators but conservators. That idea troubled me a lot. I wondered how it could be that there were Catholic, not Protestant, doctrines *everywhere* in the writings of the early Church Fathers. Were they perhaps what the apostles themselves had taught, or had they been cunningly introduced just after apostles died?

I also saw how doctrine developed in the early Church. The Trinity and the divinity of Christ were doctrines that were clearly rooted in Scripture but were not as self-evident as I had been led to believe. The full form of these doctrines, as we know them today, were not derived straight from Scripture, but are the result of centuries of deep reflection on Scripture and the oral tradition of interpreting Scripture that had been handed

[1] *History of Christian Doctrine* (Grand Rapids: Baker, 1975), 38.

on to the Church by the apostles. The 19th-century convert, John Henry Newman, became a Catholic largely because he grasped this point.

I devoured Newman's writings and a variety of other Catholic and Orthodox authors. If, during those days, somebody had asked what I thought of Catholicism I would have answered as Gandhi did when asked what he thought of western civilization: "It's a great idea. Someone ought to try it." The idea of Catholicism was intoxicating, but as soon as I began to think that perhaps it was true all I had to do to get sobered up was attend a local Mass with its banal, "Hallmark greeting card" sermons and barely audible congregational singing. The people in the pews seemed so bored and lifeless.

An oasis in the desert

But I was to face an even deeper problem. From 1982 to 1985 I experienced a clinical depression which bleached my universe of all meaning. Faith in God evaporated; love was a mirage; my hope in a beatific vision was replaced by a miserific vision.

After three years of this existential torture, as I teetered on the brink of despair, a concerned friend suggested I seek God one last time at the Trappist Abbey of Gethsemani, once home of Thomas Merton. This beautiful monastery nestled in the rolling hills of northern Kentucky, was the perfect setting for me to rediscover and reclaim my faith in Christ. The quiet liturgical rhythm of the place was like balm to my soul.

During my stay there God gathered together the frayed cords of the spiritual pain and confusion I had experienced over the last several years, and he imbued that suffering with his redemptive, purifying grace. Many hours spent in prayerful, silent solitude with the Lord allowed me to become quiet in his presence and enter into the lonely mystery of the one who once cried, "My God, my God, why have you forsaken me?" I realized that God had not forsaken me — he was there. Little by little, he led me out of the darkness and into the light of his truth. When I finished my retreat I felt refreshed, able to think clearly about what form my Christianity must take. I sensed a growing attraction to the Catholic Church, but there were still plenty of the typical Evangelical doctrinal prejudices yet in me. Though I had a lot of studying to do before I could think of becoming Catholic, something happened that galvanized me. A shove Romeward came, ironically, from the staunchly Evangelical magazine, *Christianity Today*.

I read an article that bitterly attacked Dr. Thomas Howard for his conversion to the Catholic Church. Howard was, arguably, American Evangelicalism's most talented and insightful author. A popular professor at Gordon College in suburban Boston, he was highly esteemed by his students and well-known for his writings on theological issues, especially on things liturgical and sacramental.

Christianity Today chastized Howard for what it called his "naive" acceptance of the Catholic Church's claim to have an infallible authority. How absurd, the writer argued, to acknowledge the checkered history of the Catholic Church and at the same time believe it possesses an infallible teaching authority. This attack angered me; first, because I knew Tom (the Howards and the Krestas were both Godparents to the same child), and I knew he was a man of integrity who was deeply committed to Christ and the gospel; and second, because of the intellectual hypocrisy *Christianity Today* had evinced in its article.

Just a few years earlier, *Christianity Today's* former editor, Harold Lindsell, had launched the so-called "Battle for the Bible." The International Council on Biblical Inerrancy was convened to, among other things, answer the liberal charge that there are irreconcilable contradictions in the Bible. How did *Christianity Today* reconcile those alleged discrepancies with its position that the Bible is infallible? The same way Tom Howard reconciled his acknowledgement of the problems in Catholic history with his acceptance of the Catholic Church's claim of being infallible. His arguments to establish the reliability of the testimony of the Catholic Church were the same arguments Lindsell had used to verify the inspiration and inerrancy of the Bible.

But Lindsell had another problem, perhaps one he did not see. He would not have the New Testament canon if he did not implicitly trust the teaching authority of the Catholic Church. After all, it was the Catholic Church which recognized and fixed the canon of New Testament, and Lindsell and those in his camp accept that canon.[2]

After *Christianity Today* printed my letter to the editor protesting its shabby treatment of Tom Howard, I came out of the closet, so to speak. After much prayer and study, I could no longer accept the Protestant doctrine of Scripture alone on any other than purely pragmatic grounds. The Catholic Church's authoritative role in the formation of the canon of Scripture, coupled with the lack of biblical evidence for *sola scriptura*, were the weak links in the Protestant chain that could no longer tether me. I continued somewhat half-heartedly as an Evangelical, but I was grappling with the question, "Can I follow Christ and remain a Protestant?"

In 1985, an independent charismatic church where I had done some occasional teaching honored me with a call to be its pastor. I accepted with hesitation, given the state of theological uncertainty in which I found myself. Ironically, my decision to pastor this church led me into the Catholic Church. "Mere Christianity" had ill-prepared me for the pastorate. In fact, as an adult, I had

[2] For a detailed discussion of how one can demonstrate the infallibility of both the Catholic Church and the Bible, without falling prey to the fallacy of circular reasoning, see Karl Keating, *Catholicism and Fundamentalism* (San Francisco: Ignatius, 1988), 121-133.

never been a formal member of a church until I was asked to pastor one.

How important could the Church be sincei everybody had the written Word of God for themselves? A man I still regard as a mentor, the late apologist and evangelist, Francis Schaeffer, used to say that the Reformation showed us the importance of the man of God alone (cf. 2 Tim. 3:17), with the Bible alone, guided by the Spirit alone. But as I studied Scripture that's not what I saw. The man of God is never depicted as (nor expected to be) using the Bible alone; he is called by Christ to function with authority in his teaching ministry, but only within the larger context of the doctrinal unity of the magisterium of teaching Church.[3]

Christians are never depicted in Scripture as being "lone rangers," left to decide for themselves what they think Scripture means (cf. 2 Pet. 1:20-21). Without the teaching guidance of the Church, all sorts of fanciful and erroneous interpretations of Scripture can spring up (2 Pet. 3:15). That's why Paul admonished the early Christians to always hold fast to the unity of doctrine: "I appeal to you, brothers, in the name of our Lord Jesus Christ, that all of you agree with one another so that there may be no divisions among you and that you may be perfectly united in mind and thought" (1 Cor. 1:10).

The Evangelical vision of the Church as the invisible union of all who genuinely trust in Christ seemed spectral in comparison; even a subtle form of Docetism. Docetists believed that the Word did not truly take flesh but only appeared to, the invisibilists similarly denied the materiality of Christ's Body, the Church. By refusing to accept the visible Church Protestantism denied the extension of the Incarnation.

---

[3]   Cf. Matt. 18:15-17; Phil. 1:27-28, 2:2; 1 Tim. 3:15, 4:11-16, 6:2-3; 2 Tim. 4:1-5; Titus 1:7-11, 13-14; 2:15, 3:8-10.

Ephesians 4:3 commands us to make every effort to keep the unity of the Spirit through the bond of peace. Paul hammers this point home with a series of exclamations: One body! One Spirit! One hope! One Lord! One faith! One baptism! One God and Father of all! (Eph. 4:7-13). In Acts 15 the apostles were so concerned about unity they called a plenary Church council to prevent factions from becoming permanent. Paul chides the Corinthians for naming themselves after their favorite preachers, "One of you says 'I am of Paul,' another says 'I am of Apollos,' another, 'I am of Cephas.' Isn't that evidence that you are of the flesh and not the spirit?" (1 Cor. 3:3-7).

The New Testament records conflict between believers; sharp disputes over circumcision, dining on meat sacrificed to idols, the person of Christ. And yes, the New Testament describes the sin and corruption of various Church members. But nowhere are the believers given the option of hiving off into independent splinter groups; in fact one of the few offenses that give us reason to expel a brother is the offense of causing disunity: "I urge you brothers, to watch out for those who cause divisions. Keep away from them" (Rom. 16:17). Without a visibly united Church, excommunication can't achieve its purpose: the repentance and restoration of the offender (Matt. 18:15-20, 1 Cor. 5:1-13; 2 Cor. 2:1-11). I wondered how Protestantism, which has splintered into over 20,000 denominations worldwide, could be what Jesus had in mind in John 17:21, when he said that the world will know that the Father sent the Son by the unity of his disciples. "Where is the visible expression of unity and universality in Protestantism?" I asked.

As our independent church grew and we moved to larger quarters, I found myself faced with a difficult question: "Given the biblical emphasis on the visible unity of Christ's Body, what was the justification of our separate ecclesiastical life?" I didn't know what denomination we should join — but here I was bewailing the disunity of the Church and at the same time I was leading an "independent" congregation. I felt like I had killed my mother and then complained about being an orphan.

The doctrines of "mere Christianity," the divinity of Christ, Trinity, blood atonement, authority of Scripture, etc., only take you so far and then they have to be applied to issues like church government, sacraments, church discipline, style of worship; pastoral questions such as, "Is Operation Rescue biblical?" "Is artificial insemination okay?" "Can one lose his salvation?" Who determines what is essential and what is non-essential? By what authority? Once you begin answering these necessary questions you are no longer just a Christian, you are a Baptist, or Pentecostal, or Nazarene, or Presbyterian.

To those "outside of Christ" Protestants stress that these secondary identities (dare I say, traditions) — Nazarene, Baptist, Reformed, Pentecostal, Lutheran, Anglican — are not really important. What *is* important, Protestants say, is "mere Christianity." But to those inside the circle of faith, it is exactly these secondary distinctives which form the social and theological glue that bring cohesiveness to the fellowship and distinguish you from others. They are what you fight over and divide over. For a church to retain its identity it must articulate the reason for its existence. I kept asking people what the reason was for our church's independence? Why didn't we simply merge with the Baptist or Presbyterian church down the street?

No one, myself included, had a good answer.

I also asked how it could be that Jesus would command visible unity but leave his Church without the necessarily infallible means of settling doctrinal disputes in order to maintain that unity? Would he command the impossible? And if Jesus had not given that sort of infallible teaching authority to the ministers of his Church, is it not presumptuous for a minister or a body of ministers to insist upon this or that form of church government, this or that form of baptism, or some other doctrine? That, after all, was Jesus' complaint against the Pharisees. They imposed practices, traditions of men (cf. Mark 7:6-13), for which there was no divine warrant.

I was in a quandary. Where was that teaching authority described so often in the New Testament located? Reformation Protestantism claimed the Bible alone is the only infallible rule of faith and practice. But, ironically, it was the emphasis on the Bible alone that caused all the confusion and division within Protestantism.

In addition to my pastorate, for three years I had been hosting a daily talk show on Detroit's major Evangelical radio station, WMUZ. I had the privilege of interviewing Evangelicalism's top theologians, pastors, and leaders. Many had privately shared with me their discomfort with Protestantism's perpetual splintering over petty rivalries, ambition, and doctrinal disputes; and I felt the same as they did.

On May 23, 1990, I interviewed Fr. Peter Stravinskas. Knowing I had a number of Catholic listeners who were usually overlooked in evangelical programming, I asked him to join me for an hour I dubbed "Catholic Answers to Catholic Questions." An angry caller accused Catholics of "resacrificing" Christ at Mass, in contradiction to Hebrews 7:27 and 9:28, which said that Christ's sacrifice on Calvary was "once-for-all." Fr. Stravinskas did a masterful job of explaining, right out of the Book of Hebrews, that the Mass is not a re-sacrificing of Christ. It is a re-presentation of his once-for-all sacrifice at Calvary. I don't have space here to outline his entire explanation, but I saw that the Catholic view was the biblical view.[4]

Adrenalin surged through me as I heard the refrain resounding in my brain, "My God, I'm a *Catholic*!" I felt

---

[4] A detailed study of the book of Hebrews that deals with the Sacrifice of the Mass, among other key issues, is found in Scott Hahn's eight-tape (audio) Bible study "St. Paul's Letter to the Hebrews" (available from St. Joseph's Communications, P.O. Box 720, West Covina, CA 91793).

a bit silly and imagined the Lord chuckling, "Ask not for whom the show airs, Kresta, it airs for thee."

I was both excited and troubled, as though I had been walking in the dark for a long time and then someone turned on the lights. There I was, perched on a tightrope high above the ground, already midway out. On one hand, I took heart that I had made it so far in the dark, but I trembled because I wasn't quite sure I would make it to the other side. I still regarded Marian doctrines, purgatory, artificial contraception, and other doctrinal issues as serious obstacles. Not to mention the fact that becoming Catholic would very likely mean unemployment as pastor and forfeiture of my radio show. I had wife and family, and I needed to keep a job.

But there is a time for leading and a time for quitting. To this day I miss pastoring the men and women who shared so many of their struggles and joys with me. But such trust and honor cannot be trampled on. I knew I was going to become a Catholic, and this knowledge made me an uncertain and self-conscious pulpiteer. So I decided that the only honorable thing to do was resign my pastorate, which I did in December 1990.

Things moved quickly after that. After a period of intense prayer and study of Scripture, Church history, Catholic apologetics works, and even the most formidable Evangelical anti-Catholic works I could find, I made my decision formal and re-entered the Catholic Church.

In St. Suzanne's parish in Detroit I was received back into the Church on Holy Thursday, 1992 at a Mass that was attended by my family and friends (some of those friends who were Evangelicals at the time, have since also converted to the Catholic Church). Two evenings later, at the Easter Vigil Mass, Sally and our children Alexis, Nicholas, James, and Evan, were all received into the Church as converts. What joy!

Everyone chuckled when, after being baptized, James did a little dance of happiness and excitement. In my heart, I danced too. My days of wandering were over.

How to Contact the Contributors

Patrick Madrid
P.O. Box 640
Granville, OH 43023
614-928-7767 voice
614-928-5975 fax
madrid1@aol.com

Dave Armstrong
6078 Auburn
Detroit, MI 48228
313 441-2794

Rick Conason
c/o 80 Pine Street
34th Floor
New York, NY 10005

Marcus Grodi
P.O. Box 4100
Steubenville, OH 43952
614-283-6320

Dr. Scott Hahn
Franciscan University
Franciscan Way
Steubenville, OH 43952

Al Kresta
P.O. Box 504
Ann Arbor, MI 48106
313-998-0484
credo@rc.net

James Akin
6308 Rancho Mission Rd.
San Diego, CA 92108
619-541-1131

Bob Sungenis
Catholic Apologetics Intl.
P.O. Box 2247
Columbia, MD 21045
410-489-7687
sungenis@aol.com

Tim Staples
c/o *Envoy* Magazine
Gap Knob Road
New Hope, KY 40052

Julie Swenson
282 Parkview Terrace
Suite #301
Oakland, CA 94610

Dr. Paul Thigpen
Religious Studies Dept.
S.W. Missouri Sate Univ.
901 South National Ave.
Springfield, MO 65804
517-836-5514

Steve Wood
Family Life Center
P.O. Box 6060
Port Charlotte, FL 33949
941-764-7725 voice
941-743-5352 fax

Terry Frazier
500 Providencia, #G
Burbank, CA 91501

About the Editor

PATRICK MADRID is the editor-in-chief of *Envoy* magazine, a bimonthly journal of apologetics and evangelization. He is the author of *Any Friend of God's Is a Friend of Mine* and a co-author of *Not By Scripture Alone*. He, his wife, and their children live in Ohio.

To order a subscription to *Envoy*, please contact:

Envoy **Magazine**
Subscriber Services Department
New Hope KY 40052-9989
800-55-ENVOY
www.envoymagazine.com

Free resource catalogues of materials produced by Scott Hahn, Steve Ray, Al Kresta, Patrick Madrid, and other Catholic apologists are available from:

Thy Faith, Inc.
33228 Twelvemile Road, #305
Farmington Hills, MI 48334   313-522-1262
thyfaith@compuserve.com

St. Joseph Communications
P.O. Box 720
West Covina, CA 91793   800-526-2151

Heritage of the Apostles
P.O. Box 4327
Enterprise, FL 32725   407-860-6305

Catholic Answers
P.O. Box 17490
San Diego, CA 92177   619-541-1131